Timetable and Checklist for Preparin

TOPIC/SUBJECT

☐ My subject meets the criteria of the assignm
(pp. 3–6; 15–16; 39)

☐ I have decided on an approach. (pp. 47–53)

☐ Enough sources of information are available. (p. 41)

☐ My instructor has approved the subject.

SEARCHING FOR INFORMATION

Date Due | Date Completed

☐ I followed a search strategy. (pp. 56–59)

☐ I looked for primary sources. (p. 55)

☐ I looked for secondary sources. (p. 56)

☐ I found information in books (pp. 60–65)

☐ I found information in periodicals. (pp. 60–62; 65–67)

☐ I found nonprint information. (pp. 60–62; 68; 89–99)

☐ I used computer searches. (pp. 38; 77–78; 84–87)

☐ I used sources outside of the library. (pp. 87–89)

☐ Each potential source of information is recorded
and follows appropriate conventions. (pp. 59–68)

RECORDING INFORMATION

Date Due | Date Completed

☐ I am aware of plagiarism and how to avoid it. (pp. 100–06)

☐ I evaluated each potential source. (pp. 108–10)

☐ Each note is on a separate card. (pp. 111; 128)

☐ The source is completely identified on each card.
(pp. 113–14; 129)

☐ I followed the conventions of writing the note cards.
(pp. 114–20)

☐ I made accurate summaries of information for
some note cards. (121–22)

☐ I have direct quotations on some cards. (pp. 123–25)

☐ I used paraphrases on some note cards. (pp. 122–23)

☐ Some note cards contain my personal comments,
ideas, opinions, and/or queries. (p. 125)

ORGANIZING IDEAS

Date Due | Date Completed

☐ I reevaluated my notes and selected those that allow
me to take a stand on my subject. (pp. 129–30)

☐ I wrote a useful thesis statement. (pp. 131–35)

☐ I prepared an outline in correct form. (pp. 143–47; 148–52)

☐ Every item in the outline relates directly to the
thesis statement. (pp. 143–46)

☐ The outline shows an organized progression of thought.
(pp. 137–41)

☐ I received feedback on my work thus far. (pp. 150–53)

WRITING/DRAFTING THE PAPER

	Date Due	Date Completed

- ☐ The opening of my paper leads the audience into the subject. (pp. 157–62)
- ☐ My writing is coherent. (pp. 163–64)
- ☐ Transitions connect ideas smoothly. (p. 163)
- ☐ All assertions are adequately supported. (p. 164)
- ☐ My writing is specific. (p. 165)
- ☐ Every quotation is essential to the text and is properly presented. (pp. 171–75)
- ☐ Resources, references, and quotations are integrated with my own writing in the text. (pp. 165–71)
- ☐ All sources are acknowledged and properly documented. (pp. 186–93)
- ☐ I alphabetized the Works Cited cards for sources I actually used. (p. 131)
- ☐ The paper ends with finality. (pp. 175–79)

WRITING/REVISING

	Date Due	Date Completed

- ☐ I have selected the most appropriate words for my ideas. (pp. 180–81)
- ☐ Sentences are the best that I can compose. (pp. 180–81)
- ☐ I have arranged the words and ideas in the best way I can. (p. 182)
- ☐ Spelling, punctuation, and capitalization are conventional.(pp. 181; 182)
- ☐ Documentation is accurate and consistent with the style selected. (pp. 186–201)
- ☐ Documentation is coordinated with Works Cited. (pp. 186; 188–93; 202)
- ☐ The title of the paper is specific. (pp. 183–85)
- ☐ I am satisfied with this research paper.

FINAL PRESENTATIONS

	Date Due	Date Completed

- ☐ I have followed the recommended typing or word processing format. (p. 222)
- ☐ Each page is numbered consecutively and accurately. (pp. 223–24)
- ☐ All illustrations, charts, graphs, tables, pictures, etc. are properly labeled and placed where most relevant to the text. (pp. 191–93; 225)
- ☐ The Works Cited listing (or other statement of resources) is complete and in the proper form. (pp. 105–22; 226)
- ☐ Any additional sections or materials are completed, properly identified, and put in place. (pp. 226–28)
- ☐ I have given my research paper a final proofreading and typographical errors are corrected. (pp. 221–22)

[Consult pp. 247–274 for APA and other formats.]

I turned in my research paper on _____

The Research Paper

Process, Form, and Content

Seventh Edition

The Research Paper

Process, Form, and Content

Seventh Edition

Audrey J. Roth

Miami-Dade Community College

Wadsworth Publishing Company
I(T)P™ An International Thomson Publishing Company

Belmont • Albany • Bonn • Boston • Cincinnati • Detroit • London • Madrid • Melbourne •
Mexico City • New York • Paris • San Francisco • Singapore • Tokyo • Toronto • Washington

English Editor: Angela Wrahtz Gantner
Editorial Assistant: Lisa Timbrell
Production Editor: Sara Hunsaker/*Ex Libris*
Copy Editor: Elliot Simon
Designer: Jeanne Calabrese/Lisa Berman
Print Buyer: Karen Hunt
Permissions Editor: Bob Kauser
Illustrator: Lisa Torri
Cover Designer: William Reuter
Compositor: Thompson Type
Printer: R. R. Donnelley/Crawfordsville
Cover Printer: Phoenix Color Corporation

Printed in the United States of America

4 5 6 7 8 9 10—01 00 99 98 97

For more information, contact Wadsworth Publishing Company.

Wadsworth Publishing Company
10 Davis Drive
Belmont, California 94002 USA

International Thomson Publishing Europe
Berkshire House 168-173
High Holborn
London, WC1V 7AA, England

Thomas Nelson Australia
102 Dodds Street
South Melbourne 3205
Victoria, Australia

Nelson Canada
1120 Birchmount Road
Scarborough, Ontario
Canada M1K 5G4

International Thomson Editores
Campos Eliseos 385, Piso 7
Col. Polanco
11560 México D. F. México

International Thomson Publishing GmbH
Königswinterer Strasse 418
53227 Bonn, Germany

International Thomson Publishing Asia
221 Henderson Road
#05-10 Henderson Building
Singapore 0315

International Thomson Publishing Japan
Hirakawacho Kyowa Building, 3F
2-2-1 Hirakawacho
Chiyoda-ku, Tokyo 102, Japan

Library of Congress Cataloging-in-Publication Data

Roth, Audrey J.
    The research paper : process, form, and content / Audrey J. Roth.
—7th ed.
        p.   cm.
    Includes bibliographical references and index.
    ISBN 0–534–17454–X
    1. Report writing.   2. Research.   I. Title.
LB2369.R66   1994
808'.02—dc20   94-5782

To the Teacher

What started out, many years ago, as a series of handouts to help my students fulfill the research paper assignment for one of the composition courses I taught has evolved through these seven editions. My purpose for writing, however, remains the same: to show students that by following a series of steps conscientiously and thoughtfully, they will be able to fulfill a research paper assignment. Besides applying their learning to research work for other courses, students will be able to adapt it to uses beyond school, particularly in their future vocations.

The Process

There has been much talk in recent years about process. As in previous editions, this book continues to point out to students that there is, indeed, a process to follow in preparing a research paper: searching for information in both print and nonprint sources, synthesizing what is learned with original ideas and interpretations, organizing the whole, and then writing and revising. Examples and references throughout the text continue, as they have in past editions, to show the many nonacademic uses to which this process can be applied. My aim in doing so is to show that, although the formal research paper is a school assignment, many people in all sorts of businesses and professions constantly use the processes of research. Once learned in schools, the skills will be available throughout a lifetime.

The Form

In order to make this book even more useful for students than earlier versions, instructors will note a few changes in the form of this edition. Together with Wadsworth's designers, I have sought to make the contents more accessible to students. The typefaces used and the placement of subheads will help students locate material more readily by scanning. Lists are used where they can help focus attention. Every effort was made to keep a fresh and open design. Visual and verbal instructions abound. In short, special attention has been paid to readability and easy access of information.

The Content

New editions always give an author the opportunity to find a better order and make other changes. They also give an author time to use the book with more students and to receive evaluations from more colleagues.

While the basic content of this edition remains much the same as other editions, I have been attentive to the rapid changes in student work habits and in libraries as both have switched to increased computer use. For example, CD-ROMs are more ubiquitous than they were when I wrote the last edition and the long-familiar wooden card catalog cases have often been replaced by blinking cursors and computer keyboards. Elements in Chapters 4 and 5 have been reorganized for more logical presentation. Text examples and appendices, also, continue to be updated.

This book is still dominated by the conventions of documentation recommended by the Modern Language Association in *The MLA Style Manual* (1985) and the *MLA Handbook for Writers of Research Papers*, 3rd ed. (1988), both by Joseph Gibaldi and Walter S. Achtert. They contain the forms most English and humanities instructors prefer.

However, in response to requests from some teachers, the APA style is now illustrated with an entire student-written research paper. The conventions of documentation and reference forms are those of the *Publication Manual of the American Psychological Association*, 3rd ed. (1983). Additionally, examples of APA reference forms and citations are separated from the MLA style to avoid confusion. And there is now room for information about other documentation systems less frequently used by undergraduates. Together, these materials form a separate chapter in the book, resulting in eleven chapters rather than the ten of previous editions.

What has been deemed particularly useful in past editions has been retained in this one. There continues to be emphasis on audience, from selecting a subject to incorporating that knowledge into writing and revising. Again, students are repeatedly shown how to avoid plagiarism, even during the note-taking stage. Persuasive writing continues to be stressed, so the sample research papers are in that mode. "Managing Your Time" and a "Search Strategy" form appear again, as does the long-time feature, "Timetable and Checklist" that serves as additional guidance to students.

A continuing problem for inexperienced writers seems to be integrating resources into the text of the research paper. Doing so smoothly, while maintaining the tone and style of writing, helps students overcome such difficulties. They may also practice such integrations in one of the exercises in the *Instructor's Manual* that accompanies this 7th edition.

Finally, color printing in this book plays a helpful role by highlighting various parts of the text to draw student attention to them. Also, both sample research papers have marginal notes in two colors: those in color point out the characteristics of research paper form, while those in black are notes about the content. Students can use these notes as quick guides and summaries of the sample papers and their own research papers.

The Instructor's Manual

Students often need to practice some of the skills they will incorporate into their own research papers. Therefore, the *Instructor's Manual* is available to accompany this edition. It contains exercises for student practice in such matters as selecting a subject for writing, taking notes, integrating resources with original writing, preparing works for citation, proofreading, and more. In addition to answers for teachers, there are variations on the exercises for those students who need a little extra practice and varied activities coordinated with the chapters in the text. In all, instructors will find ample material to choose from, depending on student requirements and on time available. Exercise pages in the manual may be duplicated and distributed to students.

And Thanks . . .

Books take a long time to write and revise and revise again, but authors who are lucky—as I am—have many people who help a book through to publication. Primary thanks go to my students over the years who have worked through this material, and especially to those who permitted me to include their work. They teach me more every time we start the process! Anybody who works with research materials needs a friendly and helpful librarian; Dr. Susan Byrd of the Miami-Dade Community College Kendall Campus library has been that person for me through this and other editions of the book. The people at Wadsworth Publishing Company have continued to be supportive and gentle, even when nudging this procrastinator through deadlines.

Thanks go, also, to the many colleagues whose comments and suggestions have helped me to continue improving this book. They are a long list, through these many editions, and most recently added to them are: Vicki Adams, Kent State University; Therese Brychta, Truckee Meadows Community College; Patricia Graves, Georgia State University; Alex Joncas, Glendale Community College; John Presley, Central Virginia Community College; Suzanne Shippey, St. Clair County Community College; and June Zimmerman, Alabama State University.

Books also take a lot of an author's time away from the family. Fortunately, mine is an understanding one and I again acknowledge their support, as I have in each edition. But the book, this time, is for Chuck Glass—who knows why.

Audrey J. Roth
Miami, Florida

To the Student

Writing a research paper is more than just a classroom exercise. It is an active and individual process, an ideal learning process. When you prepare and write a research paper, you search out, understand, and synthesize information and thought. In so doing, you apply many skills basic to both academic and nonacademic tasks. The research paper is, in the fullest sense, a discovery and an education that leads you beyond texts, beyond a library, and encourages you to investigate on your own. The process provides a structure, but within it you can make exciting discoveries of knowledge and of yourself. So, to produce a good research paper is both a useful and a thoroughly satisfying experience!

Students in my own classes have made many suggestions for this edition that they have found useful, and I hope they will be for you, also. For example, my students say they find the "Managing Your Time" section helpful because it addresses that common problem. The "Search Strategy" has helped keep them on track, and the "Timetable and Checklist" at the front of the book has been useful. Many students initially feel the "Process Log" is time consuming, but most agree it lets them see how they are progressing and is satisfying to look back on after the research paper is finished. Thus, these elements are continued in the 7th edition.

To keep your paper from looking like a cut-and-paste job, use the section in Chapter 7 on integrating resources into the text you write. My students have found it helps them.

They also have found that taking time to focus on a subject narrow enough to work with helps produce a successful paper. That's why the book continues to contain two chapters on this early part of the process. I hope you will use the varied suggestions in them, especially if you have free choice of a subject to write about and can explore possibilities open to you before making a final decision.

Because I know that few of you will spend the rest of your life in academe, examples and illustrations throughout the text are drawn from a variety of businesses and professions; those of you not planning to major in English will find many examples from other academic disciplines, as well. As you read them, bear in mind that although you are using this text for a school research paper, the skills you are learning and practicing will be useful to you long after this particular course is over.

New to this edition is a chapter on writing a research paper in the form recommended by the American Psychological Association, the APA. It is used in many of the social sciences and even for writing about research in the humanities. Therefore, though the teacher for this course may expect you to use the MLA form, keep this book in case future instructors expect you to produce a research paper in the APA style.

Also new to this edition is more material than the previous editions on computers and communications technology. Some of what is here about computers, databases, online searches, citations for CD-ROMs, and so on may be obsolete by the time you read this book because development and marketing in these fields seems to change almost daily. However, you can readily adapt what you read here to what is available to you.

Finally, the publisher and I have tried to make the design and typography of this edition easy to use and helpful in finding what you're looking for. Use the **index** as a reference source for the many ideas within the book. Check the **illustrations** and see how they are coordinated with full explanations in the text. Use the many **subheads** to scan for specifics. Note the number of **lists**; they point up key information and get you ready for details that follow. Look carefully at the **marginal notes** on each page of the two sample research papers: those in color call attention to forms you need to follow in your own paper, while those in black are remarks about the content of the sample research papers and can serve as a guide for writing your paper.

This book doesn't guarantee it can provide a magic formula that makes everything easy. It *does*, however, offer a procedure to follow and a framework to use in preparing a research paper. It will guide you through the entire process from choosing a subject to submitting a written paper of good quality in acceptable form. I hope you will use this book as a guide in many courses, especially if you are left completely on your own to write a research paper. (It will certainly help you!) You will probably also find this book a valuable permanent addition to your personal library.

In short, I hope this book will make research a useful part of your education and preparation for the future. I also hope that as you learn increasingly to work on your own and trust your own abilities, you will often make those personal discoveries through research and thought that are what learning and going to school are all about.

A.J.R.

Contents

TO THE TEACHER   vii

TO THE STUDENT   ix

CHAPTER 1

Starting the Research Paper   1

KINDS OF RESEARCH   1

DIFFERENCES AMONG REPORTS, DOCUMENTED PAPERS,
    AND RESEARCH PAPERS   2

WHAT A RESEARCH PAPER *IS*   3

WHAT A RESEARCH PAPER *IS NOT*   4

LENGTH OF RESEARCH PAPERS   6

FIVE STEPS TO A RESEARCH PAPER   6

    Step 1. Choosing the Subject   6
    Step 2. Collecting Information   7
    Step 3. Evaluating Materials   7
    Step 4. Organizing Ideas   7
    Step 5. Writing the Paper   8

WHY A RESEARCH PAPER IS IMPORTANT   9

WHO READS RESEARCH PAPERS—AND WHY   10

KEEPING A PROCESS LOG   11

MANAGING YOUR TIME   13

CHAPTER 2

Choosing a General Topic   14

THE TERMS "TOPIC" AND "SUBJECT"   14

QUALITIES OF A GOOD TOPIC   15

TOPICS TO AVOID   16

ASSIGNED TOPICS   19

FIELD-OF-STUDY TOPICS   19

   1. Taking Stock of What You Know   19

   2. Makes Use of Printed Aids   20

   3. Build From Your Own Interests   28

FREE-CHOICE TOPICS   29

LIBRARY CATALOGING CUSTOMS   31

   Classifications of Books (Dewey Decimal and Library of Congress)   31

   Contents of the "Card Catalog"   33

   Individual Catalog Cards   35

   Alphabetizing of Books and Periodicals   35

COMPUTER SEARCHES   38

AN ADDENDUM: DOUBLE SUBMISSIONS   39

CHAPTER 3

Narrowing the Topic   40

SOME LIMITATIONS YOU WORK WITHIN   40

   Length   40

   Materials Available   41

   Audience   41

FOCUSING ON A SUBJECT TO RESEARCH   42

   Freewriting   42

   Free Association   42

   Clustering   43

   Subdividing   43

   The Five Ws   44

   Combined Method   46

FINDING AN APPROACH   47

DECIDING ON AN APPROACH BEFORE BEING WELL INFORMED ABOUT
   YOUR SUBJECT   48

   Examining or Analyzing   48

   Evaluating or Criticizing   49

   Comparing and Contrasting   50

   Relating   50

   Arguing or Persuading   51

WORDING YOUR APPROACH   52

   A Word of Caution   53

CHOOSING A RESEARCH PAPER TITLE   53

CHAPTER 4
Searching for Information   54

THE WHAT, WHERE, AND HOW OF FINDING INFORMATION   54
PRIMARY AND SECONDARY SOURCES   55
Primary Sources   55
Secondary Sources   56
A SEARCH STRATEGY   56
The Search Strategy Record   58
RECORDING POSSIBLE SOURCES: CONVENTIONS OF PRELIMINARY CITATIONS (MLA STYLE)   59
General Conventions   60
Conventions About the Author Unit   60
Conventions About the Title Unit   61
Conventions About the Publication Information Unit   62
A. Book Publication Information   62
B. Magazine and Journal Publication Information   65
C. Newspaper Publication Information   67
D. Nonprint Publication Information   68
READING SOURCES OF PRINT INFORMATION AND WRITING PRELIMINARY CITATIONS   68
Encyclopedias   68
Reference Books and Indices: Bibliographies, Handbooks, Biographical References and More   69
The Vertical Files   73
Government Publications   74
Abstracting Services   76
Online and Card Catalogs   77
Periodical Indexes   78
Computer Databases   84
Other Sources of Print Information   87
RECORDING POSSIBLE NONPRINT SOURCES: CONVENTIONS OF PRELIMINARY CITATIONS (MLA STYLE)   89
Three Units of Information in a Nonprint Preliminary Citation   89
Radio and TV Programs   90
Interviews   91
Lectures and Speeches   92
Questionnaires, Surveys, and Polls   93
Films and Filmstrips   94
Videocassettes, Laser Discs, and Interactive Video   99
CDs, Audiotapes, Other Audios   99

CHAPTER 5

Recording Information   100

ORDERING TASKS   100

PLAGIARISM—AND HOW NOT TO COMMIT IT   100
Of Words and Ideas—And Plagiarism   101
How *Not* to Plagiarize   101
Notes That Plagiarize   102
Notes That *Don't* Plagiarize   103

COMMON KNOWLEDGE   106

READING TO TAKE NOTES   107
Previewing   107
Skimming   107
Scanning   108

EVALUATING SOURCE MATERIALS   108
Before You Read   109
When You Read   110

QUALITIES OF GOOD NOTES   111
Legibility   112
Accuracy   112
Completeness   113

CONVENTIONS OF WRITING NOTES   114
1. Quotations   114
2. Words Omitted from a Quotation   118
3. Interpolations or Commentaries   118
4. Foreign Words and Phrases   120
5. Titles Within Quotations and Sources   120

KINDS OF NOTES   120
Summary Notes   121
Paraphrase Notes   122
Direct Quotation Notes   123
Personal Comment Notes   125
Combination Notes   126

NUMBER OF NOTE CARDS   126

A NOTE ABOUT PHOTOCOPYING   127

IF YOU USE A COMPUTER   127

CHAPTER 6

Organizing Ideas   129

RECONSIDERATION TIME   129

PUTTING THE PARTS TOGETHER   130

WHAT A THESIS STATEMENT *IS*   131
WHAT A THESIS STATEMENT *IS NOT*   132
HOW A THESIS STATEMENT EVOLVES   134
HOW AN OUTLINE EVOLVES   135
WAYS OF ORGANIZING CONTENT   137
   Time   138
   Known to Unknown or Simple to Complex   138
   Comparison and Contrast   138
   General to Particular or Particular to General   139
   Problem to Solution or Question to Answer   139
   Cause to Effect or Effect to Cause   140
RELATING ORGANIZATION TO OVERALL APPROACH   140
VISUAL ORDERING—CLUSTERING AND MAPPING   141
OUTLINES   142
   Content of Outlines   143
   Forms of Outlines   147
   Conventions of Outlines   148
   Revising Outlines   150
COMPUTER AIDS TO OUTLINING   152
A FINAL CHECK   152

CHAPTER 7

Writing Your Paper   154

WHAT "DRAFTING" MEANS   154
WRITING STYLE   155
STARTING YOUR PAPER   156
   Bad Openings   161
WRITING THE BODY OF YOUR PAPER   162
   Unity and Coherence   163
   Adequate Support   164
   Emphasis   164
   Concreteness and Specificity   165
INTEGRATING RESOURCE INFORMATION   165
   1. Using Lead-in Wording   166
   2. Varying Introductory Phrases   167
   3. Documenting Information Anywhere   167
   4. Fitting Documented Material Grammatically   168
   5. Grouping Citations   169
   6. Using Paraphrases and Summaries   169

RECORDING AND PUNCTUATING QUOTATIONS   171
    Short Prose Passages   172
    Longer Prose Passages   172
    Short Passages of Poetry   173
    Longer Passages of Poetry   173
    Drama   174
COMMENT NOTES   175
ENDING THE PAPER   175
    Bad Endings   178
REVISING YOUR PAPER   179
    Word Choice and Sentence Structure   180
    Mechanics   181
REVISING ON A COMPUTER   182
SELECTING A TITLE   183

CHAPTER 8

Documenting Your Paper   186

WHERE AND HOW TO MAKE ACKNOWLEDGMENTS   186
PARENTHETICAL DOCUMENTATION: MLA (MODERN LANGUAGE
    ASSOCIATION)   187
    Conventions of Parenthetical Documentation   187
    Punctuation and Spacing in Parenthetical Documentation   188
    Identifying Sources in Parenthetical Documentation   189
DOCUMENTING VISUALS: MAPS, CHARTS, GRAPHS,
    AND TABLES   191
USING COMMENT NOTES IN ADDITION TO PARENTHETICAL
    DOCUMENTATION   193
MLA ENDNOTE DOCUMENTATION   193
    Note Numbering System   194
    First References in Endnotes: Books   194
    First References in Endnotes: Periodicals   196
    First References in Endnotes: Other Print Sources   197
    First References in Endnotes: Nonprint Sources   199
    Subsequent References in Endnotes   200

CHAPTER 9

Preparing the Works Cited List (MLA Form)   202

WHAT TO INCLUDE   202
    Conventions to Follow   203

STANDARD FORMS FOR WORKS CITED   204
  Books   204
  Periodicals   210
  Other Print Sources   212
  Nonprint Sources   217

CHAPTER 10
Final Presentation   221

MANUSCRIPT PREPARATION AND PROOFREADING   221
TYPING/WORD PROCESSING   222
PAGE NUMBERING   223
FIRST PAGE OF THE RESEARCH PAPER TEXT (MLA)   223
OUTLINE   224
THE TEXT (MLA STYLE)   224
ILLUSTRATIVE MATERIALS: CHARTS, TABLES, GRAPHS, AND OTHER
    VISUALS   225
COMMENT NOTES   225
ENDNOTES   225
WORKS CITED   226
ANNOTATIONS   226
APPENDIX   227
OTHER OPTIONS: PREFACES, STATEMENTS OF PURPOSE, SYNOPSES,
    AND ABSTRACTS   228
FASTENING PAGES   228
SAMPLE RESEARCH PAPER IN MLA FORM   229

CHAPTER 11
APA and Other Styles   247

APA FORMAT AND PAGE NUMBERING   247
APA-FORM TITLE PAGE   248
REFERENCE CITATIONS IN TEXT   248
  Acknowledging Ideas and Short Quotations   249
CONVENTIONS OF APA IN-TEXT DOCUMENTATION   249
NOTES AND ENDNOTES   251
APPENDIXES AND OTHER MATERIALS   251
REFERENCES IN THE APA FORMAT   251
  Print Resources   254
  Nonprint Resources   255

SAMPLE RESEARCH PAPER IN APA FORM   256

OTHER RESEARCH DOCUMENTATION AND REFERENCE
    SYSTEMS   272
  Footnotes   272
  Between-Line Documentation   272
  Author-and-Date System   272
  Full In-Text Documentation   273
  Numbering Sources   273

APPENDIX A

Selected List of Reference Works Available in Libraries   275

GENERAL REFERENCE WORKS   277

SCIENCE AND TECHNOLOGY   280

SOCIAL SCIENCES   282

HUMANITIES   285

VOCATIONAL STUDIES   289

APPENDIX B

Reference Words and Abbreviations   291

Index   295

Starting the Research Paper

KINDS OF RESEARCH

"Research" is more than just something you may have done for a school assignment. You have really been doing research all your life. Before you chose a school, bought a VCR, or decided on a favorite restaurant, chances are you made a careful, serious, and systematic investigation to find information you wanted. That's what research is. Nor is all research done just to assist in decision-making. You may have done research simply because you wanted to find out something about a subject you were interested in, such as fly fishing, John Lennon, collecting pressed glass, or volleyball.

Other people do research, too. Members of the U.S. Congress gather information and make investigations before determining, for instance, whether or not to change the definition and location of designated wetlands. Many people at Disney World do a lot of research (much of it at their own on-site library) on subjects such as mechanics, robotics, electricity, and costumes as they revise or plan new entertainments there.

- **Pure research** is aimed at adding new knowledge to what people have already been able to learn, even if such knowledge doesn't seem to have any immediate or practical application. It may be research done in a laboratory or by a landing vehicle scooping up surface samples from Mars.

- **Scholarly research** usually concentrates on gathering materials in existence and looking at them in new ways or synthesizing the ideas in them. You do scholarly research when you write a paper for a course; your teachers do it when they write journal articles or prepare speeches to give at their professional organizations.

- **Applied research** is the practical application of what has already been discovered or theorized. Products ranging from hosiery to carpets to fishing line are the result of people in applied research having found ways to use nylon when it was first developed in the laboratory.

- **Technical or business research** is a form of applied research used by people who have to make such practical decisions as choosing a new location for a manufacturing plant.

- **Market research**, the study of what consumers want (or say they want), results in dozens of new products and services annually. We have snowmobiles, dog-walking services, moveable shelves in refrigerators, pizza delivery, and much more that were dictated, at least in part, by market research.

- **Academic or scholarly** research is a matter of seeking out ideas and materials already found or developed by others. In this sense, the word *research* sticks close to the meaning of the prefix and root word from which it comes: "to seek out again." But in scholarly work, the researcher must put the information together in new ways—and thus make discoveries or achieve new insights. That is what you will be doing as you use this book to write an academic research paper.

DIFFERENCES AMONG REPORTS, DOCUMENTED PAPERS, AND RESEARCH PAPERS

Call it a "term paper," a "library report," an "investigative report," a "documented paper," or a "research paper"—the names are often used interchangeably, though there are some differences among them. On the other hand, they have in common the need for you to locate information on a given subject (usually in a library and, often, from additional sources) and write conclusions based on your findings.

Perhaps in elementary or high school you did some library work or even wrote a library paper. That is, you recorded facts you discovered and then handed in the results. If you only compiled information without making evaluations or interpretations about it, you were actually preparing a **report.**

Although reports are usually from one to several pages long, they may also be book length. They are very much a part of school assignments, but they are also used so often in business, industry, and government that courses are given in business and technical report writing.

A good report must document its contents, acknowledging the sources of information from which it's compiled. Therefore, the term **documented paper** or **documented report** is often used in academe. To write such a report, you find and record information and present it *without* including your own evaluation, interpretation, or ideas. Although no truly unbiased work is possible, in a documented paper you should try to present the results of your research in as "objective" a manner as you can. In order to do so, you must take notes meticulously, ascribe sources accurately, and be sure summaries and paraphrases are thorough.

Several kinds of documented papers are possible. You might *trace* the history of something, such as how windsurfing came to be accepted as an Olympic sport. Or you could *explain* a notion, such as flexible working times, perhaps illustrating the explanation with examples of how this concept has been implemented in various businesses or industries. You might make *comparisons and contrasts*, such as how the Japanese film *Seven Samurai* found new life in the United States as *The Magnificent Seven*. Or you might *examine* and report on a single feature, such as how robots are being used for difficult or dangerous jobs in the auto industry.

A **research paper** differs from a report or a documented paper in one major way: you are expected to evaluate or interpret or in some other way add to and participate in the information you gather and write about. In a research paper, you are expected to *develop a point of view toward your material, take a stand, express some original thought.*

You can do that by first narrowing down a general area and then deciding on a specific approach to take in searching for information. Later, after you have interpreted your findings or evaluated your information, that approach will be reflected in the thesis or underlying idea of your research paper. So, although you might start with an interest in sea mammals, you could focus on examining how tuna fishing nets trap and kill them. After sufficient research, you could conclude that you either were or were not persuaded by evidence you were able to find and that dolphin and other sea mammals are no longer being entrapped or that the practice has not really been discontinued. You would then incorporate your view into the thesis, and thus write your paper accordingly.

WHAT A RESEARCH PAPER *IS*

A research paper, as the term is used in this book, is an entirely new work, one you create, one that can only be found on the pages you write. It will, therefore, have a number of qualities that reflect *you*, and make it your own special creation.

1. The research paper synthesizes your discoveries about a topic and your judgment, interpretation, and evaluation of those discoveries.

Your discoveries will be mostly the ideas, knowledge, and actual words of people who have written, spoken, or made pictures about the subject you investigated. They are likely to come from both print and nonprint sources. But the special value of all that collected material is that *you weighed your discoveries and drew conclusions from them.* Your involvement will be evident because the entire research paper reflects your own ideas as much as those of anyone else who has worked on the subject.

Selecting information to use is a personal process. Deciding how to approach this information, developing a point of view toward it, and, finally, choosing your own words to present it persuasively are all highly personal activities. Therefore, the more you involve yourself in these activities, the more the resulting research paper will be your own!

2. The research paper is a work that shows your originality.

The paper resulting from your study, evaluation, and synthesis will be a totally new creation, one *you* originate. True, you will have put many hours of thought and much effort into a work that takes only a short time to read. But that is the nature of any creative endeavor. It's a real art to make the difficult appear easy, not to let an audience be aware of preparation and practice. What you read most easily is often a result of the most work. In a carefully crafted research paper, your own hand and thought—your originality—are evident.

3. The research paper acknowledges all sources you have used.

Both the words and the ideas (as well as any visuals) of others need to be documented and acknowledged. In fact, doing so is basic to research writing, and a whole series of customs or conventions has developed for crediting what you borrow from other people. You begin such acknowledgment when you start taking notes (see Chapter 5, pages 100–28). Chapter 8 explains these customs and shows you how to document your own work.

Ethical standards also demand that you acknowledge the sources that contributed to your work. Just as you develop or find information and make it available to others in your writing (or orally or on film), others have done the same for what became your sources. So, although your research paper is a new and original work, none of it would have been possible without the various sources you consulted to prepare it. Acknowledging that debt to others is only right and fair!

4. The research paper shows that you are part of a community of scholars.

Other people will acknowledge what you have done when you complete a research paper. In an academic setting, where your paper is going to be read by other students and by one or more teachers, the paper demonstrates your ability to be counted as one of a community that values research and original thought. Being part of such a group will bring you much satisfaction.

WHAT A RESEARCH PAPER *IS NOT*

If you accept the definition of a research paper that underlies this book—that it is a synthesis of your thought applied to material supplied to you by others, that it is original, and that it acknowledges source material—you will never make the mistake of attempting to hand in what is certainly *not* a research paper.

1. A summary of an article or a book (or other source material) is NOT a research paper.

A summary can't fit our definition of a research paper for two reasons: (1) a single source doesn't allow you to select materials or to exercise your own judgment, and (2) the organization can't be your own because a summary must follow the structure of the original source.

Summaries of written, visual, or audio materials have their uses—and they are important ones—but substituting for a research paper is not one of them.

2. The ideas of others, repeated uncritically, do NOT make a research paper.

By definition, the research paper has to reflect something about yourself—a synthesis, an interpretation, or some other personal involvement. To repeat, uncritically, what others have said is merely to report information already available elsewhere. For example, no amount of reading *about* a novel can substitute for reading the work yourself, any more than reading about a musical group can substitute for hearing the musicians perform.

3. A series of quotations, no matter how skillfully put together, does NOT make a research paper.

Quotations have an important place in a research paper, whether they are the words of experts in the field you are investigating or of those who are experts with words. But if your paper is nothing more than a series of quotations of other people's words, the "you" of the synthesis is missing. You yourself are not really involved in such a paper, nor does such a work give any evidence of your originality.

Moreover, quotations are likely to reflect the individual styles of their authors, so to organize dozens of quotations from different people into a coherent whole is almost impossible.

4. Unsubstantiated personal opinion does NOT constitute a research paper.

Although you are expected to inject some personal thinking into any research paper you write, you must have reasons for your beliefs and make them evident to readers. So, although individual thoughts and attitudes are valuable in certain kinds of writing assignments, the research paper is not usually one of them— unless you can support those ideas and attitudes. For one thing, the "search" aspect would be lacking. For another, a good research paper topic doesn't lend itself to opinions without extensive and factual bases.

5. Copying or accepting another person's work without acknowledging it, whether the work is published or unpublished, professional or amateur, is NOT research. IT IS PLAGIARISM.

It is morally wrong to pass off as your own any writing you didn't do. To present such work without acknowledging the source—and therefore to let someone assume it is yours when, in fact, it is not—is plagiarism. (See more about plagiarism on pages 100–06.) Turning in as your own a research paper done by someone else is indefensible, whether you accepted it from a friend trying to help you out or bought it from a company that supplies research papers to those assigned to write them in schools. There are laws against plagiarism, and in many schools any student involved in plagiarism (including the supplier of such a paper) is automatically dismissed.

On the most literal level, perhaps no word or thought is completely original; you learned it somewhere. Often only the finest line of distinction separates what must be credited in a research paper from what you can safely present without documentation. What requires crediting or documentation to avoid plagiarism and what doesn't is discussed on pages 100–07 and 114.

Showing that you can base your work on that of others is one mark of an educated person. But, obviously, presenting such materials as your own is not! Students who respect themselves and their work will certainly not be tempted to copy from anyone. Instead, they will always extend proper credit to others for ideas, as well as for specific wording.

LENGTH OF RESEARCH PAPERS

Length has nothing to do with whether a piece of work is a report or a research paper. Approach makes the difference. Writing ten pages on the differences between a Cessna 172 and a Cessna 182 would be a report; writing ten pages about why Cessna should start manufacturing the 172 again would be a research paper.

The length of a research paper may be any of the following:

- specified in advance by an assignment
- related to an instructor's expectations for course work
- determined by the complexity of the material
- governed by a student's willingness to work
- controlled by the time a student has available.

Most undergraduate college-level research papers are expected to be from 1,500 to 3,000 words (that is, six to twelve double-spaced, typewritten or word-processed pages). This book is written on the assumption that you will be working on a research paper of that length.

FIVE STEPS TO A RESEARCH PAPER

Research papers are as likely to be assigned in nursing, forestry, or accounting as they are in English, history, anthropology, or economics. Whatever the school course or subject of the paper, your **goals** will be the same:

- to learn from a study you undertake
- to present your material competently
- and to earn as high a grade (and as much personal satisfaction) as possible.

You can achieve these goals most readily if you **follow an orderly procedure from the time the paper is assigned until you turn it in.** Instead of looking for shortcuts (which often turn out to make your work more difficult), concentrate on doing each of the following steps carefully and completely. Some parts of this process may seem difficult or tedious at first, but don't worry. You'll find them easier as they become more familiar. And if some of these instructions sound unnecessary at first, remember that many people have found them the best of several possibilities.

The completed research paper, whatever its length or its subject, will be the result of your having taken only five steps.

Step 1. Choosing the Subject

Choose the right subject and you have a good chance of producing a good (or excellent) paper. Choose the wrong subject and you probably *can't* write a good research paper. This step is so important and basic to everything else you do that Chapters 2 and 3 are devoted to helping you with this task.

If you have the option of choosing your own subject, remember that specific subjects make better papers than very broad ones. "The Importance of Economics" is a title that, if descriptive, could be everything or nothing. Focusing on the economic impact of alternative manufacturing possibilities for armaments in the former Soviet Union is more specific and therefore likely to make a better research paper.

Step 2. Collecting Information

You might do most of Step 1 at your desk, but for Step 2 you need to get outside your usual study area. Your first stop will probably be a library, where you will find relevant (or not-so-relevant) materials. But plan on going *beyond* this limited research source. Query people. For instance, you might interview the manager of a shopping mall if you were writing about how architecture affects people's lives. Also, think of videotapes and videodiscs, films, the radio, computer programs, and your television set as valuable sources for information.

To complete this second step of a research paper, you will

a.   find varied sources of relevant information

b.   read, look at, and listen to what the sources contain

c.   keep a record (that is, write notes) about what you learn.

You may already have some knowledge of your chosen subject and can certainly incorporate that into your paper. But you will undoubtedly have to seek out specifically most of what you eventually want to include in any research paper you do. Chapters 4 and 5 will help you in this second step, the one in which you will be concerned mostly with the *search* part of *research*.

Step 3. Evaluating Materials

A good research paper reflects a critical attitude toward the information you collect. Evaluating information—that is, judging and weighing the usefulness of the material you've collected and determining its relevance to your subject— takes place as you formulate your own ideas about your investigation and develop an approach toward what you've been learning.

Not every piece of information you collect is equally important. As the paper begins to take shape in your mind, you may even realize that some of your notes are no longer relevant. Or you may change your outlook about an author's veracity and find that you need to do a little more research. Chapter 5 will give you some help in this step. However, be aware that much of this evaluation takes place as you work with your subject, take notes, and aim toward the next step.

Step 4. Organizing Ideas

A collection of facts, quotations, summaries, and ideas can be either meaningless or purposeful. Just as a collection of musical notes can be either random noise or a top-selling record, the work of the previous three steps can be either a hodgepodge or the foundation of a successful research paper. The difference depends on how well you put together the materials at hand.

If what you collected and evaluated is coordinated and arranged to lead logically to a conclusion, if it all makes a point that is well supported, you will have a good research paper. Therefore, putting your notes together in an organized way, such as an outline, before you begin writing the paper is crucial. Chapter 6 will help you organize material so you can begin writing.

Step 5. Writing the Paper

In this step you finally put down on paper what you have learned and what you believe about the subject of your research paper. Writing will be easier if you have carefully and thoughtfully completed all the preparatory work of the previous four steps than if you try to plunge into it without really being ready. That's not to say you won't rewrite, perhaps change the organization in some way, or decide to eliminate some ideas you planned to include. Such is the nature of writing, as you have undoubtedly learned through experience and in school courses. Many of the elements of writing noted next will seem to happen simultaneously. (That is, you may revise as you draft or even as you proofread.)

Draft a copy of your research paper as the starting point for this step. Follow your outline or other organizing guide and the aids in Chapter 7 to write out your paper. If you can use a word processing program on a computer, you'll find it most helpful to do so because it permits changes easily.

Document your paper as you draft, and be sure to keep the documentation straight as you revise. If you are following the MLA (Modern Language Association) style, as emphasized throughout this book and explained in Chapter 8, such documentation will be parenthetical and thus easy to incorporate into this early writing stage. When you finish the paper, you can prepare the list of Works Cited, as explained in Chapter 9. See Chapter 11 for APA forms.

Revise what you have written. Take a hard look at what you've said and how you've presented it. If you decide that some idea works better in a different place from where you originally put it, move it. See if you can get a better flow of thought by changing some text. (With a computer, you can move a block of text, then send it back to its original location if you don't think it works better.) Even if you're not using a word processor, be willing to make changes in what you've written. Cut and paste sections of the draft if you want to try out rearrangements.

Research on how people write has shown that most writers do some revising as they draft; confident ones may make many changes as they write. If you are *really* revising and not just prettying up punctuation and spelling, you will want to allow plenty of time to do so. Don't ignore revision because the paper is due tomorrow. Do proceed only if you're satisfied that you have said everything you want to say in the most effective way you can devise.

Edit your writing for spelling, punctuation, capitalization, and adherence to required research paper forms during the last stage of revision and before you prepare the final copy of your work in the presentation form recommended in Chapter 10. Grammar checkers and spell checkers available on many computers (and part of many word processing programs) are an invaluable help and great time saver. But remember not to depend on them blindly; even the best of them can't know the context of what you've written and certainly not what you intended.

WHY A RESEARCH PAPER IS IMPORTANT

All the skills you have just been reading about in this sketch of the research paper process—making decisions about a subject, developing an inquiring attitude, gathering information, examining it critically, thinking creatively, organizing effectively, and writing convincingly—are crucial to academic success. Learn these skills now, in preparing a research paper, and you will find yourself using them again and again in many ways and in different circumstances, both in and outside of school.

Air conditioning specialists, flight engineers, fashion designers, and nurses use these skills daily and follow this same process. So do business people, in such tasks as deciding about promoting workers or buying new merchandise. Attorneys use the same sequence of skills, whether they are preparing a murder case for courtroom trial or incorporating a new business.

Teachers don't assign research papers capriciously. Several reasons, in addition to sharpening the skills noted, commend the research paper as a popular and valuable assignment.

1. **Many kinds of writing**—from essay tests to investment brochures—require you to gather and process factual information on a specific subject, just as the research paper does. Though you may not be interested in becoming a published writer, you may well need to follow this process in writing at a future job.

2. **You will probably become a better reader** of nonfiction articles, instruction manuals, and books when you know the process by which they were developed. Most particularly, the more experience you have in understanding how ideas are organized (as you organize ideas when you write a research paper), the easier it is to see and evaluate how other people have presented their thoughts and information. Besides, understanding main ideas with their support is a key to effective reading.

3. **You will have a sense of achievement** when you work *independently* to follow through on a task and fulfill a goal—as you do in completing a research paper. You will also take satisfaction in knowing that you've done a job to the best of your ability, that you've written something well, and that you're well informed on a specific subject. Students often say that accomplishing a task they felt shaky about undertaking was particularly important to them. And not the least of personal satisfactions, of course, is having your efforts rewarded by a high grade on the assignment.

4. **You have a chance to find out about a subject** you wanted to know about or think you may be interested in. Or you may use the research paper assignment to look at something related to a course you'd like to take but have no

time to schedule. Some people who have a free choice of subjects for the re-search paper assignment use the chance to investigate something that may have a practical purpose related to their job.

5. **You learn how to use the facilities of your school and resources in the community** to support your work. Certainly, you gain confidence using the library when you do a research paper.

6. **You establish yourself as an individual**, even in a very large class, when an instructor reads your paper. Then, the teacher's concentration is entirely on you and your work.

7. **You exercise** *critical thinking* when you follow through the process of preparing a research paper. So many elements enter into critical thinking—the abilities to weigh words, to discriminate among ideas, to separate fact from opinion or assumption, to find and select relevant materials, to draw conclusions, to synthesize results—that many people believe the skill describes the characteristics of critical thinking and, indeed, of *all* education. So completing a research paper is practice in developing that form of judgment called critical thinking and is, perhaps, the most important, most desirable goal of education.

WHO READS RESEARCH PAPERS—AND WHY

Before you begin work on your research paper, you should know your audience—Who is going to read it? Will it be just the instructor for whose class you are writing the paper? Will other students in the class be reading it? Will you want to show it to your visiting relatives? Smart writers know in advance for whom they are writing so they can **choose a subject of interest to the reader** and **write in a way that will get their information to the reader.**

Although you will certainly need to choose a subject that interests you enough to work with, you will also want your prospective audience to be interested in what *you* have to say. Be less concerned that the reader is interested initially in the subject you choose than with choosing the right subject for yourself. Good work on the paper and thoughtful writing will make your work interesting reading. If you care about your topic and what you write about it, the audience probably will too.

Many research papers are read only by the student's instructor, the person who assigned the work. If that is the case for you, you can assume the instructor has an interest in a topic related to the field of study for which the paper was assigned. But if you have a free choice of topics, consider whether the instructor will want to read a paper on, for instance, ballet or auto racing. Don't make the mistake of assuming lack of interest on any topic. You might learn of an instructor's interests by examples and remarks made in class. Or you might ask outright about topic preferences by suggesting two or three possibilities for you to work on. Most teachers, however, will be glad to read about any topic, provided that the research paper is done well!

If classmates will be working with you during the research paper process, you will probably have a chance to discuss your proposed subject choices with them. You may also have the chance to help each other with drafts of your works in progress. Or you may be asked to make an oral presentation for classmates based on your research paper. Knowing your audience will help you choose a subject of interest to them. It will also let you know what level of vocabulary and sentence complexity to use.

You may also write a research paper for a family member or an employer. Fix a specific picture of that audience in your mind—not only face or physical appearance but also that reader's concerns, interests, education, language preferences or customs, usual type of reading—anything that can help you focus on the individual. Keep that person in mind all through the various steps of the research process.

Finally, think about *why* you are going to write this research paper. For a grade, of course. But future teachers, friends, or people who give scholarships for schools or organizations may also want to read your paper—or an abstract of it. Some students have found that a paper written in one course and subsequently shown to the instructor of another course served as the basis for further study or a springboard to new ideas and perspectives. You may even decide that you want to write a research paper for yourself because you want to learn something in particular!

KEEPING A PROCESS LOG

In preparing and writing a research paper, you follow the process of the five steps you read about earlier in this chapter. So it's easy to keep a **Process Log**, a **record of what you do starting now and ending with the completed research paper.**

A *log* is a record of what happened and when. The Process Log you will keep now, however, should include a bit more. Write in it, also, some brief, personal comments as you record more mundane matters. Even though entries are brief, one look at the Process Log will show you (and your instructor) what you have accomplished and where you are in the research process. When your research paper is finished, you will also have a memento of your work—something on which you can look back proudly!

Here are some kinds of entries you can put in your Process Log:

- **Thinking time**   This is really working time, because you need to think before you can work and certainly *while* you are working.

- **Study time**   Be sure you record the time you spend reading assignments in this book, for it certainly contributes to helping you with the process of writing a research paper. If you give a brief summary of what you accomplished during each study period, it will also be a memory aid.

- **Reminders to yourself**   Use the Process Log to note a follow-up you want to make or a source you want to check so that you can relate the information to what you have already done.

- **Difficulties you encounter**   No sustained work is without its difficulties or problems. The Process Log is not meant to be a record only of sweetness and light. If you have difficulty with any aspect of your work, such as all the books on your subject being out of the library or a periodical microfilm you needed being damaged and therefore difficult to read, record it in your Process Log.

- **Solutions to problems**   Don't be afraid to blow your own horn. If you solve a problem, write about it in your Process Log!

Begin keeping your Process Log **now**. The form is simple. Use the following examples. (You'll also find the Process Log format repeated on the inside back cover.

Date	Time	Entry
Write the date of the entry.	Record the time you began **and** ended what you did.	Tell what you did that was part of the research paper process. Be detailed and specific.

Some instructors will ask that you use complete sentences in your Process Log as additional practice in conventional writing. Others will be satisfied with phrases or sentence fragments. Be sure to check with your instructor to be certain about expectations.

Copy the format into a notebook, repeating it as you need additional pages. Or make a master page on a computer program from which you can print additional pages. Another convenient alternative is to make a master page and photocopy it as needed.

The following sample is from the actual Process Log kept by the student author of the MLA-style sample research paper in Chapter 10 (pages 230–46). It illustrates the sort of entries you can put in your own Process Log.

Date	Time	Entry
Jan. 18	10:30 a.m. to 12:15 p.m.	Went to the main library downtown hoping to find the biggest selection of books on environmental activism. I had a stack chosen and then discovered they were all from the reference section. Only a few were from "available" stacks. I was really ticked off at myself for not paying attention in an unfamiliar library and wasting so much time. I took notes from some of the books but then had to leave.
Jan. 23	2–2:30 p.m.	Spoke with Twilly Cannon from Greenpeace and got a quote I think I can use as a running theme.
Jan. 28	—	Finally finished reading _Silent Spring_ after all these years of hearing that it was the "catalyst of the environmental movement." I understand why now. It's explanatory and technical but in layperson's terms. I read the whole book in one sitting and took 4 pages of notes. I probably won't even use it now, but I learned a lot! She wasn't radical at all—no activist tips—she was just a scientist stating facts.
Jan. 29	10–10:20 a.m.	Tried InfoTrac in the library again. The printout will be useful when I have time to get back to the school library and look for the periodicals. It's a lot easier than writing all these Preliminary Bibliography cards by hand!

MANAGING YOUR TIME

Make your Process Log an ongoing activity. Get in the habit of writing in it whenever you do anything related to your research paper. If you wait to record one entry, you're likely to wait to record another—and another. Then you will fall so far behind it'll be difficult and time-consuming to reconstruct your activities and to pinpoint times. It's far easier, and much more productive, to make short notes as you work.

Use the **Timetable and Checklist for Preparing Your Research Paper** at the very beginning of this book to keep you on track and on time during the research process. If your instructor doesn't give you due dates for the various steps that are listed on the front pages, set your own schedule. And stick to it!

Don't procrastinate.   Work that is put off is often work never done. Or it is done sloppily and hastily. Instead of delaying what you need to do, get the work done on time—and then maybe take a break or give yourself a reward.

Realize that you will need concentrated time, even after you have all the notes you want, for thinking through organization. Most of all, you can't put off drafting and redrafting until the last minute; they take a lot of time to do successfully.

Choose a set working place and time. If you don't feel like working on a research paper after football practice or when you get home after your job, give yourself another working time. If you work better at night than in the early morning, take that into account. Just make it regular. Also, pick the place where you work best. If the library is too noisy to suit you, set your working place somewhere else.

Discipline yourself.   Most students have several courses to prepare for in a term; the course for which you are writing the research probably isn't your only one. Or you have a job or a family that takes up a lot of your out-of-school hours. You have to find the time to fit the steps of the research process into your schedule—and then make yourself do them.

Try to work regularly rather than sporadically. All-night, last-minute rush sessions don't work for most people, especially not if they want to produce a research paper they can be proud of! Rather than two six-hour sessions, rearrange your time to allow six two-hour sessions. Aim at building your research paper activities into your schedule regularly and unspectacularly; you will find that you can then do them more effectively!

Choosing a General Topic

THE TERMS "TOPIC" AND "SUBJECT"

A good topic is the beginning of a good research paper. So the rest of this chapter is about selecting a topic you can research. Chapter 3 then shows you how to narrow a topic into a subject suitable for a research paper. **In this book, the word *topic* refers to a broad range or general field of interest. The word *subject* indicates the part of a topic that is narrow enough to investigate and write about.**

EXAMPLE

"Literature" is a *topic*

"This week's best-seller fiction" is a *subject*

The subject is derived by narrowing the topic. It is still in a general stage, however, because the author has only decided on what to investigate and not yet determined an approach; nor, without reading on the subject can the author write a thesis statement.

Most research papers are assigned at the beginning of a school term and are due shortly before the term ends. Therefore, you should decide on a topic as soon as possible so you will have plenty of time to gather information, mull over ideas, write your paper, and revise it several times before turning it in. If you start when you get the assignment and don't procrastinate, you will be able to do a good job. (If you have interim due dates for various parts of the process, write them on **The Timetable and Checklist for Preparing Your Research Paper** at the very beginning of this book. If your instructor doesn't give you such dates, set them for yourself.)

When you do get the assignment to write a research paper, it will be one of three kinds:

1. **Assigned Topics** are selected by an instructor and presented to you. Often these appear as an actual list of writing subjects to choose from.

2. **Field-of-Study Topics** are those that you select, but your assignment stipulates that the topic must relate in a specific way to the course for which the research paper is assigned.

3. **Free-Choice Topics** give you broad rein to investigate any area you choose.

Sometimes topic and subject selections seem to telescope so the two processes meld into one. But in the explanations that follow later in this chapter and in the next, they are considered separately. First, before you consider the topic itself, you ought to have some notions of what will work as a research paper topic and what to avoid.

QUALITIES OF A GOOD TOPIC

Because a good topic choice sets you on the right track for a good research paper, it ought to meet the following eight qualifications:

1. The topic will enable you to fulfill the assignment.

Be sure that what you propose will do what you've been asked to do. Can you find enough information to meet the specified length? If you are choosing a Field-of-Study Topic, is it really related to the course for which you are writing it? If your instructor will deal with the topic in class, how will your research supplement what is included in the course?

If you aren't sure about a topic choice, check with your instructor, even if such approval isn't required.

2. The topic interests you enough to work on it.

You commit yourself to a lot of time and energy when you start a research paper. If you don't think you are sufficiently interested in a topic or don't feel committed to it, don't even start on it—choose another one!

3. The topic will teach you something.

A research paper isn't busywork. You should be able to learn something new from the topic you are investigating. If you don't think you will learn, choose another topic.

4. The topic is of manageable scope.

Narrowing an initial topic choice is the ultimate key to manageability. Even at the first stages, a research paper isn't the only demand on your time, so you can (and *should*) impose your own limitations on it. Remember, however, that although the topic you choose will be broad, you have the step of limiting it because you still have to select the subject to investigate.

5. You can bring something to the topic.

You have already read (on page 3) that a research paper "synthesizes your discoveries about a topic and your judgment, interpretation, and evaluation of those discoveries." That is, you put something of yourself and your ideas into the research paper, together with the material you discover. A good topic *lets* you do that.

6. Enough information on the topic is available to you.

Much of the information for your research paper will probably come from a library. So if you haven't looked through a library carefully, you should go there now and ascertain that there will be enough information available on the topic you are thinking about selecting for your research paper.

If you choose a topic recently in the news and are required to use both books and periodicals as reference sources, you may have to change the proposed topic because no book on it is yet available. There is an informational time lag. Although weekly periodicals are timely, the editors of less frequently published journals and magazines (which are often monthly or quarterly) usually select the contents many months in advance. Books take even longer—a year from submission is not unusual of a completed manuscript to its publication. Therefore, while books may supply the background for current newsworthy topics, their usefulness may be limited. Or there may be nothing available in any book on a very current topic.

Be aware that libraries select their purchases to serve a particular constituency. A community library will tend to have holdings that reflect the interests of its users and therefore general, rather than scholarly, sources. You may have to change libraries or change topics.

7. The topic is suitable for your audience.

Because you are writing this research paper for one or more readers, knowledge of that audience's reading ability, concerns, age, educational background, and known leanings or beliefs should enter into your decision about the suitability of a topic. For instance, if you propose writing on a specialized technical topic, a teacher will understand material that beginning students in the field (should they be your designated audience) could not cope with.

8. The topic lets you demonstrate all your abilities that a research paper is meant to show.

A topic too broad, too restrictive, too mundane, or too esoteric might not let you show off the extent of your ability to develop ideas, find information, evaluate and organize it, make reasoned judgments, present them convincingly, and support your statements. Be sure that the topic you decide to research will let you demonstrate all these skills.

TOPICS TO AVOID

To avoid wasting your time and effort, you should know that certain kinds of topics are unsuitable for research papers. The following eleven items (some of which are the obverse of the *good* qualities you read about on pages 15–16) is a guide to help you avoid potential problems when choosing your own Field-of-Study or Free-Choice Topic.

1. Do not choose a topic for which a single source will provide all the information you need.

You can develop an individual viewpoint, use investigative skills, evaluate materials, and organize your findings in an original way *only* if you consult several sources for information. In short, you can follow the procedures for scholarly research only if you read and study widely.

2. Do not reuse a paper you have written for another instructor.

Repetition doesn't produce new learning. Besides, to pretend you have done new work when, in fact, you have not is dishonest.

However, some instructors are willing to let you *continue* studying something you have already investigated, provided the topic warrants further research. Or they will let you examine another aspect of a topic about which you have already written a paper. Neither of these situations is the same as handing in to an instructor a paper you've already presented to someone else. Should you want to use a previously submitted research paper as the *basis* for a new one, discussing the matter frankly with your present instructor is the safest way to proceed.

3. Do not choose a topic on which you do not plan to do all the work yourself.

If anyone else does the research or any of the writing on this assignment, the work is not your own and is, therefore, not acceptable. Using material of any sort from someone else without proper and adequate acknowledgment is **plagiarism!**

4. Do not choose a topic that is too broad for a research paper.

Any topic that is the title of a book or a subject in a card catalog may be a starting place, but it is not a stopping place; you must go on to the second step, which is narrowing. After all, if a published writer needs a whole book to deal with a topic, you surely can't say much of substance about it in ten or fifteen pages.

5. Do not choose a topic about which your conclusions will be irrelevant.

A paper on how Ford should have designed the Edsel (an automobile Ford manufactured only briefly in the 1950s) is not fruitful because it doesn't matter now. Shift your thinking. If the Edsel is really a love of your life, another sort of investigation about the car might have some value. Or the subject might be relevant to special kinds of design or marketing courses or to collecting particular makes of autos.

6. Do not start work on any topic unless you think it will hold your interest long enough to complete the paper.

Research is a difficult enough assignment in itself. If you have to fight boredom with your own topic along the way, it becomes impossible.

7. Be wary of choosing a topic so neutral that you cannot express an attitude toward it.

Unless you plan a documented report, not a research paper, you will need to express some views or opinions about your material. For instance, many teachers discourage biographical papers because, unless the author has produced a work of art or an invention, initiated a business practice, or done something else for which you can get first-hand (that is, primary source information, as explained on page 55), a biography easily becomes just a compilation of what others have written.

8. Do not pursue a topic that seems to go nowhere for you.

If you have trouble narrowing a topic to a manageable subject or finding an approach (both are explained in the next chapter), perhaps that topic will prove unproductive for you. For example, if "Rotary Engines" is a topic you are determined to research but you flounder and can't seem to make progress beyond that decision, ask your instructor for help. Or drop the topic and go on to something you can work with. Another person might be able to narrow that topic and make it workable; but if you can't, you are better off making a complete change and starting something more productive.

9. Consider avoiding a topic that has been particularly popular among students.

Unless you can give a unique slant to the study or you have a special interest in pursuing such a topic, your teachers (and others who make up the audience) may be just plain bored reading yet another paper on abortion or drugs or other overexamined topics. Check with your instructor if in doubt about the advisability of researching a particular topic. Or ask a research librarian; that person receives requests for help constantly and thus knows what topics many other students have been working on.

10. Consider avoiding a highly controversial or emotional topic unless you think you can bring something new and special to it.

You may find that time and length limitations on the research paper won't let you find or present sufficient material to cover adequately a controversial topic, such as revising the federal tax structure. Similarly, avoid choosing a topic to which you have a deep emotional commitment, such as a particular religious belief, because you might not be able to be sufficiently objective or critical toward it to produce a good research paper. If you have any doubts about the advisability of working on a topic, discuss the matter with your instructor.

11. Do not choose a topic unsuited to your audience.

Some topics may offend the sensibilities of the instructor or other readers. For example, reading about various ways to investigate gory murders may not be the way your audience wants to spend its time. Writing for an audience means that you conform in some way to that audience's expectations or interests. So no matter how clever or sensational you think a topic is, don't hesitate to abandon it—or change the way you plan to treat it—if you suspect the topic might not suit your intended audience.

ASSIGNED TOPICS

An Assigned Topic is not stifling, and you should not view it as limiting. Rather, consider that it makes your beginning work easier yet provides you with many opportunities for personal expression. You will still have plenty of leeway to develop a project that depends heavily on what *you* discover and what *you* have to say on a subject.

Often an "Assigned Topic" is really a subject—an idea that has already been narrowed and is ready for investigation. Examples of such topics (or subjects) are the mathematical contributions of Leibniz or lie detector tests as a prerequisite for employment.

FIELD-OF-STUDY TOPICS

If the broad field for which you have to write a research paper is familiar to you, finding a topic to write about will be easier than if the field is entirely new. Even if the field *is* unfamiliar, you can cope if you use one or more of these methods.

1. **Take stock of what you already know.**
2. **Use printed aids to help you:**
   your textbook
   other course materials
   encyclopedias
   the library or online catalog
   periodical indexes.
3. **Build from your own interests.**

Each of these three methods of finding a topic (including the examples of printed aids) is explained in the following sections.

1. Take Stock of What You Already Know

If you have taken a course prerequisite to the one for which you have to write this research paper, you already know something about this field of study. If the field is new to you, think about what the instructor has said in giving you an overview of the course. Maybe you know something about the field from talking with friends about the class or the field. You can use all that prior knowledge as a starting place.

List some of the broad categories of information in this field of study that you already know. Suppose you have to work within anthropology. If you already know that archaeology is a branch of anthropology or that one unit in the course is about cultural anthropology, you have a good beginning.

Or write down some of the information that particularly interested you in a prerequisite course. Don't worry about organizing what you write and don't worry about spelling and punctuation; just get the ideas down on paper. By doing so, you use one method of taking stock of what you already know, and you will get a start at choosing a Field-of-Study Topic about which to write your research paper.

2. Make Use of Printed Aids to Help

Using Your Textbook

Your class textbook is a most convenient place to begin looking for a Field-of-Study Topic for your research paper. Use the many parts of a text for this help in finding a topic.

The table of contents will tell you a lot about the course and give you an overview of the field, even if you won't be studying the entire text in one term. Look over the contents, keeping alert for ideas that might interest you. Circle those you think might be interesting to pursue. Figure 1 shows the Brief Contents page of *Environmental Science*, 3rd ed., by G. Tyler Miller, Jr. (Belmont: Wadsworth, 1991), with Chapter 11, "Water Resources and Water Pollution," circled as a possible topic. Since something as broad as that is hard to work with, you should consult a more detailed listing of chapter content (which is bound to follow such a generalized listing). Figure 2 shows the specific content of Chapter 11, with headings circled that might be topics to investigate. A student might well be interested in finding out more about "Water Resource Management" or "Ocean Pollution."

The index of a textbook gives specific page locations of key ideas in a book. If you see a topic of interest listed in the index, circle it for possible Field-of-Study research, as Figure 3 shows for the index of the same text, *Environmental Science*, 3rd ed. (In some textbooks you may find that the Index is combined with the Glossary.)

A glossary lists and defines key terms used in a book. From the words listed (as in Figure 4, page 24) you can get a great deal of information about what's important in a course, even before you take it, so you can get a head start on your research paper by selecting one such term.

The bibliography of a textbook is another place to look. You may find in this listing of resources an author has used or recommends some title of a book or periodical article intriguing enough to encourage you to look into that particular subject. Some books have lists often called "Further Reading" at the ends of chapters; they can help as any other bibliography might.

BRIEF CONTENTS

PART ONE
HUMANS AND NATURE: AN OVERVIEW 1
Chapter 1
Population, Resources, Environmental
Degradation, and Pollution 2
Chapter 2
Cultural Changes, Worldviews, Ethics,
and Environment 21

PART TWO
BASIC CONCEPTS 35
Chapter 3
Matter and Energy Resources:
Types and Concepts 36
Chapter 4
Ecosystems: What Are They and How Do They
Work? 59
Chapter 5
Ecosystems: What Are the Major Types
and What Can Happen to Them? 86
Chapter 6
Human Population Dynamics: Growth,
Urbanization, and Regulation 115
Chapter 7
Environmental Economics and Politics 147
Chapter 8
Hazards, Risk, and Human Health 170

PART THREE
AIR, WATER, AND SOIL RESOURCES 185
Chapter 9
Air Resources and Air Pollution 186
Chapter 10
Climate, Global Warming, Ozone Depletion,
and Nuclear War: Ultimate Problems 209
Chapter 11
Water Resources and Water Pollution 232
Chapter 12
Soil Resources and Hazardous Waste 266

PART FOUR
LIVING RESOURCES 293
Chapter 13
Food Resources 294
Chapter 14
Protecting Food Resources: Pesticides
and Pest Control 313
Chapter 15
Land Resources: Forests, Rangelands, Parks,
and Wilderness 329
Chapter 16
Wild Plant and Animal Resources 354

PART FIVE
ENERGY AND MINERAL RESOURCES 377
Chapter 17
Perpetual and Renewable Energy Resources 378
Chapter 18
Nonrenewable Energy Resources 408
Chapter 19
Nonrenewable Mineral Resources
and Solid Waste 441
Epilogue
Achieving a Sustainable-Earth Society 463
Appendixes A1
Glossary A4
Index A16

Fig. 1. A brief table of contents page.
Source: G. Tyler Miller, Jr., *Environmental Science*, 3rd ed. (Belmont: Wadsworth, 1991) xii.
Reprinted by permission of the publisher.

Chapter 11
Water Resources and Water Pollution   232

11-1 Supply, Renewal, and Use of Water
       Resources   232
11-2 Water Resource Problems   236
11-3 Water Resource Management   240
11-4 Major Forms of Water Pollution   248
11-5 Pollution of Streams and Lakes   249
11-6 Ocean Pollution   251
11-7 Groundwater Pollution and Its Control   254
11-8 Controlling Surface Water Pollution   256

Fig. 2. A detail of a table of contents.
Source: G. Tyler Miller, Jr., *Environmental Science*, 3rd ed. (Belmont: Wadsworth, 1991) xv.
Reprinted by permission of the publisher.

The preface or *introduction* of a textbook is more than just a summary of contents; it is usually the author's way of leading you into the subject of the course or book. Read it and you may be able to use some of the ideas it contains to suggest a topic for research.

Appendices may also be helpful to you in finding a topic. In *Environmental Science*, 3rd ed., one appendix lists "Publications, Environmental Organizations, and Federal and International Agencies." Another lists "Major U.S. Resource Conservation and Environmental Legislation."

Authors included in an anthology may suggest people whose work bears investigation for a Field-of-Study Topic.

Using Course Materials

Some courses are taught from several books that are either assigned or recommended rather than from a single book. Or you may receive a suggested reading list. You can use any of these sources in the same way you can use your textbook to help you choose a broad Field-of-Study Topic.

If you are given a course syllabus (whether or not the course has a textbook), look through it, also, at the beginning of the term and draw information from it about what the course will cover. Use the syllabus as an additional start in deciding on a topic for your research paper.

Air pollution, 18
    acid deposition (*see* Acid deposition)
    controlling, 200–207
    effects of, on human health, 197–99, 207
    effects of, on living organisms and materials, 197–200, *201*
    emissions of, in U.S., *189*
    fossil fuels and, 1ء1, 189–97, 411, 414, 418
    individual's role in reducing, 206
    indoor, 189, 190–91 *192*
    in Mexico City, *129*
    outdoor, 188–89
    primary/secondary, *188*
    protecting forests from, 345
    radon gas, 190–91
    smog, 189–94
    urban heat islands, 131, *132*
Air quality standards, U.S., 200–202
Air-to-air heat exchangers, 190, 387
Alaska
    Exxon Valdez oil spill in, 258–59
    oil deposits in, 411
    oil exploration in Arctic National Wildlife Refuge, 367
Albers Technologies Corporation, 384
Alfven, Hannes, 437
Alien species, **80**
    introduction of, 361, 362, 363
Alley cropping, **276**
Alligator, ecological significance of, 81
Alpha particles, 43
Altitude, **88**
Aluminum, recyling, 456
Amazon Basin, *127*, *292*
    deforestation fires in, as seen from space, *331*
    development/destruction of, 332–33
Anemia, 300
Animal(s). *See* Wild plant and animal resources
Animal manure, **278**
Annual plants, **63**
Annual rate of natural population change, **116**
Antarctic
    food web in, *73*
    ozone hole over, *224*
Ants, control of, 326
Aquaculture, **306**
Aquatic ecosystems, **65**, 95–103
    coastal zone, 96–98
    effects of air pollution on, 195, 200
    freshwater, *67*, 98–102
    inland wetlands, 102–3

B

Baby boom generation in U.S., 123, *124*
Background ionizing radiation, 43, 44
Bangladesh, flooding in, 237–38
Barrier beach, 97, *98*, *99*
Barrier islands, 98, *99*, 219
Bathyal zone in oceans, *96*
Beaches, 97–99
Benign tumor, **179**
Benthic zone, *100*
Berry, Thomas, 28, 29
Beta particles, **43**
Beverage container deposit laws, 456
Bhopal, India, pesticide disaster, 317
Biodegradable pollutants, **12**
Biodiversity. *See* Biological diversity
Biofuels
    converting biomass to, 399–401
    major types of, *397*
Biogas, 399
Biogeochemical cycles, **62**, 63, 75, 112
    human disruption of, 187
Biological amplification, **319**
    of pesticides, 317, *318–19*
Biological community, **65**
Biological control of insect pests, 320–22
Biological diversity, 7, 108, 209. *See also* Ecological diversity; Genetic diversity; Species diversity
    effects of global warming on, 217–19
    health report on, 11
    importance of/crisis in, 7
    in tropical forests, *334*
Biological evolution, **107**
Biomass, 397–401
    burning agricultural and urban waste as, 399
    burning wood and wood wastes as, 398
    converting solid, to liquid/gaseous biofuels, 399–401
    energy plantations for, 399
    fuelwood crisis in LDCs, 335–37
    versatility of, as fuel, 397–98
Biomass energy plantations, 399
Biome. *See* Terrestrial ecosystems
Biosphere, **59**, *60*
Biotic development. *See* Ecological succession
Biotic ecosystem components, **66**–70
Birds, effect of pesticides on, 319
Birth control

Fig. 3. **Section of an index.**
Source: G. Tyler Miller, Jr., *Environmental Science*, 3rd ed. (Belmont: Wadsworth, 1991) A16.
Reprinted by permission of the publisher.

biosphere   The living and dead organisms found near the earth's surface in parts of the lithosphere, atmosphere, and hydrosphere. See also *ecosphere*.

biotic   Living. Living organisms make up the biotic parts of ecosystems. Compare *abiotic*.

birth rate   See *crude birth rate*.

bitumen   Gooey, black, high-sulfur, heavy oil extracted from tar sand and then upgraded to synthetic fuel oil. See *tar sand*.

breeder nuclear fission reactor   Nuclear fission reactor that produces more nuclear fuel than it consumes by converting nonfissionable uranium-238 into fissionable plutonium-239.

calorie   Unit of energy; amount of energy needed to raise the temperature of 1 gram of water 1°C. See also *kilocalorie*.

cancer   Group of more than 120 different diseases—one for most major cell types in the human body. Each type of cancer produces a tumor in which cells multiply uncontrollably and invade surrounding tissue.

capital goods   Tools, machinery, equipment, factory buildings, transportation facilities, and other manufactured items made from natural resources and used to produce and distribute consumer goods and services. Compare *labor, natural resources*.

carbon cycle   Cyclic movement of carbon in different chemical forms from the environment, to organisms, and then back to the environment.

carcinogen   Chemical or form of high-energy radiation that can directly or indirectly cause a cancer.

carnivore   Animal that feeds on other animals. Compare *herbivore, omnivore*.

carrying capacity   Maximum population of a particular species that a given habitat can support over a given period of time.

chromosome   A grouping of various genes and associated proteins in plant and animal cells which carry certain types of genetic information. See *gene*.

chronic effect   A harmful effect from exposure to a toxic substance or disease-causing organism that is delayed and usually long-lasting. Compare *acute effect*.

clearcutting   Method of timber harvesting in which all trees in a forested area are removed in a single cutting. Compare *selective cutting, seed-tree cutting, shelterwood cutting, whole-tree harvesting*.

climate   General pattern of atmospheric or weather conditions, seasonal variations, and weather extremes in a region over a long period—at least 30 years. Compare *weather*.

climax community   See *mature community*.

coal   Solid, combustible mixture of organic compounds with 30% to 98% carbon by weight, mixed with varying amounts of water and small amounts of compounds containing sulfur and nitrogen. It is formed in several stages as the remains of plants are subjected to intense heat and pressure over millions of years.

coal gasification   Conversion of solid coal to synthetic natural gas (SNG), or a gaseous mixture that can be burned as a fuel.

coal liquefaction   Conversion of solid coal to a liquid fuel such as synthetic crude oil or methanol.

coastal wetland   Land along a coastline, extending inland from an estuary that is flooded with salt water all or part of the year. Examples are marshes, bays, lagoons, tidal flats, and mangrove swamps. Compare *inland wetland*.

coastal zone   Relatively warm, nutrient-rich, shallow part of the ocean that extends from the high-tide mark on land to the edge of a shelflike extension of continental land masses known as the continental shelf. Compare *open sea*.

Fig. 4. Detail of a glossary.
Source: G. Tyler Miller, Jr., *Environmental Science*, 3rd ed. (Belmont: Wadsworth, 1991) A5. Reprinted by permission of the publisher.

Skimming Encyclopedias

Certainly, you are now beyond the stage of rushing to an encyclopedia and copying out an entry to serve as a "research topic." Most encyclopedias deal only generally with any item included. However, there is value for you in skimming an encyclopedia on the field of a course (or on a related field) for the overall view it will give you and for its broad perspective. From that quick overview may well come a topic idea for your research paper.

More than just the entry itself, many encyclopedia articles have **cross-references** (that is, listings of related articles in the same encyclopedia). Some of them may be topics you want to look into—or that suggest still other ideas to you.

Another way to use an encyclopedia article to help you find a topic for research is to consider the **major divisions of an entry** as a starting place. Finally, a **bibliography** at the end of an encyclopedia entry will introduce you to still more ideas. Some of the books listed, or others by the same authors, may be in the library you are using or can be obtained through an interlibrary loan system. Either use the titles in a bibliography as topic ideas or use the books as additional sources, drawing ideas from their tables of contents, introductions, indexes, or other features.

Other related articles

Air force
Air force, United States
Airmail
Airport
Careers (Transportation)
Federal Aviation Administration
Great-circle route
Jet propulsion
Jet stream

Manufacturing
National Aeronautic
 Association
National Air and
 Space Museum
Radar
Test pilot
Transportation

Fig. 5. Listing showing cross-references in an encyclopedia.
Source: "Aviation." *The World Book Encyclopedia* 1991 ed. Reprinted by permission of the publisher.

Outline
I. The aviation industry
  A. Aircraft manufacturing
  B. General aviation activities
  C. Airline operations
  D. Airport operations
  E. Aviation support industries
  F. Recent developments
II. Aviation agencies and organizations
  A. Aviation agencies in the United States
  B. Canadian aviation agencies
  C. The International Civil Aviation Organization
  D. Other aviation organizations
III. History of the aviation industry
IV. Careers in aviation
  A. Jobs in general aviation
  B. Jobs with airlines and airports
  C. Jobs in the aircraft industry
  D. Jobs with government agencies

Fig. 6. Major divisions of an encyclopedia entry in outline form.
Source: "Aviation." *The World Book Encyclopedia* 1991 ed. Reprinted by permission of the publisher.

Bibliography

Barrett, Gary W., and Rosenberg, Rutger, eds., *Stress Effects on Natural Ecosystems* (Wiley 1981).

Beaumont, Peter, *Environmental Management and Development in Drylands* (Routledge 1989).

Bernarde, M. A., *Our Evolving Environment* (Wiley 1989).

Brock, Neeley W., and Gary, Blau, eds. *Environmental Exposure from Chemicals*, vol. 2 (CRC Press 1985).

Chanlett, Emil T., *Environmental Protection*, 2d ed. (McGraw 1979).

Daly, Herman E., and Umana, Alvaro F., eds., *Energy, Economics, and Environment* (Westview Press 1981).

Duffus, John H., *Environmental Toxicology* (Halsted Press 1980).

Henry, Glynn, and Heinke, Gary W., *Environmental Science and Engineering* (Prentice-Hall 1989).

Kay, David A., *Environmental Protection* (Allanheld, Osman & Co. Pubs. 1983).

Shea, Cynthia P., *A Vanishing Shield: Protecting the Ozone Layer* (Worldwatch Inst. 1988).

Fig. 7. Bibliography at the end of an encyclopedia entry.
Source: "Environment." *Encyclopedia American*, Int'l Ed. 1992.
Reprinted by permission of the publisher.

Online Catalogs and Card Catalogs

The library you will be using for your research may have the familiar card catalog drawers, a printed catalog, or an online computer catalog—or a combination of these. (See more about catalog customs on pages 31–39.) Increasingly, libraries are being computerized, either individually or in consortia, and you will find information you seek at a computer terminal.

Catalogs are of two different kinds:

- **Divided catalog,** containing entries for each book divided in three ways: by subject (which will help you to find a topic), author, and title

- **Dictionary catalog,** which lists all book holdings of that library alphabetically

Whichever kind of library catalog you work with, you can use it to help discover a Field-of-Study Topic.

If you work in a library with computer terminals for students, you can call up on a screen the subjects held in memory. Although using the online catalog is faster than going from drawer to drawer and flipping through catalog cards, it doesn't have the same "feel" as browsing through cards in search of a topic.

Begin looking in the catalog for subject headings having to do with the content of the course for which you will be writing the research paper. Whatever you find will, of course, be very broad: accounting, space, pollution, environment. Then look at a few of the books you identify through the catalog under the subject

```
                           (Record 11 of 62)                              LINCC
      AUTHOR: Daly, Herman E.
       TITLE: For the common good : redirecting the economy toward community,
              the environment, and a sustainable future
   PUBLISHER: Beacon Press, c1989.
    SUBJECTS: Economic development--Environmental aspects.    Environmental
              policy.


   ##     ---- Call Number -------- Volume     Material   Location

   1     330.1 D153f                           Book       MDCC/KEN



   Press (RETURN) to display holdings at other locations.
   Type in a LINE # for additional information on a copy.
   Enter:    B          to Backup.
             F          to see the Full title record.
             REL(F7)    to see RELated headings.
   >>
                                              Enter ? (RETURN) for HELP.
```

Fig. 8. Printout of an online catalog screen.

headings; go through them, as already suggested in the earlier section above on using your textbook as a source of ideas.

Don't overlook the potential of "see also" catalog listings to help you even more. They refer you to related subject headings where you can find even more books to consult (see Figure 8); use them as just noted to help you find a topic to write about.

Periodical Indexes

Many million more words are printed in periodicals than in books, so you will find them helpful in choosing a Field-of-Study Topic for research. Each discipline has many specific indexes. *Education Index*, *Chemical Abstracts*, and *Book Review Index* are just a few; many others are listed in Appendix A, "Selected List of Reference Works Available in Libraries" beginning on page 275. These indexes are particularly helpful for those seeking academic or business information. There are also general indexes such as the *New York Times Index* or the familiar *Readers' Guide to Periodical Literature* that will help you find topics to write about. Consult, particularly, the principal headings or divisions in an index. Many indexes have "see also" listings as regular entries, so additional ideas are available to you.

Check several volumes of an index and be sure to look at one or more related topics with a volume to be sure you get a broad range of ideas to work with.

3. Build From Your Own Interests

One of the most satisfying ways of selecting a Field-of-Study Topic is to relate the field you have to work with to what you already know or have special interests in, either vocational or avocational. Then you can study something you already care about or something you may find useful.

A Personal Inventory

Begin by making a Personal Inventory. That is, draw four columns on a piece of paper and put one of the following headings at the top of each. Then, under each heading, write as many individual items as you can.

Know and Care About (Include hobbies, clubs, special events, scouting badges earned, favorite kinds of music, previous school courses, and so on.)

Special Concerns (List things you think about, ideas that intrigue you, and more.)

Vocational Interests (Include a satisfying job you now have or careers you are considering.)

Like to Learn About (Give free rein to your imagination for this listing.)

EXAMPLE

Know and Care About	Special Concerns	Vocational Interests	Like to Learn About
motocross	acid rain	nursing	gun control
racing	child care	aviation	ocean pollution
hair styling	space travel		destruction of
astronomy	drinking laws		rain forests
			sailboating

Be honest with yourself on these lists; they're for your own use. Make each list as long as you can, but don't make choices at first. Use memories, free association, whatever techniques you can to add items to each of the four lists. Obviously, you won't be able to use many items (nor will they all make sense with what you're going to do next). But think of the store of resources you'll have for other courses, for writing assignments, and for your job résumé!

Making Relationships

Use your Personal Inventory list as a starting point to arrive at a Field-of-Study Topic for your research paper. At the top of a sheet of paper write the name of the field or course for which you must write the research paper. Then draw a vertical line down the center of the page. Choose a word from one of the lists you just made and write it to the right of the line. On the left side of the line, make a list of words related to the course for which you need to write the research paper. Use words from the table of contents of a textbook, special terms you know, or words arrived at just by thinking about the material in the course. Now you are ready to start making relationships to help you find a Field-of-Study Topic.

EXAMPLE

LITERATURE   [course for which you will write this research paper]

[literature-related words]

1. authors

2. novels

3. nonfiction

4. plays   [special interest]
                                                       airplanes
5. eras

6. poems

7. countries

8. adventures

By combining each word in the left column with the word on the right, you can arrive at related ideas that will serve as general topics for the research paper.

EXAMPLE

1. authors + airplanes = pilots who have written books

2. novels + airplanes = novels about flying

3. nonfiction + airplanes = books about development of the aviation industry or about special-purpose aircraft

4. plays + airplanes = plays or movies about flying or flyers

5. eras + airplanes = flight in mythology of ancient cultures

6. poems + airplanes = poetry about flying or by pilots

7. countries + airplanes = stories about flying, true or fictional, from different countries

8. adventures + airplanes = written records of great adventures undertaken by pilots

If the relationship you're looking for doesn't work out for a particular word, try another from one of the lists in your Personal Inventory. Be creative, be inventive, be imaginative in making relationships!

FREE-CHOICE TOPICS

If you have free choice of a topic, suddenly all of human knowledge is open to you! The trick is to pinpoint just one part of it to work with, and the best way to do that is to examine several possibilities systematically before choosing what is most appealing to you. Here are seven possibilities to help you make that choice.

1. Expand a familiar area.

Choose a topic or area about which you already know something but would like to know more. Instead of breaking completely new ground, you will then have a chance to increase your learning in an organized way.

EXAMPLES

- You did some reading on medieval beliefs about witchcraft on your own and want to know about contemporary attitudes toward it.
- You studied about the Mayans in a history course but would like to know more about them.

2. Look to an area new to you.

EXAMPLES

- An article about the future mentioned *cryogenics*. What is it all about?
- Grimmelshausen is the name of an author you saw on a bookshelf. It's such an unusual name. Who is or was that person?
- You've always meant to find out about the history of jazz.
- People on space missions these days perform many different kinds of experiments. What are some of them? What practical applications may result?

3. Try a textbook.

Look through a textbook you own or one in the library on some subject you care about or that holds special interest for you. Look through the table of contents, index, glossary, bibliography, appendices, or preface. Use the same methods for choosing a Field-of-Study Topic described on pages 19–29.

4. Work from your strengths.

Take stock of your strengths and abilities and use one of them as the basis for your research paper. If you haven't already read page 28 on making a Personal Inventory, do so now and make such an inventory. Use the following listing for your categories:

- what you know and care about
- special concerns or intriguing ideas
- vocational interests
- what you want to know more about
- outstanding or significant personal experiences
- things you do well

List words and phrases (never mind about complete sentences here!) under each of these headings. Don't stop to evaluate as you write; just get the ideas down on paper.

Every item on each list represents a personal strength because each is prompted by you. Use the items as starting places to find topics you care enough about to study further.

5. Become a browser in the library.

Walk around and see what's available to you—but within a structure you set up, in order to save time and wandering. You might decide to look at periodicals and academic journals that are out on open shelves and scan the titles of articles in them for topic ideas. If *Omni, Ms, Ebony,* or *Car and Driver* are already familiar to you, try looking through titles that are new to you, such as *American Crafts, Modern Healthcare, Changing Times, Journal of Atmospheric Sciences,* or *Mental Retardation.* In them, you may find articles that suggest topics you will want to investigate.

Another kind of purposeful browsing is to take a cue from the "Selected List of Reference Works Available in Libraries" (Appendix A, page 275). The library you are working in may not have all the works listed there, but you can check off the titles that seem of interest; if the volumes are available you can skim through them on the lookout for topics you care to investigate further.

6. Try brainstorming.

Write down all sorts of names, subjects, places, events, or whatever else comes to mind. Or enlist the aid of a friend—because people often generate more ideas for themselves when they work with somebody else—and then turn on a tape recorder to catch the list of words and ideas both of you say. Then, either check off likely research prospects on your written list or write down research possibilities when you play back the tape. Narrow the list to two or three topics before heading for the library to find reference works on them. Perhaps that's the way you will arrive at a research topic.

7. "Get inside" the library catalog system.

To understand most completely the riches available to you in a library—and therefore available to you as Free-Choice Topics—you should understand the cataloging systems used to make books and periodicals accessible to you. Such customs are explained in the next section of this chapter.

However, for now you should be aware that you can "get inside" your library to look for a topic idea by beginning with books. If the library you use has an open-shelf system, start to look through a particular section of books until you find a topic that strikes your fancy for research. If the library doesn't have open shelves, you will have to do your browsing for interesting-looking titles in the catalog and then request books that seem likely prospects for topic ideas.

You could also consult either a general or specialized periodical index (see some titles in Appendix A, page 275), depending on the sort of paper you plan to do. Be aware, however, that if you are required to use books as a reference source in your research paper, some entries in a periodical index may be so new or current that there are not yet books on that specific topic.

LIBRARY CATALOGING CUSTOMS

Classifications of Books

Whether the library you work at lists its books on cards, a computer, microfilm or microfiche, or a print catalog, all its holdings will be arranged either by the **Library of Congress** classification system or by the **Dewey Decimal** classification system. Both systems classify books—and, thus, knowledge or possible writing topics—in broad categories, each of which is then subdivided into progressively smaller or narrower groups.

The Library of Congress Classification System

[Note that there are only twenty-one groups in this system; the letters I, O, W, X, and Y are omitted.]

A	General works and polygraphy	M	Music
B	Philosophy and religion	N	Fine arts
C	History and auxiliary sciences	P	Language and literature
D	History and topography	Q	Science
	(except America)	R	Medicine
E *and* F	America	S	Agriculture and plant and animal
G	Geography and anthropology		industry
H	Social sciences	T	Technology
J	Political science	U	Military science
K	Law	V	Naval science
L	Education	Z	Bibliography and library science

The Dewey Decimal Classification System

[Note that each class is identified by a three-digit number in this system devised by Melvil Dewey.]

000–099 Generalities

100–199 Philosophy and related

200–299 Religion

300–399 The social sciences

400–499 Language

500–599 Pure sciences

600–699 Technology (Applied science)

700–799 The arts

800–899 Literature and rhetoric

900–999 General geography and history

Each classification system is further divided. In the Library of Congress system, the second subdivision is indicated by a letter added to the primary letter; further subdivisions are given a numerical range. (See Figure 9.) In the Dewey Decimal system, each division is subdivided into groups of ten numbers, and each of *them* is further divided to accommodate books of greater specialization. (See Figure 10 on page 34.)

In using these classifications, even at the third level, all you can get is a large selection of Free-Choice Topics for research. For example, "South American History" or "Reptiles and Birds" are fine topics for books, but not for student research papers. Whatever topic you choose from these classifications will have to be narrowed further into a suitable subject, as explained in Chapter 3.

H
SOCIOLOGY

HM   Sociology (General and theoretical)
        101–121 Civilization. Culture. Progress
            Cf. CB
        201–219 Social elements, forces, laws
        251–299 Social psychology
HN   Social history. Social reform
        30–39 The church and social problems
            Cf. BR 115.S6
        Social groups
HQ   Family. Marriage. Home
            16– 471   Sex relations
            750– 799 Eugenics. Child culture, study, etc.
            1101–1870 Woman. Feminism
            1871–2030 Women's clubs
HS   Associations: Secret societies, clubs, etc.
HT   Communities. Classes. Races.
            101– 381   Urban groups: The city
            401– 485   Rural groups: The country
            851–1445   Slavery
            Works on slavery in the United States of America
                are classifies in E441-453.
HV   Social pathology. Philanthropy. Charities and corrections
            530– 696 Social welfare
            697–4630   Protection, assistance and relief of special classes
                according to age, defects, race, occupation, etc.
            4701–4959 Protection of animals

Fig. 9. Library of Congress second-level classification.
Source: *Library of Congress Classification*: 8.

Contents of the "Card Catalog"

The card catalog—that is drawers of 3- × 5-inch cards, each representing a book
in a library—are undoubtedly familiar to you. The term *card catalog* is being used
here, even if the library in which you will work has an online (that is, computer)
or microform catalog. Printed catalogs are bound volumes in which pages show
reproductions of the same cards that would otherwise be in the traditional library
drawers. The following information applies to any books a library holds.

Every book in a library's collection is listed in its card catalog.

• **Fiction** books each have two cards in the catalog: one by title and one by
the author's name. Collections of short stories may also have **additional cards**
headed by titles or authors within a book.

• **Nonfiction** books each have at least three cards in the catalog: one by subject, one by title, and one by author's name. They may also have additional cards

Second Summary*
The Hundred Divisions

000 Generalities
010   Bibliography
020   Library & information sciences
030   General encyclopedic works
040
050   General serials & their indexes
060   General organizations & museology
070   News media, journalism, publishing
080   General collections
090   Manuscripts & rare books

100 Philosophy & psychology
110   Metaphysics
120   Epistemology, causation, humankind
130   Paranormal phenomena
140   Specific philosophical schools
150   Psychology
160   Logic
170   Ethics (Moral philosophy)
180   Ancient, medieval, Oriental philosophy
190   Modern Western philosophy

200 Religion
210   Natural theology
220   Bible
230   Christian theology
240   Christian moral & devotional theology
250   Christian orders & local church
260   Christian social theology
270   Christian church history
280   Christian denominations & sects
290   Other & comparative religions

300 Social sciences
310   General statistics
320   Political science
330   Economics
340   Law
350   Public administration
360   Social services; association
370   Education
380   Commerce, communications, transport
390   Customs, etiquette, folklore

400 Language
410   Linguistics
420   English & Old English
430   Germanic languages   German
440   Romance languages   French
450   Italian, Romanian, Rhaeto-Romanic
460   Spanish & Portuguese languages
470   Italic languages   Latin
480   Hellenic languages   Classical Greek
490   Other languages

500 Natural sciences & mathematics
510   Mathematics
520   Astronomy & allied sciences
530   Physics
540   Chemistry & allied sciences
550   Earth sciences
560   Paleontology   Paleozoology
570   Life sciences
580   Botanical sciences
590   Zoological sciences

600 Technology (Applied sciences)
610   Medical sciences   Medicine
620   Engineering & allied operations
630   Agriculture
640   Home economics & family living
650   Management & auxiliary services
660   Chemical engineering
670   Manufacturing
680   Manufacture for specific uses
690   Buildings

700 The arts
710   Civic & landscape art
720   Architecture
730   Plastic arts   Sculpture
740   Drawing & decorative arts
750   Painting & paintings
760   Graphic arts   Printmaking & prints
770   Photography & photographs
780   Music
790   Recreational & performing arts

800 Literature & rhetoric
810   American literature in English
820   English & Old English literatures
830   Literatures of Germanic languages
840   Literatures of Romance languages
850   Italian, Romanian, Rhaeto-Romanic
860   Spanish & Portuguese literatures
870   Italic literatures   Latin
880   Hellenic literatures   Classical Greek
890   Literatures of other languages

900 Geography & history
910   Geography & travel
920   Biography, genealogy, insignia
930   History of ancient world
940   General history of Europe
950   General history of Asia   Far East
960   General history of Africa
970   General history of North America
980   General history of South America
990   General history of other areas

*Consult schedules for complete and exact headings

Fig. 10. Dewey Decimal second-level classification.
Source: *Dewey Decimal Classification and Relative Index*, 20th. ed., v.2: x.
Reprinted by permission of the publisher.

headed (and filed) by as many alternate subjects as seems practical. For instance, a book about trees might be listed under such subject headings as "trees," "forestry," and "ecology."

Because catalog cards are made to help you locate information, they may also be headed by a **translator's name** or an **author's pseudonym**.

Audiovisual holdings are usually represented by cards in the general catalog of a library, thus making it easier for you to find nonprint sources of information if not necessarily helpful to determining a research topic. (Audiovisual and computer materials may, additionally, be cataloged in a separate section, such as one from which they may be borrowed or used.)

Government documents held in a library are also listed in its card catalog. They, too, may also be cataloged in a separate section, depending on the quantity of such documents a library has.

Individual Catalog Cards

The **author card** is basic to the catalog and is the prime entry card for each book in a library. When a book is published in the United States, copies of it are sent to the Library of Congress in Washington, D.C. The author card is printed there or by other library-supply sources; your library purchases the card from one of them.

Libraries use that basic card to make their own title, subject, and other heading cards by typing the appropriate information above the author's name. The title is usually typed in black and the subject in red. Each library also adds a classification number at the top left corner of the card, following guidelines of whichever system it uses, the Library of Congress or the Dewey Decimal. (See Figure 11.)

"See also" cards are additional cards for help both in finding a topic and in searching out information for your research paper. They are found in the card catalog at the end of a subject section.

Alphabetizing of Books and Periodicals

Usually, books in a card catalog and entries in periodical indexes are filed alphabetically according to author, title, or subject. Here are some other uniform practices of library cataloging.

1. If the same word is applicable to a person, place, subject, or book title in a dictionary catalog, the cards follow that same order.

EXAMPLE

Washington, George   *(the person)*

Washington, D.C.   *(the place)*

Washington Square   *(a book title)*

Obviously, this practice can be applicable only to a dictionary catalog (which lists all holdings in alphabetical order according to card headings) and not to a divided catalog (where authors, titles, and subjects are in separate groups).

Author
card

```
            Rifkin, Jeremy.
363.70525
G796     The Green lifestyle handbook / Jeremy
         Rifkin, editor. -- 1st ed. -- New York :
         H. Holt,c1990.
         xxii, 198 p. ; 19 x 24 cm.
         "The 1001 ways you can heal the earth" --
         Cover.
         "An Owl book."
         Includes bibliographical references.
         ISBN 0-8050-1369-5 (pbk. : alk. paper)

         1. Environmental protection--Citizen
         participation.  I. Rifkin, Jeremy.  II.
         Greenhouse Crisis Foundation.
FMMD    02 MAY 91   10828260  FYMSac  89-26944
```

Title
card

```
363.70525
G796     The Green lifestyle handbook / Jeremy
         Rifkin, editor. -- 1st ed. -- New York :
         H. Holt,c1990.
         xxii, 198 p. ; 19 x 24 cm.
         "The 1001 ways you can heal the earth" --
         Cover.
         "An Owl book."
         Includes bibliographical references.
         ISBN 0-8050-1369-5 (pbk. : alk. paper)

         1. Environmental protection--Citizen
         participation.  I. Rifkin, Jeremy.  II.
         Greenhouse Crisis Foundation.

FMMD    02 MAY 91   20828260  FYMStc  89-26944
```

Subject
card

```
         ENVIRONMENTAL PROTECTION--CITIZEN
            PARTICIPATION.
363.70525
G796     The Green lifestyle handbook / Jeremy
         Rifkin, editor. -- 1st ed. -- New York :
         H. Holt,c1990.
         xxii, 198 p. ; 19 x 24 cm.
         "The 1001 ways you can heal the earth" --
         Cover.
         "An Owl book."
         Includes bibliographical references.
         ISBN 0-8050-1369-5 (pbk. : alk. paper)

         1. Environmental protection--Citizen
         participation.  I. Rifkin, Jeremy.  II.
         Greenhouse Crisis Foundation.
FMMD    02 MAY 91   10828260  FYMSsc  89-26944
```

Fig. 11. Title, subject, and author cards for the same book.

2. Abbreviations, such as "St.," "Dr.," "U.S.," and "19th cent." are filed as if they were spelled out: "Saint," "Doctor," "United States," "Nineteenth century," and so on.

If you were looking for the book *St. Thomas and the Future of Metaphysics* and didn't know the author, you would look for "Saint Thomas . . ." in the card catalog.

3. Listing is alphabetical word by word and letter by letter to the end of each word.

It is *not* simply letter-by-letter listing in either a card catalog or a periodical index. (Note that the article "the" is overlooked in alphabetizing, although it is written in the normal place.)

EXAMPLE

Actual Catalog Order	*Not*
North Carolina	North Carolina
North Dakota	Northcote
Northcote	North Dakota
The Northwest Wind	Northwestern
Northwest	The Northwest Wind

4. Names or words beginning with *Mac* or variations—such as *Mc* or *M'*—are all listed as though they began with *Mac*.

EXAMPLE

Proper Catalog Order

Mach

McHale

MacHenry

Machiavelli

5. Foreign prefixes with names (such as "de," "van," or "von") are not used in alphabetizing. Instead, listing is by last name, with the prefix following.

EXAMPLE   Beethoven, Ludwig van

English names beginning with "De" or "Van" are listed by that prefix.

EXAMPLE   DeWitt, John

Spanish names are listed by the patronym (father's family name) although they often include the mother's maiden name. A place name is often added to an individual's name, according to Spanish custom, but it is not used for alphabetizing.

EXAMPLE   Cervantes Saavedra, Miguel de

6. Titles that begin with "A," "An," or "The" are alphabetized by the second word.

Articles are ignored for alphabetizing purposes but usually shown following a comma at the end of the title.

EXAMPLE   *Adventures of Huckleberry Finn, The*

7. Acronyms appear before words that are spelled out.

Thus, "OPEC" will be listed before "oil" in both a card catalog and a periodical index.

8. Subjects—except history—are subdivided in alphabetical order.

EXAMPLE

Songs   *[subject]*

    Ballads

    Carols

    Children's songs

    Drinking songs   *[subdivisions]*

    Folk songs

    Madrigals

    Popular songs

9. History is subdivided according to eras or time.

EXAMPLE

Gt. Brit.—History (By Period)

    Roman Period, 55 B.C.—A.D. 449

    Anglo-Saxon Period, 449–1066

    14th Century

    War of the Roses, 1455–1584

COMPUTER SEARCHES

As already noted, many libraries now list their books in machine-readable formats. Most also subscribe to at least one periodical index, such as *InfoTrac*, or other online catalogs or CD-ROMs that list documents on several databases, such as *Readers' Guide to Periodical Literature, Social Sciences Index, Business Periodicals Index, Applied Science and Technology Index,* and others. Thus, instead of looking through boxes of a card catalog or bound volumes of periodical subject listings, you may be able to access that information at computer terminals in a library or dormitory. Although it is convenient to have a general idea of what sort of information you're looking for and thus make a computer search for a Field-of-Study Topic, you may also want to do so for a Free-Choice Topic by following the suggestions in the previous section on "Free-Choice Topics." Once you are familiar with computers in a library, you will develop the knack of using them with as much ease as any other catalog system.

AN ADDENDUM: DOUBLE SUBMISSIONS

If you have two research papers assigned in the same term, you may want to consider choosing a topic suitable for both of them. For example, a paper for a psychology class may be on a topic that is also acceptable for an education course; one prepared for an English class might be on a topic suitable to fulfill a research assignment in electronics or art history. You may find that both teachers will permit the same paper to be submitted to them, feeling that a top-notch job on one paper is preferable to a half-hearted or hurried job on two of them.

Or, with the permission of both instructors, you could choose the same topic, perhaps use the same sources—but tailor each paper for a different course.

If you consider a dual submission of either sort, **consult the instructors involved, explain your reasoning, and get permission** before making any final topic choices. Realize, too, that in a dual submission you may have to use different forms of documentation (depending on the standards of the academic discipline for which you write each paper) and you will have to submit to the grading criteria of two different people—all the more reason for planning ahead with your instructors.

Narrowing the Topic

SOME LIMITATIONS YOU WORK WITHIN

Deciding on a topic is the starting point for writing a research paper, but you need to narrow it to a **specific subject** before starting to gather information. To make that determination, you particularly need to take into consideration three limitations that are "givens" and within which you must work:

1. the required length of the paper you will write
2. the source material available to you
3. the audience who will read your paper.

1. Length

If your assignment for the research paper doesn't include a statement of expected length, you will have to use your own judgment. Be guided by the sort of work you expect of yourself, the time available to fulfill the assignment, and the importance you and your instructor put on the individual research paper. (As you already read on page 6, this book assumes you are preparing a research paper of 1,500 to 3,000 words, or about six to twelve double-spaced typewritten or word-processed pages. Use your judgment, based on time and expectations, for papers of other lengths.)

The subject you decide on, after narrowing a topic, should have sufficient range and depth to show your work as that of a serious student and enable you to deal *adequately* with what you choose. Just don't choose a subject so broad that you must be superficial to fit it into the required length. A literary research paper on playwright Arthur Miller is too broad to work with; better to narrow it to biographical elements in one of his plays, such as *A Memory of Two Mondays*. Similarly, the topic of geriatrics is not limited enough, even if you decide to investigate recent developments in the field; you'd still have a book-length work. Better to narrow it still further, such as to studying how pets can help older people.

Although many people seem to have trouble limiting the range of a subject, it's also possible to choose one so specialized or esoteric that you need to devote several pages of background information to accommodate the audience before you can begin to write about the subject. Such imbalance doesn't leave you enough space to say anything substantial in your paper.

2. Materials Available

You must be able to locate, *conveniently*, enough information for a paper you want to write. School libraries try to have materials for the work of their students, so the library is probably your best beginning source of information. However, budgets always limit a library's acquisitions. For example, if you attend a school where engineering and natural science courses are primary, you may not find enough materials on art or music to make possible extensive research on those subjects.

Print Materials

Before you decide definitely on a subject for your research, **go to the principal library you plan to use.** If you didn't use its facilities to arrive at a topic for research, you should look through the online or card catalog now to make sure information is available. Also, look at relevant periodical indexes. Both books and periodicals will give you ideas of how to narrow a topic. In the periodical indexes, especially, check to be sure that the library has some of the items listed that may be needed for research on the subject you plan to work with.

If you have trouble finding information in a library, check with a librarian; each is a specialist in helping students locate materials. If you still can't find the right kind of information, adjust the scope of your proposed subject.

Nonprint Materials

Investigate the availability of nonprint materials before you make a final decision on your subject. As explained in Chapter 4 (pages 88–89), not all research sources are in print or in a library. Unless you are asked to do just a library search, most instructors are happy to have you demonstrate your ability to find and work from varied sources. Interviews may be useful. What you hear on radio or see on television may be relevant. You may even plan to write letters of inquiry if you have enough time to wait for answers. Videotapes in a library or in private collections may be useful. Traditional or interactive computer programs may also be counted among nonprint sources of information.

3. Audience

You already know that from the very beginning of the research paper process you must consider who will read what you write (see pages 10–11). Even the earliest considerations of narrowing a topic to a workable subject should be done with your readers in mind: who they are, what they know, what they'd be interested in knowing, and how they will respond to what you write.

In some classes, students work collaboratively at various stages or make oral presentations about their final research papers. If yours is such a class, you can get help from classmates at this stage, because they will be your audience.

FOCUSING ON A SUBJECT TO RESEARCH

Occasionally, the topic you choose will immediately bring to mind a specific subject, a part of that broad category you want to investigate. If that happens, you're lucky. Most people have to narrow the topic and many have trouble limiting it to workable proportions. Yet finding a specific subject is crucial to a successful research paper. If you have trouble limiting or focusing on a subject, try one (or all) of the five methods explained here.

- freewriting
- free association
- clustering
- subdividing
- the five Ws

Freewriting

Sit down with a blank sheet of paper in front of you, take pen or pencil in hand (or sit before your typewriter or computer keyboard), and start writing whatever comes into your head about the topic you selected. Don't plan or try to think ahead; don't worry about spelling or punctuation. Just write without stopping. That's freewriting.

Freewriting helps you get thoughts out of your system and down on paper. Writers often use the method to find out what they know or think about a subject, for it taps sources of information deep within them.

When you use freewriting to help you narrow from topic to research subject, you look over what you've put down in freewriting and see if you've written something that will help you focus on a subject. Or, if not a subject, see if you can find a word or phrase narrower than the topic. Then use that as the starting point for another freewriting session. (Have someone time your writings, if you wish.) The second—or third—time may be the charm and you will find a subject to work from.

Free Association

Free association is used in many problem-solving situations—and narrowing a topic to a suitable subject for research is certainly a problem to be solved. Free association (sometimes also called *brainstorming* when you do it orally and with other people) is the practice of writing down words or phrases that occur to you as they come to mind and without worry about order, spelling, usefulness, applicability, or any other matter of judgment.

Begin by writing down the topic you selected, and underneath it list everything that comes to mind. Make the list as quickly as you can just by letting your mind rove over every idea the topic suggests.

E X A M P L E

Environment

whales	elephants
endangered species	rain forest
Africa	South America
toxic waste disposal	future of planet
global warming	Sierra Club
activists	acid rain
logging	international conference

From this list you could choose a subject, but it might be too broad. So another listing made by free association is in order. This time, begin with one of the words or phrases from the first list.

E X A M P L E

Activists

stop animal poaching	buy up lands
study whales	Greenpeace
nonviolence	confrontational tactics

The student whose research paper appears on pages 230–46 followed these two procedures and, because she had participated in a nonviolent protest on an environmental issue, she decided to research the subject. Such free association may also lead you as easily to a research subject.

If the free association method doesn't produce a subject suitable for your research paper, you might go to the library with an "almost" subject and refine or limit it after browsing through some periodical indexes (which will, generally, give you something more specific than will an online or card catalog).

Clustering

In clustering, you write down your ideas in a way that shows their relationships. Begin by putting your topic in the center of a page, enclose it in a small circle, and then start your imagination or "stream of consciousness" working. As ideas occur to you, arrange them in relation to one another with more circled words and more lines showing which ideas stem from which others. See page 44.

Subdividing

Another organized way to narrow a topic is to divide it into progressively smaller units. Continue subdividing the topic you've chosen until you reach a subject you are interested in researching. Sometimes several possibilities for a research paper emerge only after a few levels of subdividing.

Example of clustering.

Subdividing looks—and is—somewhat more structured than clustering. In the latter, you can move anywhere at any time. However, subdividing requires a more ordered thinking process as you write down possibilities. Also, remember that nothing can be divided into just one part; you must have at least two parts in order to make a subdivision.

The Five Ws

Asking questions—"What about . . . ?" or "What if . . . ?" or others—is still another way of narrowing a topic to a subject you can work with. You might simply ask yourself (or write down) those questions that occur to you about the topic you start with. You could assume the role of someone who knows nothing about the topic and ask questions to elicit information you'd like to have.

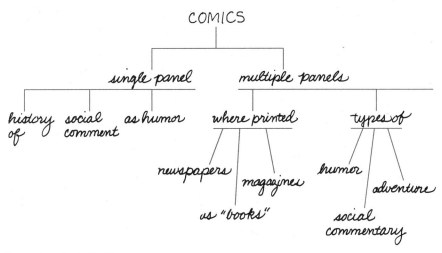

Example of subdividing.

Or you can develop questions in an organized way by adapting the journalistic tradition that good reporting means covering the five Ws of a story: **who, what, where, when,** and **why.** These key words lead to the complete coverage of a subject being reported, so if you use them as guides, they can help you find a useful research subject.

Who?   people

What?   problems, things, ideas

Where?   places

When?   times (i.e., past, present, future)

Why?   causes, reasons, results, conditions

To use these five Ws as a help in finding a subject, write your topic at the top of a page. Under it write each of the five W words as headings and fill in appropriate words or phrases. Or list the questions and leave room next to each, as in the following examples, so you can fill in answers to them.

EXAMPLE 1

Television   (the broad topic)

Who?   show hosts

              power structure

              directors

              Arsenio Hall

What?   news

              violence

              religious networks

              commercials

              home VCR tapes

Where?   remotes

studios

satellite transmissions

When?   future of cable

commercial beginnings

Why?   persuasive power

education

selling to children

role in elections

Some of the words listed in Example 1 are still too broad for a ten-page paper and need further narrowing. Use the same five Ws method again, as in Example 2. But this time begin with one of your "answer" words from the first level.

EXAMPLE 2

Television Violence   *(taken from "What" list)*

Who?   actors

audience

What?   effects of violence

types of

Where?   cartoons

news

"cop" series

specials

When?   prime time

Saturday mornings

Why?   psychology

realism

audience

On the basis of this further narrowing, you might decide to investigate the psychology of audiences wanting to see violence on television programs, or you might decide to study the effect of violence in cartoons on young children.

Combined Method

You may already have noticed that these are not exactly "pure" categories. That is, free association is probably used in the 5Ws, or brainstorming may be what yields clusters.

Barbara Howell, the student who wrote the sample research paper in Chapter 10 (pages 230–46), actually arrived at her subject by combining the methods you have been reading about. She started with a Free-Choice Topic of interest—ecology—and narrowed it in several steps.

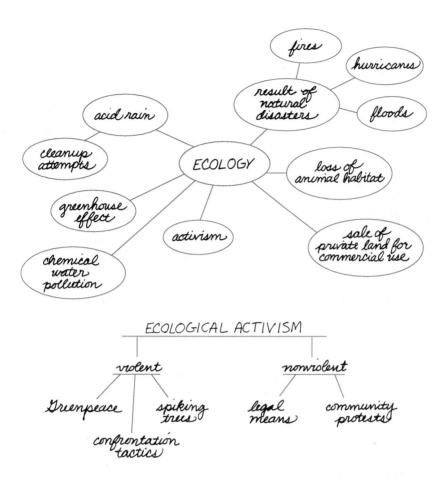

The train of thought seemed to be about nonconfrontational tactics in preserving the environment, a notion reinforced by Ms. Howell's previous involvement in local efforts to preserve lands. The title of her paper, "Nonviolent Tools for Environmental Activists," evolved as she followed through on the approach she decided to use.

FINDING AN APPROACH

Deciding on an approach to your subject *doesn't* mean deciding on a thesis statement before doing the research. To do so would mean you'd already decided what to say and therefore didn't expect to learn anything from this whole process. Rather, the early choice of an *approach* is a matter of focusing energy and ideas, so you can do good work with greater ease, make intelligent decisions during the information-gathering process, and read what will be most useful to you.

Many times the approach will be defined for you by the assignment. For instance, if the instructor specifies that you produce a persuasive or argumentative paper, the decision is made for you. But if the choice is up to you, make it at this stage and you will have three advantages:

1. **You will be able to exercise your critical thinking abilities to select information more carefully.** That is, having an advance idea of what information needs to be included will set you to looking for it and not wasting time on nonessentials.

2. **You will know what kind of support you need for the ideas you will deal with.**

3. **You will start to develop some notions of how to present your information.** That is, you will begin early to get a feel for how to organize your paper.

DECIDING ON AN APPROACH BEFORE BEING WELL INFORMED ABOUT YOUR SUBJECT

If you are not familiar with the subject you plan to research (or one close to it), get a quick overview of it by looking at an encyclopedia article, by consulting at least one periodical index to find the titles of articles people are writing about it, and by looking through some books on the subject. Skim, but don't read these sources closely yet. (The skill of skimming for ideas is explained on pages 107–08.) When you have this fuller sense of what you will be working with, you can make an intelligent choice of approach. Choosing from one of the following approaches will be helpful.

Five Possible Approaches to a Research Subject

1. **Examine or analyze the subject,** looking at various aspects of it and viewing it from more than one perspective.

2. **Evaluate or criticize the subject,** thus making a judgment about some quality of it.

3. **Compare and contrast things or ideas,** showing how both similarities and dissimilarities exist or are evident when someone looks closely at the subject.

4. **Establish relationships among ideas,** showing how they may have drawn from each other or how they are related in other ways to each other.

5. **Argue for or against something** and try to persuade the audience to agree with you.

As you will note in the following explanations and examples, it's not always possible to make clear-cut distinctions among the five ways of approaching a topic. A paper concerned with *examining* a subject may also involve some *comparison*. *Comparison and contrast* are essentially types of *relationships*. However, if you decide on a primary approach to your subject at the outset, you will find it easier to work purposefully and to gather only related material—and thus save yourself time and effort.

Examining or Analyzing

Examining a subject is like putting it under a microscope so you can see its details and look at them individually. You can examine anything from a single event to an entire political system or scientific theory. *Analyzing* something means looking at it closely enough to see what its components are and how it is put together. Thus, when you examine a subject you are almost always also analyzing it. Here are some kinds of examinations or analyses you might undertake as exemplified by approaches to subjects:

- **Stylistic devices** such as in a work of literature

  EXAMPLES

  - *Tom Jones* as a picaresque novel
  - political satire in *Gulliver's Travels*

- **Intellectual, scientific, or sociological background** of a person or a historical period

  EXAMPLES

  - Boris Yeltsin's evolution from Communist to non-Communist leader
  - economic considerations in the reunification of Germany
  - scientific developments needed to make satellite communications possible

- **Variations or revisions,** especially of a work of art or a philosophical idea

  EXAMPLES

  - Picasso's development of *Guernica*
  - differences in versions of "Sailing to Byzantium"
  - major changes in the idea of Communism from Marx to Mao

- **Evolution** of a business practice

  EXAMPLES

  - growth of television "programs" that are really paid advertising
  - solar heaters as a growth industry

If you decide to examine or analyze a subject for your research paper, don't fall into the trap of just enumerating information, thus ending with a report rather than a research paper. Remember that, according to the definition on page 3, you need to bring your own thoughts to what you learn through research.

Evaluating or Criticizing

An *evaluation* is a judgment about a subject after it has been studied at some length. *Criticism* means weighing or judging the quality of something, and should include both positive and negative commentary. (Contrary to popular belief, criticism is *not* just fault-finding.) Some kinds of evaluative or critical approaches you might take are:

- **Evaluate individuals, works, or ideas** in order to make judgments about them.

  EXAMPLES

  - effectiveness of seat belt laws
  - computer games as learning tools

- **Criticize works or ideas.**

  EXAMPLES

  - practical results of experiments performed during space shuttle missions
  - ethics of the death penalty

Comparing and Contrasting

To compare is to find similarities; *to contrast* is to find differences. The two words define different approaches, but they are generally used together to give a fuller view of a subject than either can provide alone. Another reason for the usual linking of the two verbs is that there must be some similarity established before a contrast is possible. For instance, though the Democratic and Republican party platforms differ during national election years, they can be compared and contrasted because both will deal with many of the same national and international issues. Some examples of comparing and contrasting approaches are these:

- **Works of art**, either with similar works or with the same one in different times or different media

  EXAMPLES

  - views of the novel *1984* when it was published and in the year 1984
  - *High Noon* and *Shane* as archetypal western films
  - Goethe's *Werther* and the opera of that title by Massenet
- **Views of an individual**

  EXAMPLES

  - how Malcolm X is treated in *The Autobiography of Malcolm X* and in its film version
  - how three political columnists saw the role of President Jimmy Carter in bringing Sadat and Begin together
- **Ideas**

  EXAMPLES

  - mayoral and city managerial governments
  - viewpoints about underwater oil exploration
  - nutritional values in three popular diets
- **Events**

  EXAMPLES

  - fiction and nonfiction accounts of military actions during Operation Desert Storm
  - peace-keeping efforts after a city's riots as viewed by police, psychologists, and social workers

Note that comparison and contrast is usually, but not necessarily, limited to two elements.

Relating

People learn by establishing relationships between what they already know and what is unfamiliar. Therefore, if you decide to undertake a research project that establishes (or explores) relationships, you will need to show how something the audience knows is related to something you presume is new to it. In fact, if you think back over what you have just read about comparison and contrast (and, to a lesser degree, about examining and evaluating as approaches), you will see that the ability to perceive and establish relationships permeates much of what you do in deciding on any sort of approach to a research paper assignment.

If you set out to approach your subject specifically as a matter of establishing relationships, you might select one of the following kinds of relationships:

- **A theory and its practical application**

  EXAMPLES

  - medieval beliefs about numerology and their influence on European church architecture
  - Mendelian theory as used in the selective breeding of cattle
  - language learning theories applied to possible understandings of how marine mammals communicate

- **A person's work or thought and life**

  EXAMPLES

  - autobiographical elements Hemingway incorporated into his stories set in Africa
  - what Cesar Chavez, the labor leader, may have learned from Gandhi

- **Specific events or attitudes**
  - uses of the "suicide machine" and conventional attitudes about euthanasia
  - how the American Revolution influenced the French Revolution

Arguing or Persuading

When you try to *persuade* someone to believe or act in a particular way, you are *arguing* your case. One school of thought is that as soon as you take a stand on a subject—as you must do to make yourself part of a research project and to determine an approach toward a subject—you automatically begin persuading your audience. However, argumentation and persuasion are generally organized differently from the other approaches you have been reading about.

All good writing supports the principal points its makes, but there is usually more emphasis on logical support using evidence in an argumentative or persuasive approach. ("Logic" is reasoning without fallacies—that is, without errors.) Evidence of your own critical thinking ability is that you can convince a careful reader by choosing what you need to include in an argument and then unfolding the material in an orderly way.

Although you will probably not take a position in deciding on an argumentive or persuasive approach until *after* you have done some research on a subject and know where you stand on it (or what you believe you can successfully convince your audience about), you should know that several kinds of possibilities exist. You could:

- **Defend a position** that has already been taken.

  EXAMPLES

  - secession as the only solution the South saw to problems it faced prior to the Civil War
  - money spent on space exploration as money well spent

- **Justify an action.**

  EXAMPLES

  - frequent changes in auto designs
  - federal monies allotted to feeding and housing the homeless

- **Prove or support a belief.** In order not to make a decision about what stand you will take before doing research on the subject, you will probably want to consider an approach that begins with "if."

  EXAMPLES

  - if nonacademic "scholarships" ought to be called by another name
  - if tests given for entry into schools or academic programs really measure learning
  - if horror movies are harmless to people viewing them

WORDING YOUR APPROACH

When you find an approach to your subject, you are focusing on a principal idea that you might develop in your research paper. Rather than depend on re-membering the wording, **write it out and put it in front of you when you work.** Memory is short, and too many things demand your time and thoughts during the several steps of the research process. It's easy to forget what you haven't written down. But you'll stay on track with your approach written out and available to look at from time to time.

Make your approach statement a two-part phrase, with the narrowed subject to research as one part and the approach as the other.

EXAMPLES

Approach	*Narrowed Subject*
examine ways an individual can overcome........................obesity	
argue for or against self-help programs that provide..............housing for the poor	
compare and contrast the book, the ballet, and the film of ....<u>Peter Rabbit</u>	
analyze local efforts to find jobs for...........................Haitian immigrants	

Note that **none of these sample subjects or approaches is in the form of a question.** You will have plenty of questions to ask yourself as you begin collecting information, and you should save questions until then so you can try to answer them through your research. Therefore, if you find yourself thinking in terms of a question, simply rephrase it into a statement.

E X A M P L E

Question	*Rephrased as Statement*
How has Richard III been depicted in two different eras?	Richard III as depicted by Shakespeare and by twentieth-century historians *(approach: comparison and contrast)*

You wouldn't know before finding information on the subject whether that depiction was similar or different, so the wording of this approach would have to remain general.

A Word of Caution

Even if you've taken the time to perform all this part of the research process, including skimming some related print materials (as described on pages 107–08), you *may* find you've chosen an approach that you can't work with. Or you may find that, once you start collecting information, the approach you expected to use isn't feasible. Rather than stick with something that won't work out well, don't hesitate to find another approach based on your early information gathering or on a conference with your instructor. There's no need to commit yourself to a direction that will prove unproductive.

CHOOSING A RESEARCH PAPER TITLE

Sometimes the wording you select for your approach will sound very much like the title for a paper. It may even end up as the title. However, don't be too quick to choose the title; that is a decision you need not make until the end of your writing.

If you do feel more comfortable working from a title than from a subject stated as an approach, then by all means write one down so you don't forget it. Many professional writers, in fact, say they work best when they start writing from a title.

Titles for research papers don't have to be clever or provocative. In fact, since your paper will be an academic one, and since most academic writing has descriptive titles, you should probably follow suit. The advantage of a descriptive title for this sort of paper is that it immediately signals the audience what to expect.

Searching for Information

THE WHAT, WHERE, AND HOW OF FINDING INFORMATION

No doubt about it: we live in "the information age." Reams and reams are added to the storehouse of print information daily, and new ways of storing sounds and images make nonprint resources ever more numerous and accessible. As one working on a research paper, you need to know:

1. **What** kind of information to look for
2. **Where** to find it
3. **How** to cite or acknowledge it

What you need to look for depends on the subject you are studying and the extent of knowledge you bring to it. Therefore, the more selective you have been in choosing a subject and an approach, the more focused you will be as you look among the various resources available. Know in advance what you are expected to search out. Will it be periodicals as well as books? Nonprint as well as print? Primary as well as secondary sources? (These last two terms are explained in the next section.)

Where to look for the information will not be overwhelming if you organize your search and follow an orderly pattern. To that end, study the section that follows, called "A Search Strategy" (beginning on page 56), and then use the "Search Strategy Record" beginning on page 58.

How to record what you find is actually done in two steps. First, you should make preliminary citation cards that show all the possible sources of information. The MLA (Modern Language Association) style of citing sources consulted for your research paper is used predominantly in this book and is logical and specific in detail [although the APA (American Psychological Association) style as well is explained on pages 247–56 and illustrated on pages 257–71]. If you keep referring to this book, it isn't hard to follow. Nobody expects you to memorize its many conventions; just know where to locate the models this book contains.

To write a preliminary citation card, follow the general conventions explained on pages 59–67; specific kinds of preliminary citation cards are explained and illustrated on pages 79–98. If the source you need to write a card for is not detailed in this chapter, follow the appropriate model shown in Chapter 9, pages 204–20.

Be sure to write the call numbers of books and the locations of other library information (and the library name if you work at more than one) in the top left corner of every preliminary citation card you write. Doing so will save frustration and wasted time when you need to find these sources to consult and take notes from.

Second, you will need to consult these sources systematically and take notes on what you find in each that may be useful in preparing the paper. Chapter 5 shows you how to record that information.

Be guided by the headings and subheadings in this chapter if you want to work your way easily through the complexities of these conventions.

PRIMARY AND SECONDARY SOURCES

You should know the difference between primary and secondary sources of information so that, to whatever extent possible, you can include both kinds in your search strategy. Desirable as they are, primary sources may not always be available to you. Or the limited time you have for some research assignments makes obtaining them difficult or impossible. On the other hand, there is danger in relying too heavily on secondary sources, especially if you ignore the materials on which they are based or the possible slanting they reflect. (Read more about evaluating source materials on pages 108–11.)

Primary Sources

These come straight from the people or works you are researching and are, therefore, the most direct kinds of information you can collect. Your research should rely on them when they are available, because they are firsthand observations and investigations. Examples of primary sources are Neil Armstrong's report of his moon walk, or President Nixon's writing or speaking about his decision to resign. Other kinds of primary sources include the following:

- **Diaries, notes, journals, and letters**
- **Interviews**
- **Autobiographies**
- **Works of art you are writing about**, such as novels, poems, short stories, plays, films, paintings, sculpture, librettos, and musical scores
- **Spoken or written works by someone who participates in an event or discovery**, such as a recording of a president's television address and the observations of an astronomer
- **Many public documents**, such as the *Congressional Record* or publications of the U.S. Bureau of the Census Statistics

Use your ingenuity to locate primary sources for your research subject. For instance, to find out about the psychological strain of living with AIDS, primary sources might include interviews with AIDS patients and their caretakers.

Secondary Sources

These are one step removed from the original and are often an examination of a study someone else has made on a subject or an evaluation of, commentary on, or summary of primary materials. Some examples of secondary sources are:

- **Critical (i.e., evaluative) reviews or commentaries**
- **Biographies**
- **Second-person reports**

EXAMPLES

Primary Sources	*Secondary Sources*
about Abraham Lincoln	
Lincoln's letters, speeches	Carl Sandburg's books on Lincoln
about Carl Sandburg	
Sandburg's books on Lincoln	a biography
Sandburg's letters and journals	
about misuse of government funds	
reports and records of disbursements	newspaper stories about the issue

Check secondary sources carefully by going back to their primary sources if possible. View materials skeptically and critically. And never, *never* rely solely on anyone's review of a book, play, or other written work without reading that work yourself!

A SEARCH STRATEGY

Given the wide array of resources available to you for research, both print and nonprint, both inside a library and outside it, you need to be organized and selective in order to accomplish your task. Smart researchers set up a **strategy to discover what resources are available**. In the course of making such a search, you will also discover whether or not your subject and approach will yield required information. If you find at this early stage that they won't, you can make a change or variation before you've invested a lot of time and energy.

The record to keep for each resource you locate while following your search strategy is called a **preliminary citation card**. It is "preliminary" because each card records *potential*, though not necessarily ultimately usable, information. Some materials you locate during this initial search will not be available to you, and some will not be relevant to what you seek or, eventually, incorporate into your paper. **Preliminary citations contain information about the author, title, publication, *and location* of each potential source of information**. They will be used for three purposes:

1. To locate and consult the resources you've identified and want to read or view or listen to in order to take from them information for your paper
2. To simplify documenting the text of your research paper
3. To prepare the Works Cited list at the end of your paper

A library is the best starting place to look for information. But be sure to think in terms of nonprint material (and resource people), too. This chapter gives you an overview of some of the most useful resources, details places to find information, and shows you how to make preliminary Works Cited cards for what you locate. The section immediately following this gives you a form to use a **Search Strategy Record**—as a help in organizing your search for information. Use it to keep your research moving and on target by filling in the appropriate dates.

Involve a **librarian** at an early stage of your search strategy. Nobody knows more about the resources of a library than the people who have been specially trained to help students use them. In fact, at most colleges and universities the librarians have faculty status, thus attesting to their function as teachers.

At this stage, don't plan on reading the sources you locate except, perhaps, for skimming encyclopedia articles for overviews because you'll already have the proper volumes open. Concentrate first on locating the resources.

The most effective search strategy begins with finding general reference information and then moves to more specific materials. For most people that means starting in the reference room or section of a library—but it can also mean contacting people in the community who might give you needed information. Included in the reference section you will find encyclopedias, general and specialized dictionaries, almanacs, handbooks, maps, atlases, directories, bibliographies, indexes, and biographical reference books. Your search strategy should include consulting the following:

- **Encyclopedias**, for the overviews they offer
- **Bibliographies**, to find books and other sources, sometimes unexpected, on your subject
- **Handbooks**, to give you additional general information
- **Online or card catalogs**, to locate relevant books and, from descriptions of them, to get an idea of their contents
- **Periodical indexes (that is, listings of magazines, discipline journals, and newspapers)**, for sources of up-to-date as well as retrospective information on your subject. Many of these are now available on CD-ROMs that are accessible through computer searches.
- **Other print sources**, such as corporate reports or letters
- **Computer databases**, usually for access to periodical information, but often for books and newsletters, too
- **Abstracting services**, to find many sources not listed elsewhere
- **Government documents**, especially in libraries designated as repositories
- **Nonprint sources**, such as slides, movies, audiodiscs and -tapes, videodiscs and -tapes, and filmstrips. These may be listed in the general catalog of a library, but sometimes they're cataloged only at a media center.
- **Computer programs and interactive videos**, either listed in a general catalog or at a media or computer center.

The Search Strategy Record

Fill in the "dates checked" on this record sheet as you follow the search strategy for your research paper. Be sure you make preliminary citation cards (samples for each category of information are in this chapter) whenever you find any sources that seem as if they'll be useful. Then use this record for the following purposes.

1. **Make sure you have fulfilled the requirements of the assignment.** For instance, if you were supposed to include both magazines and journals as resources and didn't locate any journals, be sure there are none with relevant contents. Otherwise, you can either rectify the problem or consult with your instructor about it.

2. **Share your preliminary citation cards with classmates who know the contents of this book and your assignment.** That way, you can get an outside view of your research paper work thus far.

3. **Ascertain that you are ready to move ahead to the next step in the research process.**

RESEARCH PAPER SEARCH STRATEGY RECORD

SUBJECT: _____

AUDIENCE: _____

Date Checked

General Reference Information

Encyclopedias	_____
Reference books and indexes	_____
Bibliographies	_____
Abstracting services	_____
Handbooks	_____
Other	_____
(names) _____	

Other Print Information   _____

Online or Card Catalog   _____

Periodical Indexes

For magazines	_____
For journals	_____
For newspapers	_____

Computer Databases   _____

Government Documents   _____

Other Print Information   _____

Nonprint Sources

Radio or TV programs _____

Interviews _____

   Appointments made: Yes ___ No ___

Lectures and speeches _____

Questionnaires, surveys, polls _____

   Plans made: Yes ___ No ___

Films/filmstrips _____

Videotapes/videodiscs _____

CDs/audiodiscs/audiotapes _____

Other Sources

(names) _____

_____

_____

POSSIBLE PRIMARY SOURCES *(list below)*:

_____

_____

_____

_____

RECORDING POSSIBLE PRINT SOURCES: CONVENTIONS OF PRELIMINARY CITATIONS (MLA STYLE)

Well-written preliminary citation cards keep you from retracing your steps or spending additional time as you move ahead in the research process. Use the same care in writing preliminary citation cards that you do in all other academic and scholarly work. Unless you can carry a portable computer into a library with you, **record the citations in ink on 3- × 5-inch cards**.

Research papers follow many conventions of formatting, spacing, punctuation, and other details. Nowhere is that evident more quickly than in the citations you will use in your Works Cited list. By following those conventions when writing the preliminary citation cards, you make your later work easier.

On page 60 you will see some **general conventions** about preliminary citation cards. They are followed on pages 60–65 by **conventions that apply to author, title, and publication units**. How those three units will appear on preliminary citation cards **for print sources** is illustrated on pages 70–88 and **for nonprint sources**, including a special section about "publication" citations, on pages 91–98. If you don't find an example here of citation information you need to record, check the specific examples on pages 204–20 or use the index of this book to find a description that covers what you want to find.

General Conventions

1. **Use hanging indentation**. That is, the first line of each entry begins at the left-hand margin and continues to the right margin you set. Each succeeding line is indented five spaces from the left margin, but continues as far as needed to the right margin.

EXAMPLE

```
Hanging indentation looks like this. It is the opposite of
    normal paragraphing. However, it makes the first word
    of a citation easy to read or to find in a list.
```

2. **There are three units to each citation: author, title, and publication. Each unit ends with a period. However, if an author uses any initials, the period after the last initial substitutes for the period to conclude the unit. If a title ends with a question mark or exclamation mark, let it substitute for the period**. Allow two spaces after the periods (or other end marks), just as you do in typing regular text.

EXAMPLE   **Auden, W. H.**   [Comment: This poet usually uses just initials for his given and middle names.]

"How Fair Are Airline Fares?"

Wonderful to Behold!

3. **Allow one space after any comma or colon**, just as you do in regular typing.

EXAMPLE   **The Research Paper: Process, Form, and Content**

4. **Long poems appearing in book form, such as *Paradise Lost* or *The Rime of the Ancient Mariner*, are treated as books**.

5. **The Bible and the names of books within it are not underlined**. The King James Version is assumed unless you state otherwise.

Conventions About the Author Unit

1. **The author's surname appears first, followed by a comma, then the given name(s) and a period. Record the information exactly as you see it in the source from which you take the preliminary citation**. Some catalogs give an author's complete name, including all given names, even when the person ordinarily uses initials for all but the surname. Periodical indexes usually show only initials for given names. Later, if you consult that source, correct the preliminary citation card to conform to the author's choice of name usage in print or film.

EXAMPLE   **Roth, A. J.**   [on preliminary citation card, later corrected to **Roth, Audrey J.** as shown on the title page]

2. If there are *two or more authors*, only the name of the first one shown is reversed; the others are written in normal first-name then last-name order. The names are joined by the word "and," preceded by a comma.

EXAMPLE   Altshuler, Thelma, and Richard Paul

                Janaro.

3. If a work has *three authors*, put a comma instead of the word "and" between the first and second persons' names. Use the "and" following a comma after the second person's name.

EXAMPLE   Heertje, Arnold, Francis W. Rushing, and

                Felicity Skidmore.

4. If a work has *four or more authors*, record only the first person's name and use the Latin abbreviation "et al." (meaning "and others") to signal that there are additional authors. The period that shows abbreviation of the second word becomes the period at the end of the author unit.

EXAMPLE   Maimon, Elaine P., et al.

Conventions About the Title Unit

1. **Titles of books, pamphlets, magazines, newspapers, radio or television programs, videotapes or -discs, full-length films, plays, operas, and computer software are underlined.** Later, when you type them in a Works Cited list, you either underline them or use italics. Subtitles (that is, wording following a colon) are considered part of the title.

EXAMPLE   <u>You Just Don't Understand: Women and Men</u>

                <u>in Conversation.</u>

2. **Titles of poems, short stories, essays, articles in newspapers or magazines or journals, chapter titles within a book, individual radio or TV episodes in a series, songs, lectures, and speeches are enclosed in quotation marks. Put the period ending the title unit *inside the quotation marks*.** If the title already contains wording in quotation marks, use single quotation marks where the double marks appear in print.

EXAMPLES   "Underground."   [title of a short story]

                " 'Look at Me When I'm Talking to You!':

                Cross Talk Across the Ages." [title

                of a chapter in a book]

                "The Scapegoat in 'The Lottery' and in

                Life." [title of a short story within the title of

                an essay]

3. **Capitalize the first letter of each word in a title (except articles, conjunctions, or prepositions), even if all lowercase letters or all capitals appear in the information from which you get the title.**

EXAMPLE

Title appearing in an index: Caution is the watchword

Title as you should write it: "Caution Is the Watchword."

4. **Special cases of titles**:

   a. If *a book is a revised or has a numbered edition or some other variation,* end the underlining at the last letter of the title, put a comma, then abbreviate (but do *not* underline) the special information. Some common designations, used alone or in combination as required, are: rev. (revised), alt. (alternate), ed. (edition). Remember that the period after the abbreviation suffices as the period to end the title unit.

   EXAMPLE   The Research Paper: Process, Form, and

   Content, 7th ed.

   b. If *the title of a book contains the title of another work that is usually underlined,* underline the title of the book but neither underline nor put quotation marks around the second title.

   EXAMPLE   Focus on Rashomon.

   [*Rashomon*, the title of a feature length film—which is normally underlined—is the subject of a book for which it's also part of the title.]

   c. *Titles normally put in quotation marks are so recorded if they appear within titles that are underlined.*

   EXAMPLE   Sourcebook for "Snows of Kilimanjaro."

   [The book (underlined) is about the short story (in quotation marks).]

Conventions About the Publication Information Unit

Here there are variations depending on whether you are recording information about a book (section A, below), a periodical (sections B and C that follow), or a nonprint source (see page 89).

A. BOOK PUBLICATION INFORMATION

Record the city where the publisher is located (but not the state) followed by a colon, the publisher's name (see details about streamlining names on pages 63–65) **followed by a comma, and the copyright date of the book**. The unit ends with a period, of course.

EXAMPLE   Belmont: Wadsworth, 1994.

1. **For the place of publication**:

   a. Add an abbreviation for the name of a foreign country, except Canada, which you identify by abbreviating the province in which a publisher is headquartered.

   EXAMPLES

   Fr.   [for France]

   Alb.   [for Alberta, Canada]

b. If you can't find a place of publication (either for the preliminary publication card or for the final Works Cited list), write "n. p." for "no place" where the city would ordinarily appear.

c. If several cities appear for a publisher's location, use the first one or the featured one (often shown by being printed in boldface or in a larger type size) on the list.

E X A M P L E

The source lists: "• San Diego • New York • Chicago • Austin • London

• Sydney • Tokyo • Toronto"

You write: **San Diego**

2. For the name of the publisher:

a. The names of book publishers are recorded in abbreviated form, usually consisting of the first word of a company title. See "Streamlining Publishers' Names" beginning at the bottom of this page .

b. If no publisher is given, write "n. p." after the colon where the publisher's name is usually written.

3. For the date of publication (i.e., the copyright date):

a. If several copyright dates are given (showing publication dates of several editions of the book), record only the most recent one.

E X A M P L E   The source lists: "©1990, 1987, 1984, 1980"

You write: **1990.**

b. If no copyright or publication date is given, write "n. d." after the comma where the copyright date is usually written. The period at the end of that abbreviation suffices as the period concluding the unit.

c. Do not confuse the date of a printing with the copyright date. Some books are reprinted a number of times and you may see something like "5th printing, 1992"; the copyright date is usually an earlier year and is preceded by the copyright symbol, ©.

Streamlining Publishers' Names

In the interest of streamlining publication information, both the MLA (Modern Language Association), upon whose conventions this book is primarily based, and the APA (American Psychological Association) adopted a shortened form to record the names of book publishers. Therefore, instead of using a complete name and such an abbreviation as "Co.," "Inc.," or "Ltd.," you may now use just one or a few words.

In each list that follows, the column on the left shows the full name of a publisher and the column on the right shows how that information should appear on a preliminary Works Cited card and in the Works Cited listing of your research paper. Anyone looking at these words can easily find the complete company name by consulting a reference book, a librarian, or anyone familiar with publishing companies.

1. **The first name or word suffices to identify a publisher whose company title may include several names or words.**

   EXAMPLES   Farrar, Straus & Giroux, Inc.   `Farrar`

   Bedford Books of St. Martin's Press   `Bedford`

   St. Martin's Press, Inc.   `St. Martin's`

   Pocket Books   `Pocket`

   The Free Press   `Free`

   Prentice Hall Co.   `Prentice`

2. **If the publisher's name is that of one person** (the first and last name or initials and last name), **record just the last name.**

   EXAMPLES   R. R. Bowker Company   `Bowker`

   Alfred A. Knopf, Inc.   `Knopf`

   G. P. Putnam's Sons   `Putnam`

3. **Omit business abbreviations** (such as "Co.," "Inc.," or "Corp."), **articles, and descriptive words** (such as "Press" and "Publishers") that are part of the publisher's full name.

   EXAMPLES   Wadsworth Publishing Co.   `Wadsworth`

   Clark Boardman Co., Ltd.   `Boardman`

   George Allen and Unwin   `Allen`
   Publishers, Inc.

4. **University press publications are recorded by the name of the university together with the initials "U"** (for University) **and "P"** (for Press or Publishers). No periods are required after the letters.

   EXAMPLES   Oxford University Press   `Oxford UP`

   Princeton University Press   `Princeton UP`

   University of Chicago Press   `U of Chicago P`

   The Johns Hopkins University Press `Johns Hopkins UP`

5. **Use standard abbreviations for words that are part of a publisher's name.**

   EXAMPLES   Harvard Law Review   `Harvard Law Rev. Assn.`
   Association

   Academy for Educational   `Acad. for Educ. Dev.`
   Development, Inc.

6. **Use familiar capital letter combinations if the name of a publisher is customarily known by them.**

   EXAMPLES   U.S. Government Printing Office   `GPO`

   National Council of Teachers of English   `NCTE`

However, if you believe readers may not know the acronym or letter combination, use abbreviations.

E X A M P L E   **Mod. Lang. Assn.,**   rather than MLA

B. MAGAZINE AND JOURNAL PUBLICATION INFORMATION

Record the title of the publication (underlined), the date of the publication (followed by a colon), and the pages on which the article appears. Leave one space after the title and one space after the colon.

Magazines and journals number pages either annually (that is, by volume year) or by individual issue. There are differences in the way you write a preliminary citation card (and, therefore, a Works Cited entry) for each type. See the section in this chapter titled "Magazine and Journal Page Numbering Systems" on pages 65–67.

E X A M P L E   **AOPA Pilot July 1993: 120.**

1. **All months except May, June, and July are recorded in the traditional three- and four-letter abbreviations.**

   E X A M P L E S   **Feb.   May   July   Sept.   Nov.**

2. **Do not use the word "pages" or any abbreviation for it. The location following a colon shows these are page numbers.**

   a. If the article is on successive pages, record the first and last page numbers with a hyphen between.

   E X A M P L E   **: 86-90.**

   b. If the article is *not* on successive pages, record only the first page followed by "+." Articles that have advertising or other text separating their pages are not on successive pages.

   E X A M P L E   Write   **: 56+.**   [shows that the article begins on page 56 but continues on other pages, such as 58 and then 93]

   c. If the article begins and ends with three-digit page numbers, the first of which is the same, no repetition is needed. However, if the first digit changes, record all of them.

   E X A M P L E S   Write   **: 235-42.**   or   **: 198-202.**

Magazine and Journal Page Numbering Systems

Publishers number periodical pages *either* by issue *or* by volume year. The two kinds of pagination (i.e., page numbering) are recorded differently on preliminary citation cards and in the subsequent Works Cited listing for that resource. Therefore, be sure to follow the appropriate custom for any article you are recording.

Paging by issue.   This means that each time the magazine or journal is published, the issue begins with page 1 and numbering continues until the end of that issue. Most general magazines are paged this way (such as *Time, Newsweek,*

Ebony, Car and Driver), and some academic and professional journals are (such as *The Annals of the American Academy of Political and Social Science*). The clue to paging by issue when you locate a resource in an index is that issues past the beginning of the year will have fairly low page numbers. (Ignore the volume number for such index entries when you write the citation.)

EXAMPLE

Here is the way the entry appeared on the *Magazine Index* computer search screen:

```
Crossing the line: when faced with threats to the
environment, some people turn to civil disobedience. by
Rick Searle il v19 Nature Canada Spring '90 p22(4)
```

COMMENT: Page 22 in a Spring edition suggests there may have been a Winter edition and is a clue that each issue of the magazine begins with page 1. Therefore, the volume number is omitted on the preliminary citation card, which thus should look like this:

```
Searle, Rick. "Crossing the Line: When Faced with Threats
    to the Environment, Some People Turn to Civil
    Disobedience." Nature Canada Spring 1990: 22+.
```

Later, when you look at the actual resource that you've recorded on each preliminary citation card, check to be sure your inference about the page numbering system is accurate. If not, see the example on page 210 to include volume and issue numbers.

Paging by volume.   This is also called **continuous pagination** or **successive pagination**. The system is used frequently in academic and professional journals, though only occasionally in general-interest periodicals. It means that page 1 will appear only once during a 12-month cycle: in the first issue of the publication's volume year. Thereafter, the pagination will continue through the volume year.

EXAMPLE

Quarterly Journal Paginated by Volume

Volume 16	published in January	contains pages 1 through 128
	published in April	contains pages 129 through 256
	published in July	contains pages 257 through 390
	published in October	contains pages 391 through 578
Volume 17	published in January	contains pages 1 through 211
	published in April	contains pages 212 through 401
	(and so on)	

The publication unit for a citation from a magazine or journal with successive pagination puts the volume number after the periodical's title; it is followed by the year, in parentheses, and then a colon and page numbers.

EXAMPLE

Anderson, Claire J., and Giovanna Imperia. "The Corporate
Annual Report: A Photo Analysis." The Journal of
Business Communication 29 (1992): 113-28.

(Remember that the first of three digits of a page number may be omitted, as it is here, rather than be repeated.)

Magazines and journals plan their publishing (and their finances) on an annual basis, and the publications for a year are called a "volume." Usually the volume year is the same as a calendar year (that is, running from January through December). But a volume year may be the same as a customary academic year (September through June), as it is for some academic journals, or even the same as a company's fiscal year (perhaps from July through June).

Issues of a magazine or journal usually begin with Volume 1 in the first year of publication, and succeeding years increase accordingly. So if you see "Volume 30" on a magazine or journal, it is probably the thirtieth year of that publication. (That doesn't always hold true, however. The July 20, 1992, issue of *Time* shows as Volume 140, and the magazine certainly hasn't been in existence for 140 years.)

C. NEWSPAPER PUBLICATION INFORMATION

Record the name of the paper (underlined), the date of publication (in date, month, year order), the name of the edition, the section of the newspaper, and the page(s) on which the article appeared. Put a comma after the year, a colon after the name of the edition, and a space after each of these parts or the punctuation mark following them. The unit concludes with a period, of course.

EXAMPLE

Miami Herald 14 Nov. 1992, final ed: B2.

1. **Omit an article that is part of the name of a newspaper, even if it appears on the masthead.**

EXAMPLE

The title of the paper on the masthead reads: *The Miami Herald*

You record it as   Miami Herald

2. **If the name of the city is not part of the name of the newspaper, supply it in square brackets. If you need to add the state as further identification, use the two-letter postal abbreviation.**

EXAMPLES

Times-Picayune [New Orleans]

Monitor [Concord, NH]

3. **Articles that are continued, but not on successive pages, are signified with a "+" after the beginning page number.**

EXAMPLE

Write   : A1+.

D. NONPRINT PUBLICATION INFORMATION

Nonprint sources vary so greatly that the "publication" information you must include about them will also vary. However, in general, you may presume that the distributor or location of a work should appear, as should such relevant information as the medium (CD-ROM, videotape, and so on), timing, whether it's in color or not (if the material is visual), and anything else that will tell someone reading the information details of the source. See pages 89–99 for more details.

READING SOURCES OF PRINT INFORMATION, AND THE WRITING OF PRELIMINARY CITATIONS

The rest of this chapter, as already noted, will detail the contents of various sources of materials that you can consult, and show how to read entries (if they might be confusing) and how to "translate" that information into a preliminary citation card. The order follows the format of your Research Paper Search Strategy Record.

Almost all the printed information you will need for a research paper will probably be found in a library. Print, however, may take more than the traditional book or newspaper form. When you use an online computer database, the result of your search will appear as on-screen print or will be printed out as hard copy; for convenience, then, it too, is considered a print source.

You should also seek out nontraditional sources of print information, when possible and appropriate, such as corporate reports, product specification sheets, and responses to letters of specific inquiry. See the section on pages 212–15 for more details.

Encyclopedias

An encyclopedia *is not* a place from which to get a whole paper (although, unfortunately, some people believe it is). But it *is* a source of material that will give you enough of a general view of a subject to start from in your research and in your understanding of the subject you selected. Two different kinds of encyclopedias are available. Consult both, if possible.

A **general encyclopedia** gives a broad picture of many subjects that students usually work with. If you want to know whether a particular encyclopedia covers the subject you're looking for, consult the index (which is usually in the last volume of a set). However, the contents of most encyclopedias are arranged alphabetically, so you can also check directly to find if the subject you're looking for is available.

The *Encyclopedia Americana* and the *World Book Encyclopedia* are familiar to most students and are good for background information; there are also bibliographies with most entries. (See Figure 7 on page 26.) The *Academic American Encyclopedia* is known for its fine graphics that supplement the print entries.

The *Encyclopaedia Britannica*, though a general encyclopedia, has always been considered strong in the humanities. It is arranged differently from other encyclopedias, for it comes in three units. The *Micropaedia* is ten volumes, indicated by roman numerals, containing ready reference material and an index. Use it first when you look for information, because it will either contain what you are looking for or tell you where to find more information in the *Macropedia*. The nineteen volumes of the *Macropaedia*, each designated by an arabic numeral, give knowledge in depth and will probably be the second you use most. The one-volume *Propaedia* gives a general outline of knowledge; its entries are probably too broad for you to consult for the kind of research paper this book is about, but they provide a good overview and direction for more specific sources. Should you use this encyclopedia as a resource, note that the specific unit used is considered part of the book title, in this way:

Encyclopaedia Britannica: Micropaedia. 1985.

A **subject encyclopedia** probably exists for whatever field you're working on. Consult it for more detailed and restrictive discussions of a subject. The content of most subject encyclopedias is arranged alphabetically. Some examples of the kind and range of subject encyclopedias available are *The Encyclopedia of Crime and Justice, The Encyclopedia of World Art, The McGraw-Hill Encyclopedia of Science and Technology*, and the *New Grove Dictionary of Music and Musicians* (which is actually a twenty-volume encyclopedia). Other subject encyclopedias are listed in Appendix A, "Selected List of Reference Works Available in Libraries," on pages 275–90.

When you write a preliminary citation from an encyclopedia, be sure you find the *author* of an entry so you can record that information on your citation card. Many encyclopedia articles are signed; if only the author's initials appear at the end of an entry, the person's full name can usually be found listed within the volume (or another volume within a set).

As in any work that is organized alphabetically, **do not write volume or page numbers** as part of the citation. Figure 12 is a sample of a preliminary citation card for an encyclopedia, with the spacing marked for you in color.

Reference Books and Indexes: Bibliographies, Handbooks, Biographical References, Vertical File, Government Publications, and More

Most of these materials will give you more information than you need for a preliminary citation card (that is, sometimes sizes of pages or notes of illustrations) and not show it in the form you need (such as no quotation marks or capitals for titles). Making the transition to record it on your card is easy if you follow the formats presented in this chapter.

- A **reference guide** such as Eugene Sheehy's *Guide to Reference Books* identifies all sorts of reference books by field, so if you decide to check his book, you will be led to other sources quickly. Figure 13 shows a portion of a page from this book as an example of the kind of sources it indicates.

- A **bibliography** will help you find additional source listings to consult in your search for information. Many are newly issued or updated so that recent publications on a specific subject or in a particular publication are readily

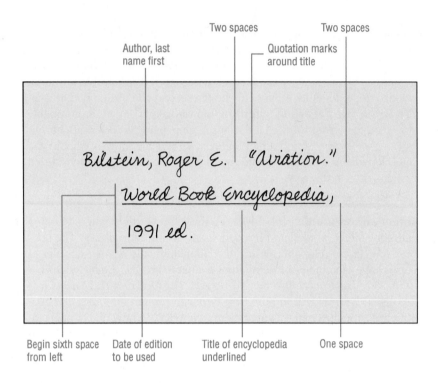

Two spaces   Two spaces

Author, last   Quotation marks
name first   around title

Bilstein, Roger E.   "aviation."

World Book Encyclopedia,

1991 ed.

Begin sixth space   Date of edition   Title of encyclopedia   One space
from left   to be used   underlined

Fig. 12. Preliminary citation card for an encyclopedia entry.

available. For instance, the *Bibliographical Index: A Cumulative Bibliography of Bibliographies* lists, by subject, all books and journal articles containing at least fifty bibliographic citations of works that have been published separately or that have appeared as parts of books, pamphlets, and periodicals. Figure 14 illustrates how "see" listings, in addition to other entries, can lead you to other pages in the index for further sources of information to include in your preliminary citations.

- A **directory** that, despite its name, may be helpful is the *Encyclopedia of Associations*. It tells which reference books identify organizations and institutions in a field. Its particular use for students preparing research papers is that from it you can find names and addresses to write to—or fax or phone—for special kinds of information.

- A **biographical reference book** will be helpful in finding out about persons mentioned in your research or about the author of material on your subject. *Who's Who in America, American Men and Women of Science, Contemporary Authors, Dictionary of National Biography* (usually referred to as DNB), and other volumes will give you dates of birth and death, nationality, and information about occupations. The *New York Times Bibliographical Service* is also helpful. The *Biography and Genealogy Master Index* lists 350 current and retrospective indexes and is much used for biographical research.

Air pollution

Bibliography

Davenport, Sara Jeannette and Morgis, G. G. Air pollution; a bibliography. Wash., Govt. Prt. Off., 1954. 448p. (U.S. Bureau of Mines. Bull., no.537)   **EJ138**

3,902 entries, with abstracts, from many sources arranged by subject. Covers nature and origin of air pollution, composition of air pollutants, effects of air pollution, control of air pollution, legal aspects, etc.

A complementary listing of research projects in air pollution was provided by the U.S. Division of Air Pollution's series, *Guide to research in air pollution* (1st–6th eds., 1953–66; title and issuing agency vary).   Z6673.D36

U.S. Air Pollution Technical Information Center. Odors and air pollution; bibliography with abstracts. Wash., 1972. 257p. (Air Programs Office. Pubn. AP-113)   **EJ139**

"The abstracted documents are thought to be representative of available literature. . . ."—*Introd.* Classed arrangement with author and detailed subject index. International coverage with English abstracts. Titles of foreign-language works are given in English followed by the original title. One of a number of annotated bibliographies in the issuing agency's publications series.

U.S. Division of Air Pollution. Air pollution publications; a selected bibliography, 1955/62– . Wash., U.S. Dept. of Health, Education, and Welfare, Public Health Service, Div. of Air Pollution, 1963– . (U.S. Public Health Service pubn. 979)   **EJ140**

A revision and extension of the first issue was published 1964 (covering 1955/63). Later issues cover 1963/66 (publ. 1966); 1966/68 (publ. 1969).

Classed arrangement with author and subject or title indexes. Includes references, with abstracts, mainly to journal articles, but also to books, monographs, report literature, and conference papers. Covers mainly English-language publications.   Z6673.U44

Fig. 13. Section of a page from Sheehy.
Source: Eugene P. Sheehy, *Guide to Reference Books*, 10th ed., ALA, 1986: 1251.

- **Indexes** in various subjects will also prove helpful sources for locating titles of works you may want to read for information. For example, if you are doing research about essays and other writings within longer works, you could consult the *Essay and General Literature Index*. A section from it appears as Figure 15. It lists, by subject and author, and occasionally by title under catchwords or significant phrases, material you can't find in book titles alone. In addition to a person's works, it lists secondary sources about a person's life or work and published criticism of an individual work. At the end of that index is a list of the publishers and dates of the books shown in the many entries, so you can have additional help in locating what you want to consult.

Environmental health engineering *See* Sanitary engineering
Environmental impact analysis
    See also
    Environmental impact statements
Jenks, Dennis. Recent publications in planning. (CPL bibliography, no294-296) Council of Planning Librarians 1993 3v
Parkin, James. Judging plans and projects; analysis and public participation in the evaluation process. Avebury 1993 p179-96
Toward improved accounting for the environment; edited by Ernst Lutz. World Bank 1993 incl bibl
        Alaska
Tornfelt, Evert E. Special theories of environmental assessment; a decade of an Alaskan perspective. Stephen Tornfelt Memorial Fund 1992 incl bibl
Environmental impact evaluation *See* Environmental impact analysis
Environmental impact statements
    EIS: digests of environmental impact statements. Cambridge Scientific Abstracts. See issues
Environmental law
    See also
    Natural resources—Law and legislation
Miller, E. Willard (Eugene Willard), and Miller, Ruby M. Environmental hazards; toxic waste and hazardous material: a reference handbook. ABC-CLIO 1991 p149-238
Environmental law, International
Rogers, Adam. The Earth Summit; a planetary reckoning. Global View Press 1993 p339-42
Environmental literature
Miller, Joseph Arthur. The Island Press bibliography of environmental literature. Island Press 1992 396p
Environmental management *See* Environmental engineering; Environmental law; Environmental policy
Environmental monitoring
    See also
    Environmental impact analysis
    Pollution—Measurement
Earth observations and global change decision making; a special bibliography; [by the] National Aeronautics and Space Administration. (NASA SP, 7092) National Aeronautics & Space Adm. Scientific & Tech. Information Div. 1991 93p

Fig. 14. Portion of a page in the *Bibliographical Index: A Cumulative Bibliography of Bibliographies*. Note the many cross references to other parts of the book.
Source: *Bibliographical Index: A Cumulative Bibliography of Bibliographies*, (New York: Wilson, 1993) 313.

People writing about literature often use *Poetry Explication* as a resource. It is an index containing explications of individual poems and criticism of them that appeared in books and periodicals. *Granger's Index to Poetry and Recitations* is another source you might consult if you are working with poetry.

Sources similar to the above are *20th Century Short Story Explication* and the *Short Story Index*.

If your subject falls within the area of the social sciences, you could look at the *Social Sciences Index*. In addition to the article titles shown under subject headings, additional headings are suggested in "see also" listings.

Many other indexes are helpful in yielding information; some of them available in most libraries are listed in Appendix A, beginning on page 275.

Mozart, Wolfgang Amadeus, 1756-1791
    About individual works
      Don Giovanni
      Pack, R. On desire and sublimation. (*In*
      Pack, R. The long view: essays on the
      discipline of hope and poetic craft p163-70)
Mr. and Mrs. Smith (Motion picture)
    Polan, D. B. The light side of genius:
    Hitchcock's Mr. and Mrs. Smith in the
    screwball tradition. (*In* Comedy/cinema/
    theory; ed. by A. S. Horton p131-52)
MSI *See* Movimento Sociale Italiano
Mücke, Dorothea E. von
    Virtue and the veil of illusion
    Contents
    Classical tragedy and Bildungsroman
    The epistolary novel and bourgeois
      tragedy: an ideal daughter and an ideal
      father
    'Julie ou la nouvelle Héloûise': the
      mother and the state
    The project of Anschaulichkeit in the
      mid-eighteenth century
    The project of Bildung in German clas-
      sicism and neo-humanism
Mueller-Vollmer, Kurt
    Staël's Germany and the beginnings of
    an American national literature. (*In* Ger-
    maine de Staël; ed. by M. Gutwirth, A.
    Goldberger, and K. Szmurlo p141-58)
Muhammadanism *See* Islam

Fig. 15. Section from *Essay and General Literature Index.*
Source: *Essay and General Literature Index,* (New York: Wilson, June 1992) 127.

Such standards as *Business Periodicals Index, Biological Abstracts (Biosis),* and *Applied Science and Technology* are among the many available on computer databases as well as in print volumes.

- The *Public Affairs Information Service Bulletin* (PAIS) gives a brief summary of articles it lists from 1,400 periodicals as well as from government documents. Thus, it's obviously a good source to search for preliminary citations.

The Vertical File

The pamphlets, booklets, and other informational items that can't be classified as either books or periodicals are maintained by many libraries in their vertical files. *The Vertical File Index: A Subject and Title Index to Selected Pamphlet*

```
CURR. SUDOC:  EP 1.89/2:600/S 3-86/018
SUDOCS NBR.:  EP 1.89/2:600/S 3-86/018
REPORT NBR.:  EPA/600/S 3-86/018
OCLC NBR.:        18952183
AUTHOR:       Anderson, J. W. (John Wayne)
TITLE:        Sources, fates, and effects of aromatic
              hydrocarbons in the Alaskan marine environment
              with recommendations for monitoring strategies
PUBLISHER:    Corvallis, OR : U.S. Environmental Protection
              Agency, Environmental Research Laboratory,
DATE:         [1986]
DESCRIPTION:  2 p. ; 28 cm.
NOTES:        Caption title.
NOTES:        At head of title: Project summary.
NOTES:        Distributed to depository libraries in
              microfiche.
NOTES:        "Apr. 1986."
NOTES:        "EPA/600/S3-86/018."
SUBJECT:      Hydrocarbons--Alaska.
SUBJECT:      Polycyclic aromatic hydrocarbons.
SUBJECT:      Marine ecology--Alaska.
SUBJECT:      Biotic communities--Alaska.
SUBJECT:      Environmental monitoring--Alaska.
CO-AUTHOR:    Neff, Jerry M.
CO-AUTHOR:    Boehm, P. D.
CO-AUTHOR:    Corvallis Environmental Research Laboratory.
ENTRY NBR.:   00888022
ENTRY NBR.:   (DGPO)89005934
ITEM NBR.:    431-L-12 (microfiche)
FORMAT:       book
```

Fig. 16. A. Example of a screen printout from a CD-ROM search of government documents.
Source: Impact Co. Government Document Catalog Service, 1994.

Material tells where and how to order additional materials. You may make preliminary citation cards on the basis of this index and send for what's listed if you have enough time and want to do so. Otherwise, check the current file in your library to see if the material you want is already in its collection.

Government Publications

These are a rich source of information because the government is the country's leading publisher. Besides all sorts of free pamphlets you can send for (and which are often advertised on television), many libraries regularly receive copies of the *Congressional Record*, the official daily report of proceedings of open sessions of Congress. The *Congressional Quarterly*, issued weekly and as an almanac, is a reliable news source for a summary of congressional activities.

The National Archives and Records Administration may also have something useful for you. Inquire by mail to Washington, D.C. But if you live in or near

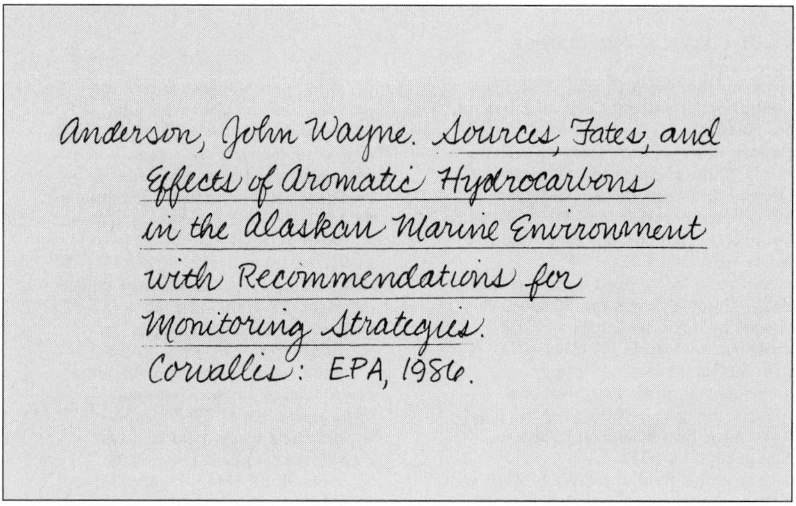

Anderson, John Wayne. Sources, Fates, and Effects of Aromatic Hydrocarbons in the Alaskan Marine Environment with Recommendations for Monitoring Strategies. Corvallis: EPA, 1986.

Fig. 16. *B*. Preliminary citation card from a CD-ROM computer screen.

Boston, New York, Philadelphia, Atlanta, Chicago, Kansas City, Fort Worth, Denver, Los Angeles, San Francisco, or Seattle, you can visit one of the National Archives field branches. Lists of publications and ordering information are readily available, and some public libraries hold microfilmed copies of records from the National Archives. There are now also many presidential libraries that hold documents from that person's time in public office; one may be accessible to you.

If you have access to one of the approximately 1,400 libraries designated as a "depository library" for government documents, you have an added bonus in quick access—through microforms and computer as well as in print volumes—to seemingly limitless information and publications generated by the United States government. Congressional Information Services publishes indexes of bills, reports, documents, treaties, executive reports, publications, and public laws. So many items are available that documenting them can be difficult; in fact, there is even a book titled *The Complete Guide to Citing Government Documents*, by Diane L. Garner and Diane H. Smith (Bethesda: Congressional Information Service, 1984).

In the *Monthly Catalog of United States Government Publications* you will find the titles and prices of all publications available from government agencies. Since you are only looking for sources of information at this point in the process, you will find in it subject, title, and author information or indexes that are potentially useful. Many items listed in the catalog may already be in the library you are using for research; others you may have time to send for.

The library you are using may subscribe to the *Congressional Quarterly*'s weekly *Editorial Research Reports*, a publication helpful if you are looking for sources of information on an issue of current national significance.

Index of Subjects and Names

Coyote and Berryessa Creeks, Calif, flood control project, Army Corps of Engrs rpt, 90 H640-1

Delaware River channel dredging project, Army Corps of Engrs rpt, 88 H640-1

DOE nuclear facilities compliance with environmental regulations, 90 H561-32.1

DOE nuclear facilities, environmental and safety issues, 88 S311-15.4

Ecorse Creek, Mich, flood control project, Army Corps of Engrs rpt, 90 H640-8

El Portal hydroelectric project environmental issues, 87 S311-44.2

"Environmental Effects of Energy Development in the Artic National Wildlife Refuge: A Critique of the Final Legislative Environmental Impact Statement", 88 S311-1.1

"Environmental Studies for Washington and Oregon Relative to Lease Sale Planning Area 132", 90 H181-80.6

Falfurrias, Tex, flood control project, Army Corps of Engrs rpt, 88 H640-3

FERC programs oversight, 89 H361-157.1

Forest and rangeland resources mgmt planning draft environmental impact statement, comments, 87 H161-12.4, 87 H161-12.5

Glen Canyon Dam, Ariz, interim flow release constraints estab, 90 H443-40, 90 S313-59

Guadalupe River channel navigation project, Army Corps of Engrs rpt, 88 H640-4

Idaho wilderness study areas land use

Mont wilderness study areas land use classification, judicial review ban, 87 H443-63, 88 H161-13, 88 S311-74

Natl Environmental Policy Act environmental impact assessment requirements, Fed agencies compliance, 88 S321-29, 88 S323-14

Natl Environmental Policy Act implementation, oversight, 87 H561-34

Natl forest mgmt and timber sales policies oversight, 88 H441-12.5, 88 H441-12.8

Natl forest timber sales in Oreg, 89 H161-30.3

NC coastal waters gas exploration plan, environmental impact statement requirement, 89 H563-7

Nev wilderness study areas land use classification, judicial review ban, 87 H441-4, 87 H443-77, 87 S311-8, 88 H441-42, 88 S311-18

Nogales Wash and tributaries, Ariz, flood control project, Army Corps of Engrs rpt, 90 H640-4

North Fork Kentucky River flood control project, Army Corps of Engrs rpt, 87 H640-13

NYC mail processing facility expansion, community concerns, 90 H621-30.1

Oakland, Calif, harbor deep draft navigation plan, Army Corps of Engrs rpt, 87 H640-8

Ocean woodburning site designation in NY Bight, environmental issues, 90 H561-34.3

Fig. 17. U.S. House and Senate documents and years are shown in this section of subject and name index from the CIS (Congressional Information Service). Other sections of this index give you annotations on items you select to look at further.
Source: *CIS/Four-Year Cumulative Index.* Bethesda, (1987–1990) 925.

Abstracting Services

Short summaries of what has been written—both published and unpublished—on a subject are found in various abstracting services. A look under appropriate headings in an abstracting service publication lets you see what sort of material is available and decide if you want to make a preliminary citation card for a work. The abstract itself is most likely also available on a computer database or on a microform (that is, on microfilm, microfiche, or microcard). Although abstracting services are a rich source of information, *never substitute an abstract for your own complete reading of the original source!* Make a preliminary citation card as part of your search for resources. Later, discard it if you can't locate the original piece of writing, no matter how promising the abstract seems.

Psychological Abstracts, Science Abstracts, Abstracts in Anthropology, Historical Abstracts, Biological Abstracts, and many others will lead you to titles of journal articles or books that might be useful and from which you can make preliminary citation cards. Other such specialized abstracting services are listed in Appendix A, "Selected List of Reference Works Available in Libraries," beginning on page 275.

Dissertation Abstracts International (titled just *Dissertation Abstracts* should you have occasion to consult it for volumes before 1969) records the dissertation subjects and titles of all doctoral degrees awarded. *DAI* is divided into Series A for humanities and social sciences, Series B for the sciences, and Series C for European dissertations. Although most of these dissertations remain unpublished, copies may often be borrowed through interlibrary loan from the library at the institution that awarded the degree; ask a librarian to request it for you. Doctoral dissertations are an interesting source of information, for they represent both research of past work and original contributions by the author. You get the benefits of both—plus sources of information listed by the writer.

ERIC (Educational Resources Information Center) is a good place to look if your research has anything to do with education. Cataloging is by special collection, such as Reading and Communication Skills, Higher Education, Counseling and Personnel Services, Urban Education, and others. ERIC documents are available in many libraries in microform, or through DIALOG (a computer database service), or they may be ordered as regular page copies.

Online and Card Catalogs

Increasingly, libraries have transferred their lists of holding to online (that is, computer) catalogs. However, many still—or also—maintain their catalogs on cards in banks of long drawers. Printed catalogs are also in use; they are bound volumes in which pages show reproductions of cards that would otherwise be in the more traditional drawers. So are microform catalogs, which have the information on cards reduced to such minute size that the sheets must be read with a special device that enlarges the information, and CD-ROM catalogs containing information on discs that look like videodiscs but project the information onto a computer screen. *Card catalog* is the term used here, but substitute for it the kind of catalog you will be using in your library for research.

Audiovisual or government document holdings are also sometimes represented by cards in the catalog. Preliminary citation cards you write from them, however, will follow the format for the particular medium, not that for a book.

As you read in Chapter 2 (page 26), the holdings of a library are either in dictionary or divided catalog format. Each book in a library's collection is listed in its card catalog, so it is a prime source to search and make preliminary citation cards on the basis of titles you find there.

- **Fiction** books each have two cards in the catalog: one by title and one by the author's name. Story titles within a book of collected stories may also be recorded on their own catalog cards.

- **Nonfiction books** each have at least three listings in the catalog: one by subject, one by title, and one by author's name. They may also have additional cards headed (and filed) by alternate subjects.

Additional cards or entries for books may be headed, and filed, by the name of a translator, by a writer's pen name, or by other ways the librarians devise to help you locate information.

For the **preliminary citations forms for books shown in the card or online catalog**, follow the conventions described on pages 60–68. Pay particular attention to the spacing after periods, commas, and colons—and be sure to end the citation with a period. And remember to write the call number or letters in the top left corner of the card. If you write each preliminary citation card properly, you will have all the information you need to enter sources on the Works Cited listing at the end of your research paper.

Figure 18 shows a typical preliminary citation card for a book by a single author. However, when you record a book from the card catalog that has multiple authors or a translator or an editor, or represents any other special situation, remember to use the examples in Chapter 9, pages 204–20, as models.

Periodical Indexes

Any publication that appears at regular intervals (daily, weekly, monthly, semi-annually) is called a *periodical*. General-interest magazines, trade papers, academic journals, newspapers, and special-interest magazines (such as *College English, Advertising Age,* and *American Indian Art Magazine*) are periodicals, and thus articles published in them will be listed in one or more periodical indexes.

Because periodicals are published at least several times a year, you will find more current information in them than you will in books, which are often years in the writing and which usually take a year from manuscript completion to publication. Also, you will find a wider variety of information in periodicals because each issue can represent the thinking of several authors.

The **entries in periodical indexes** may vary from one another, but in the front of each issue of such an index you will find a list of periodicals represented in it, a key to the abbreviations used for their titles, and other information about the entries. Be sure to look at that information, for there are variations among the different indexes. However, most follow similar conventions, listed next, together with what they mean to you in preparing your preliminary citation cards.

Conventions Usually Found in Periodical Indexes

- **Subjects are divided and titled in as many categories as the compilers of that index believe will be helpful for you to locate information easily**. Look under several headings to find all the material you can use on your chosen subject.

- **The names of authors are usually recorded by surname and initials**. Record them that way on a preliminary citation card. However, when you look at that particular resource, be sure to change the name on the card to reflect the way that person (or persons) actually uses her or his name; you will need *complete names* should you use this card for a Works Cited list.

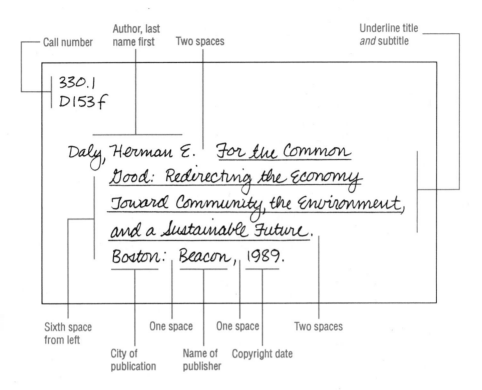

Fig. 18. Preliminary citation card for book by a single author.

- **Titles are not enclosed within quotation marks, nor is each word capitalized**. Remember, however, that when *you* write the title of an article on a preliminary citation card (and in a Works Cited list) it must be *enclosed within quotation marks* and the first letter of each word except articles, prepositions, and conjunctions is *capitalized*.

- **Abbreviations in the entry will show whether the piece is abridged, condensed, illustrated, or includes maps or diagrams**. Since such information is *not* entered in the Works Cited, there is *no need* to put it on the preliminary citation card.

- **The title of the periodical in which a piece appears is usually abbreviated and isn't underlined, though it may be italicized**. Remember, however, to *underline the complete title* of the periodical on your preliminary citation card. If you're not sure of the actual name of the publication, check the abbreviation listing at the beginning of the index you are using.

- **The volume number of each periodical precedes a colon in its entry**. Record the volume number in the preliminary citation entry *only* if the publication has continuous pagination, as explained on pages 65–67. (However, you may want to note the volume number in the lower right corner of the preliminary citation card because in some microfilm collections the drawers holding the film rolls are labeled by volume number.)

- **All page numbers on which an article appears will be shown in an entry**. However, record them according to the convention shown on page 65: two sets of numbers joined by a hyphen if the article is on successive pages or one number and a plus sign if the article is not on successive pages.

- **Publication dates are often shown in one- or two-letter abbreviations**. You must record them on the preliminary citation card with the *conventional abbreviations* (three letters, except for Sept.) and spelling out for May, June, and July.

Magazine Indexes

Magazine indexes still appear in familiar volume formats, but increasingly are seen in libraries as computer databases, which are detailed in the next section on pages 84–87. Magazines include many aimed at a general audience (such as *Newsweek* and *Psychology Today*) and others that appeal to a specific audience (such as *Tropical Fish Hobbyist* and *Metropolitan Home*).

Probably the most familiar of all periodical indexes is the *Readers' Guide to Periodical Literature*, published since 1900. (See Figure 19.) It indexes, by subject and author, articles appearing in more than one hundred general magazines, some of them on scientific subjects, and has a separate author listing for book reviews. Twenty-one issues of the *Readers' Guide* are published every year, monthly in February, July, and August, but semimonthly the rest of the year. These issues are put into cumulative form quarterly and annually. By all means consult the *Readers' Guide* if you think information on your selected subject is available in it. But be aware that many academicians consider it inappropriate for any but the most superficial and general research material. Instead of depending on it, consider it *just one of many indexes* in which you can find sources of information for your research paper.

Journal Indexes

Journals are usually published less frequently than mass audience magazines and are directed to narrow interests, often in particular professions or academic disciplines. Their circulations are thus smaller than those of magazines, but people read them for more specific information and often for reports of research in that discipline. *Personnel Journal, The Negro Educational Review, Foreign Affairs*, and *Signs (The Journal of Women in Culture and Society)* are examples of journals. Many journals are the publications of organizations in special subject areas, as are *College Composition and Communication* (the journal of the Conference on College Composition and Communication) and *The Journal of Southern History* (the publication of the Southern Historical Association).

The contents of specialized and technical periodicals, including scholarly journals, appear in many indexes. The variety of their titles will give you some idea: *Education Index, Business Periodicals Index, Cumulative Index to Nursing and Allied Health Literature, Applied Science and Technology Index*, and *Book Review Digest*.

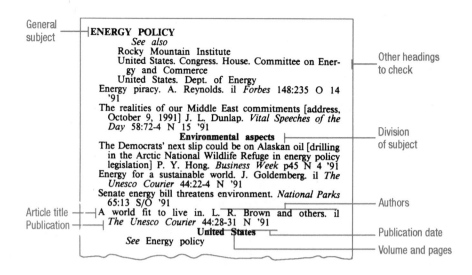

General subject

ENERGY POLICY
  See also
  Rocky Mountain Institute
  United States. Congress. House. Committee on Energy and Commerce
  United States. Dept. of Energy
  Energy piracy. A. Reynolds. il *Forbes* 148:235 O 14 '91
  The realities of our Middle East commitments [address, October 9, 1991] J. L. Dunlap. *Vital Speeches of the Day* 58:72-4 N 15 '91
    Environmental aspects
  The Democrats' next slip could be on Alaskan oil [drilling in the Arctic National Wildlife Refuge in energy policy legislation] P. Y. Hong. *Business Week* p45 N 4 '91
  Energy for a sustainable world. J. Goldemberg. il *The Unesco Courier* 44:22-4 N '91
  Senate energy bill threatens environment. *National Parks* 65:13 S/O '91
  A world fit to live in. L. R. Brown and others. il *The Unesco Courier* 44:28-31 N '91
    United States
    See Energy policy

Other headings to check

Division of subject

Article title
Publication

Authors

Publication date

Volume and pages

Fig. 19. A. Page from *Readers' Guide* marked to show how to read entry.

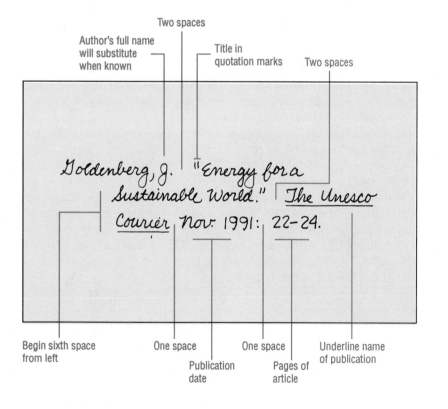

Two spaces

Author's full name will substitute when known

Title in quotation marks

Two spaces

Goldenberg, J. "Energy for a Sustainable World." The Unesco Courier Nov. 1991: 22-24.

Begin sixth space from left

One space

One space

Publication date

Pages of article

Underline name of publication

Fig. 19. B. Preliminary citation card for a *Readers' Guide* listing.

The *Social Sciences Index* and the *Humanities Index* (formerly together and at one time called the *International Guide to Periodicals* and later by the cumbersome title of *A Guide to Periodical Literature in the Social Sciences and the Humanities*)—which you may have to consult in your information search—are good sources of information about articles in foreign magazines and in a variety of specific and scholarly publications. See the sample entries in Figure 20.

The *General Sciences Index* is one of the newest indexes, containing articles published only since 1978. However, since it indexes about one hundred journals in the basic sciences (physics, biology, paleontology, and more), you should consult it if your research subject is in the natural sciences.

If you are curious about periodicals related to your research subject, you will be interested in looking at *Magazines for Libraries* (3rd ed. by Bill Katz and Barry G. Richards). There, labeled by subject, you will find an annotated list of 6,500 periodicals selected from 65,000 titles! To find out where the contents of each periodical is listed, consult *Ulrich's International Periodicals Directory*. Also, see the titles of other periodical indexes listed under the subject headings in Appendix A, pages 275–90.

Newspaper Indexes

Newspaper indexes are your richest source of current events and other newsworthy information that never appears in other kinds of periodicals. Chief among newspaper indexes is *The New York Times Index*. Figure 21 shows how to understand it and how to write a preliminary citation card for an article. So many libraries have copies of this newspaper on microfilm that if you get a preliminary citation from this index, chances are you will be able to find the precise reference when you're ready to read it and take notes.

Many other well-known newspapers in this country are indexed, especially since the 1970s, and copies of the papers are often available on microfilm in libraries. Among them are the *Index to the Chicago Tribune, Index to the Los Angeles Times, Index to the San Francisco Chronicle, Index to the Washington Post*, and (since 1949) *Index to the Christian Science Monitor*. Indexes to foreign papers, such as *The Times* (of London) *Official Index*, are also available in many libraries, and you may have occasion to consult them. And if your research subject has anything to do with business, you ought to look at the *Index to the Wall Street Journal*.

Facts on File, published weekly, is a world news digest that will give more information. It also has a cumulative index.

If you're looking for local coverage of a news event, you may want to use *The Gale Directory of Publications* (formerly *Ayer's*) to locate a newspaper you might not otherwise know exists. This index is geographically organized and gives information about daily and weekly newspapers as well as about consumer, business, technical, trade, professional, and farm magazines.

When you write a **preliminary citation card for a newspaper article**, look for clues about the edition and section of the paper on which it appeared. Although you may not be able to find such information until you search out the article, do record it at that time on your card, for it should be included in the final Works Cited entry for a newspaper article.

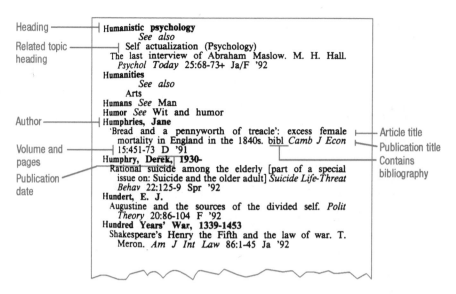

Heading — Humanistic **psychology**
            See also
Related topic — Self actualization (Psychology)
heading   The last interview of Abraham Maslow. M. H. Hall.
            Psychol Today 25:68-73+ Ja/F '92
          Humanities
            See also
            Arts
          Humans *See* Man
          Humor *See* Wit and humor
Author — **Humphries, Jane**
            'Bread and a pennyworth of treacle': excess female — Article title
            mortality in England in the 1840s. bibl *Camb J Econ* — Publication title
Volume and — 15:451-73 D '91
pages   **Humphry, Derek,** 1930- — Contains
            Rational suicide among the elderly [part of a special — bibliography
Publication   issue on: Suicide and the older adult] *Suicide Life-Threat*
date   *Behav* 22:125-9 Spr '92
          Hundert, E. J.
            Augustine and the sources of the divided self. *Polit*
            Theory 20:86-104 F '92
          Hundred Years' War, 1339-1453
            Shakespeare's Henry the Fifth and the law of war. T.
            Meron. *Am J Int Law* 86:1-45 Ja '92

Fig. 20. A. Page from *Social Sciences Index* with diagram of how to read it.

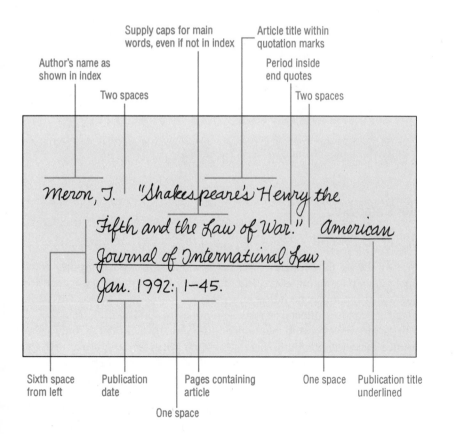

Fig. 20. B. Sample preliminary citation card for a *Social Sciences Index* entry.

ENVIRONMENT. See also
Air Pollution
Land Use Policies
Noise
Water Pollution
Weather
   Some industries are responding to increased activity by
states on environmental matters by rushing to Washington
seeking uniform Federal rules; as result of Federal inaction,
many important environmental policies are being set at
state level, often to dismay of industries affected; students
of government say anti-regulation, free-market orientation
of Reagan and Bush Administrations produced power
vacuum on some environmental issues and that states have
moved to fill void; examples of some actions taken by
states (M), Ap 1,D,1:1
   Study by researchers at National Institute of Neurological
Disorders and Stroke suggests mass burials of virus-plagued
livestock may result in long-term contamination of
environment since some viral-like substances can remain in
soil for at least three years after infected animals are buried
(Science Watch) (S), Ap 2,C,6:4
   Pressure on Mexico to curb pollution has emerged as key
issue in proposed free trade accord among United States,
Mexico and Canada; environmental groups want Mexico's
environmental promises written in to any pact; photos (M),
Ap 14,IV,4:1
   Top environmental officials from Mexico assure California
officials that American companies would find no sanctuary
south of border from pollution controls; say enforcement has
increased five-fold in last two years and that any company
seeking to relocate to Mexico would have to comply with
emission standards at least as strict as where it came from
(M), Ap 18,A,20:5
   List of activities focusing on environmental issues in
celebrations of Earth Week, Ap 19,C,19:1
   Sayville is host town for Long Island's celebration of
Earth Day; events described; photos (The Talk of Sayville)
(M), Ap 21,XII-LI,1:1
   Op-Ed article by Sen Frank Lautenberg on environmental
consumerism, or 'green' marketing, which is likely to be one
of most popular movements in 1990s; says many products
have false or misleading claims on their labels about being
environmentally safe; says most consumers are willing to
look for 'environmentally safe' products or packaging, but
businesses must be required to make only truthful claims on
their product labels (M), Ap 22,A,17:1
   Several advertising agencies plan environmental
awareness drives (S), Ap 22,D,9:4

See card
at night

Fig. 21. A. Part of a page from *New York Times Index.*

Computer Databases

   As you may know from using a personal computer, a *database* is a collection
of records about a particular subject that has been brought together and organized for easy access. One special reward of being able to use a computer database is that you get a printout at the end of a search that eliminates the need for
you to hand write what may be rather long lists.

   Typically, a vendor collects, reports, and organizes information from one or
more sources and makes it available to print users but, by contract, to only a single computer database company. The latter then puts the data into a form for
electronic storage and retrieval, if it is not already in that form, and builds indexes
within its system to aid rapid searching. As you certainly know, the amount of information generated daily is staggering (for example, the contents for the database ZOOLOGICAL RECORD come from approximately 6,000 journals); that it
is now quickly available to every researcher could not even have been dreamed of
a generation ago.

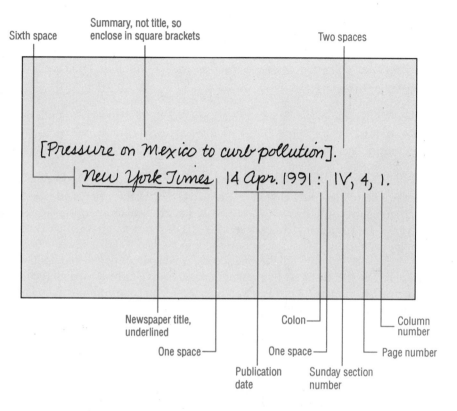

Fig. 21. B. Preliminary citation card for a *New York Times Index* entry. Article title not printed.

Libraries usually have two kinds of databases from which you can locate sources of information for your research. One is on a CD-ROM (compact disc read only memory), on which information is compiled and stored under useful headings. Just as in a periodical index, the disc is sent to the library, and you access it directly on a computer screen. The content on such discs is updated frequently, so you will get the most current information on this sort of database. Moreover, many such CD-ROM databases include various kinds of periodicals, saving you from searching in several locations. Because the library subscribes to this service, it is usually free to users.

InfoTrac II is a popular database accessible in many libraries; its Academic Index indexes the last four years of 200 magazine and 200 academic journal titles and the last six months of the *New York Times* newspaper. InfoTrac, another version, indexes the last four years of over 900 business, technical, and general-interest periodicals, the current year of the *Wall Street Journal*, the last six months of the *New York Times*, and more than 700 legal publications. Wilsondisc, another CD-ROM, contains the last four years of *Humanities Index*, *Social Sciences Index*, *Business Periodicals Index*, and *Readers' Guide Abstracts*. Newsbank, another such computer database, gives access on microfiche to over 500 U.S. newspapers as well as the full text of over 500,000 articles.

A second kind of database is one that transmits information over telephone lines, as a fax does. Therefore, there is a time charge for both requesting and receiving information, so when a library is charged, the cost is usually passed along to the student initiating the search. It may be from $5 on up, depending on the time taken for a search of databases in the system used, the type and amount of material requested (from simple bibliographic entries to complete texts), and thus the transmission time used. (Some college libraries now include a limited subscription to a database, such as DIALOG, as part of their operating expenses and do not require students to pay separately for simple searches.) Most database searches do require the help of a librarian who knows the access codes and who has training in how to narrow searches based on particular descriptors.

DIALOG Information Retrieval Service is the largest database of its kind and is online with many libraries; it subscribes to more than 300 databases, which are then available to you through this one source. Among other popular computer databases are ORBIT, BRS (Bibliographic Retrieval Service) Information Technologies, and Mead Data Central, which has LEXIS (perhaps the best-known legal database) and NEXIS (which is for news and public affairs). THE SOURCE has regularly updated business and general news, including abstracts of business magazine articles, and *NewsNet* has information from 200 specialized newsletters as well as wire services online. Some of these databases are interlocked. For example, NTIS (National Technical Information Service), an agency of the Department of Commerce, holds more that 2,500 databases, data files, and computer programs. Its Bibliographic Database is available through BRS, DIALOG, Mead, and System Development Corporation.

Not only libraries subscribe to databases; so do student clubs and dormitory groups, as well as business and professional people and some individuals who want to access the databases directly from home or office. For example, KNOWLEDGE INDEX is a service of DIALOG that offers low-cost access to more than 17 million summaries during evenings and weekends, when most DIALOG subscribers are not calling upon its facilities and when telephone rates are lower. If you have access to such subscribers, or are already one yourself, you may be able to bypass the library and make your computer search from another terminal.

Barbara Howell, the student whose research paper appears on pages 230–46, used DIALOG for more sources of information than InfoTrac II elicited. Within seconds after the request was made from Florida, a search was made at DIALOG in California and 27 likely sounding citations were printed out in the Florida library. The titles were scanned and requests for annotations were made from likely looking ones; these were immediately printed on the library computer. (See Figure 22.) No requests for full texts were made, because Ms. Howell decided to look for the actual articles herself, although full texts can be ordered from some databases. They may then either appear on the computer screen and be printed out immediately or, often, be mailed, to save money; such hard copy sent is called "off-line."

A **preliminary citation card from a database** or computer information service treats the author, title, and publication units as you would any other peri-

```
Diringer, Elliot; Snyder, George; Bancroft, Ann; Israel, Bill
San Francisco Chronicle (SF) Sec A, p 1, col 1  Jun 11, 1990

   As   environmentalists   plan   anti-logging  demonstrations  throughout
Northern   California   for   "Redwood   Summer,"   local   authorities,   timber
companies and other citizens anxiously hope the events will be nonviolent.
? ss s5 and s6
               341   S5
             59842   S6
        S9      11   S5 AND S6
? t 9/6/1-11

   9/6/1     (Item 1 from file: 40)
   0191745   Enviroline Number: *88-011250
   FARMING WITH AHIMSA: INTEGRATED RURAL DEVELOPMENT IN SRI LANKA,

   9/6/2     (Item 2 from file: 40)
   0165037   Enviroline Number: 83-003792
   THE ECO-PRANKSTERS,

   9/6/3     (Item 3 from file: 40)
   0129074   Enviroline Number: 78-003968
   THE POLITICS OF PLUTONIUM,

   9/6/4     (Item 4 from file: 40)
   0124581   Enviroline Number: *77-006571
   THE  CLAMSHELL  ALLIANCE:  GETTING  IT  TOGETHER; ANTI-NUCLEAR FERMENT IN
   EUROPE,

   9/6/5     (Item 1 from file: 484)
   01444494            91043026
   No Second Warning

   9/6/6     (Item 2 from file: 484)
   01278184            90528044
   Running for Congress Under Greens Banner
```

Fig. 22. Section of a DIALOG search printout.

odical information. However, it is prudent to add a *fourth unit* acknowledging where you obtained this information, in case you should have to check back on it. Do so as Figure 23 shows, allowing two spaces after the end of the publication unit, then recording the name of the database service where you found the citation, the file number you consulted, and the item number (ending with a period, of course). The latter information will not be needed, of course, if the source is ultimately used in the Works Cited list of the research paper.

Other Sources of Print Information

1. **Corporations, agencies, and professional organizations** publish reports, pamphlets, booklets, charts, maps, and more materials that libraries either don't know about or couldn't catalog and store if they obtained it. Consider making arrangements to gather such materials as you think may be relevant to your subject. For example, you might write to an auto manufacturer if you are researching auto safety or to an organization such as Habitat for Humanity if you are looking for information on low-cost housing. Be on the lookout for free offers of information, and send for what seems relevant. The *Vertical File Index* will lead you to some such material. You may not be able to write a preliminary citation card for this sort of resource unless you know a title you seek or until the material arrives.

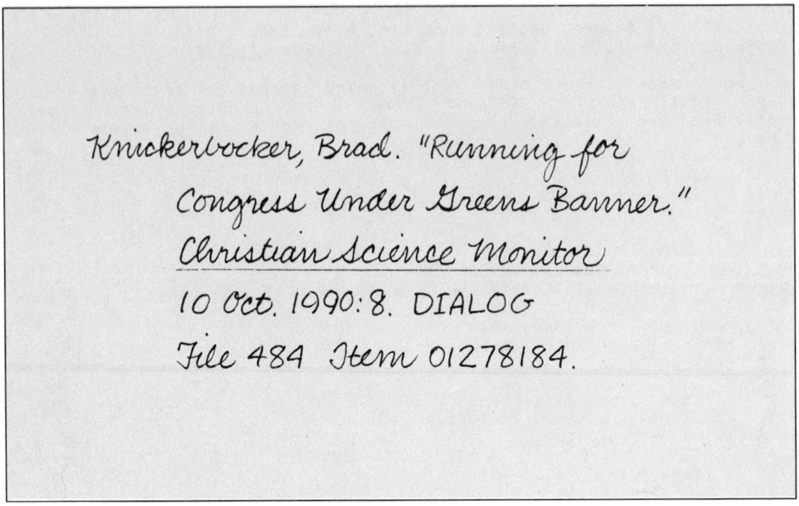
Knickerbocker, Brad. "Running for Congress Under Greens Banner." Christian Science Monitor 10 Oct. 1990: 8. DIALOG File 484 Item 01278184.

Fig. 23. Preliminary citation card from DIALOG printout.

2. **Specialized library collections in museums, historical societies, legal or medical or engineering groups, and others** are available in many cities. Find out if any is in the one where you are and, if your subject is one that lends itself to those available, take advantage of them. Make your preliminary citation cards based on what you find when you visit the collection.

3. **Interlibrary loans** are sometimes a possibility. With the growth of academic consortia and online computer links, it is easier than ever before to discover what exists outside the library you happen to be working in and to take advantage of such shared resources.

4. **Letters from an individual or an organization** can give you certain information you want for your research paper—provided you initiate such correspondence early enough to receive a reply. Send a brief letter containing *specific* questions. Also, you stand a better chance of a response if you address a particular person within an organization by name or, at least, by title. A librarian can help you locate the name and address of the person you should address.

   You won't always receive an instantaneous reply, but you may be pleasantly surprised at how many busy or well-known people are willing to take time to write someone working on a well-defined school project. The letters you receive may result in excellent help for your research and even provide you with some primary source material.

Work on the assumption that you will hear from whomever you have written to, and make a preliminary citation card containing any information you have to start with. Use the format for the resource as illustrated on pages 204–20 in Chapter 9.

RECORDING POSSIBLE NONPRINT SOURCES: CONVENTIONS OF PRELIMINARY CITATIONS (MLA STYLE)

The notion that all research sources are in a library is certainly outmoded! You do so much learning through what you hear and see, in addition to what you read, that you should certainly seek nonprint sources of knowledge in your Search Strategy. Besides, if you ever have occasion to do research in your vocation, you will quickly discover not only that not all sources are in a library, but also that using print sources may not be enough. You may have to interview people, watch a traffic flow, or otherwise rely on information that isn't written out and stored somewhere.

Public and academic libraries increasingly have video- and audiotapes available for loan. Schools invariably have media collections or media centers where such materials are housed and perhaps cataloged. Or they may be cataloged together with a library's print holdings. Often, library or media specialists can order special materials for your use from other collections or even from outside sources.

The extent to which such information sources are useful to you depends on the subject you're researching. In this section you will be reminded of many such sources—including such prosaic ones as your own radio and television—and see examples of how to make preliminary citation cards for the various nonprint media.

Three Units of Information in a Nonprint Preliminary Citation

Preliminary citation cards of nonprint sources carry the same three units of information as do print resources and in the same order: author, title, and publication information. The principal reason for recording publication information is so that anyone wanting to read, see, or hear a source you use in your research paper may do so. However, there is considerable variety in the kind of publication information you must record for nonprint resources, depending on the particular medium.

Pictures, if they are printed, can obviously be located in a book, pamphlet, or periodical. You consider a museum or other location where a painting or sculpture may be seen as its "publication information." Movies or even television programs can often be viewed, so they may be considered as "published." However, "publication information" for radio broadcasts and unrecorded speeches or lectures can only tell where you heard them.

Conventions of Nonprint "Publication Information"

In this section are some general guidelines about what may loosely be called publication information for some kinds of nonprint resources. Details about specific media are in the Works Cited examples on pages 217–22; consult them for models of how to record that information on your preliminary bibliography cards.

1. The **producer**, either a company or individual, of a video or other nonprint resource is considered its "publisher."

2. The **distributor** of a nonprint source is also noted as publication information.

3. The **copyright date** may be known and recorded. If none is shown, the year of production is regarded as copyright.

4. **Technical information** is recorded as if it were publication details. Indicate if the source is on video- or audiotape, is a CD or a 16-mm film, appears in black and white or color, and so on.

5. **Running time** is considered part of the technical information.

In the following example, for which no author is available in a film catalog and which thus can't appear on a preliminary citation card, all but the title comprise the publication information. Note that periods separate the producer and distributor (and copyright date) from the technical information.

EXAMPLE

Fastest Planes in the Sky. Nova. WGBH Collection. Films for

the Humanities & Sciences, 1991. VHS 60 min. color.

Radio and TV Programs

Using this source for information may be elusive—but rewarding. Although your advance warning to watch or tape-record a program may not be much more than a notice in that morning's newspaper, students often discover that radio and television carry a wealth of good material broadcast during a search for research paper sources. So be alert to every such possibility. And if you happen to turn on a broadcast that's useful to your study but that you didn't know about in advance, you can always write out a card that, instead of being a preliminary citation, turns out to be a Works Cited card.

A **preliminary citation card** for a radio or television program will include the title of the program, the name of a person or the persons featured, and whatever production or broadcast information you can get. There are enough variations that you should use the information above about "publication information" as a guide and examples on pages 215 and 218 to help with a particular format you need. See an example in Figure 24.

If you audiotape or videotape a program, you can use playback to get the names of people involved in production and broadcast as well as other facets of preparation that you will need to record on the card. If you don't tape the program, be alert for the names of people whose function you know will be needed in a citation.

Sometimes videotapes of regular programs, including those of news shows, are available for purchase. Less expensive, and usually just as useful for your own research purposes, are transcripts (that is, the written scripts) of TV programs.

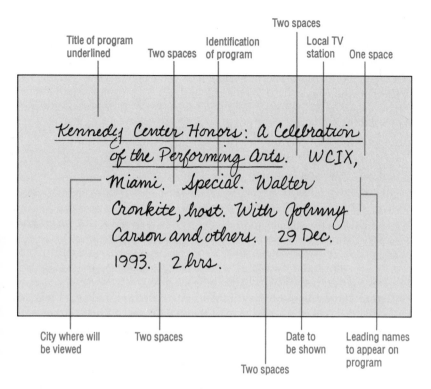

Two spaces

Title of program
underlined   Two spaces   Identification
of program   Local TV
station   One space

Kennedy Center Honors: a Celebration of the Performing Arts. WCIX, Miami. Special. Walter Cronkite, host. With Johnny Carson and others. 29 Dec. 1993. 2 hrs.

City where will
be viewed   Two spaces   Date to
be shown   Leading names
to appear on
program

Two spaces

Fig. 24. Preliminary citation card for a TV program. (Names of producer and director may be added after viewing the program.)

If needed information slips by you, call the radio or televison station (if it's a local one) on which something was broadcast and ask for the names of people involved or other information to help you to complete a preliminary citation card.

Interviews

Sometimes you can find published interviews of people of consequence in the subject you are researching. Occasionally, you can find a recorded audio or video interview; or you may listen to one on the radio or observe one on television. If the interview is one you happen upon on radio or TV, simply make a Works Cited card that contains the same information as other interview cards, but with the interviewer's name and call letters of the station plus the date heard/seen as identification. One enterprising student called the White House and was rewarded by receiving the transcript of a presidential press conference—an interview—on the subject she was working on! Usually, though, the most useful kind of interview for your own research may be the one you set up yourself, either in person or over the telephone.

The person to interview may be an expert in the field you are researching. Or you may simply need some kind of personal response from individuals. You can set up either kind of interview(s) easily, for most people are willing to help students get their homework finished. If you don't know people (or others who know them), you might find those to interview merely by looking in the phone book for people in specific jobs or businesses. At schools you will find faculty members who are bound to be specialists and who you can interview. Most of all, be creative about who you can find to talk with and where you can locate them.

One big advantage of an interview is that you can, to some degree, control the conversation. That is, you can ask the person you interview to repeat or clarify. Or you can move the conversation in a different direction by the questions you ask and the responses you make during the conversation. Remember, too, that an interview will often give you a primary source to work with.

Make an interview worthwhile for your research by adhering to the following guidelines:

1.   Have good reasons for asking a person or persons for an interview. And know in at least a general way what kind of information you're seeking through the interview.

2.   Call or write in advance for an appointment specifically for the interview.

3.   Be well prepared for the interview. (Take a cue here from radio and television personalities such as Larry King and Barbara Walters.) Know the subject you will talk about sufficiently well to ask intelligent and useful questions. Know the interviewee well enough to know what kinds of questions that person will be able to respond to.

4.   Prepare at least the key questions in advance, and be sure you control the interview in such a way that you get responses to the questions most important to your needs. Avoid asking questions that can be answered merely by "yes" or "no."

5.   Record both questions and answers accurately. A tape recording that is later transcribed is excellent, if the person you interview agrees to allow you to tape. (*Always* ask permission to tape-record a person.) Experienced interviewers use both notes *and* a tape recording for maximum accuracy—especially for any quotations that might be used.

6.   After the interview, be courteous enough to let the interviewee know what you decide to actually use in your paper, especially if you want to include any quotation.

A **preliminary citation card** for an interview should be written at the time you set the appointment. (If, for any reason, the day of an interview is changed, be sure to make the change on your card. And, of course, if the interview is canceled, discard the card.) See the example in Figure 25 for a card on a personal interview. Substitute the word "telephone" for "personal" in order to state accurately your method of conducting the interview.

Lectures and Speeches

You may have occasion to attend a lecture or speech (or hear one broadcast or listen to a recording of one) that relates to the subject you are researching. Class lectures are also categorized this way for purposes of research. Recording

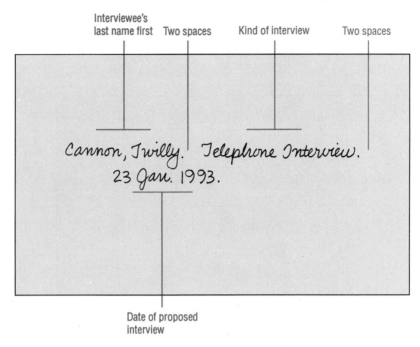

Interviewee's last name first   Two spaces   Kind of interview   Two spaces

Cannon, Twilly. Telephone Interview. 23 Jan. 1993.

Date of proposed interview

Fig. 25. Preliminary citation card for a personal interview. Note whether it will be in person or by telephone.

during a live presentation (except in a class where a teacher gives permission) is usually prohibited, but you should listen especially closely for points the speaker makes that are most relevant to your research concerns. Also, take complete and careful notes.

If you have the opportunity to ask questions of the speaker, either as part of an open forum or informally after the presentation, you will have an even better chance of gathering information from this source.

A **preliminary citation card** is possible if you know in advance that you will be listening to a speaker on material related to your research. Figure 26 is an example of such a card.

Obviously, there is no publication information on an oral presentation. However, the more details you can give, the more useful the citation will be to you in writing information you garner from it and in developing the subsequent Works Cited listing. For example, if the speech was a keynote or a closing address, note it on your citation. Also, see the example on page 216 in Chapter 9.

Questionnaires, Surveys, and Polls

One kind of primary and original research you may wish to use is a questionnaire, a survey, or a poll that you prepare, administer, evaluate, and use in your research paper. Rarely do you have time to develop extensive statistical studies or write a computer program to handle the data from the results of any such studies, even though that may be your object or inclination. At any rate, you should

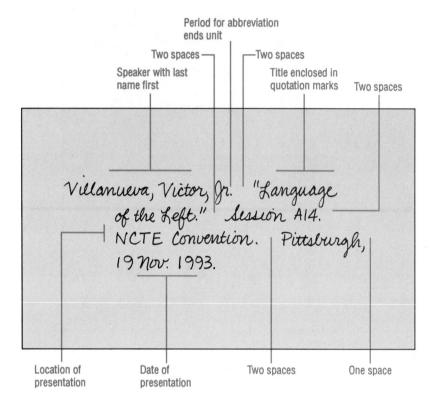

Fig. 26. Preliminary citation card for a speech or lecture.

consider using these methods as sources of information if you think one or more will be helpful to your research and to the paper you will write. Know, too, that if you elect to use any of these sources, the effectiveness of each depends on carefully framed questions and on the people you select to respond.

If you seek written responses to a questionnaire, technically you are probably using a written source. But for purposes of your research paper (and of this book), consider them among the sources of nonprint information. The category into which you put it is certainly less important than the material you can develop from these sources.

Write a **preliminary citation card** when you decide to develop a questionnaire, survey, or poll. Use slightly different forms, depending on whether it was answered anonymously or by people who signed their names. Of course, if many people answer your questions, you can't cite them all as sources. And, in fact, you yourself are the author if you use an original questionnaire. Figure 27 shows the form of a preliminary citation card for a questionnaire; use the same form for a survey or a poll, changing only the word that describes which of them you will use.

Films and Filmstrips

New films that libraries order are invariably on videotape, and that has been standardized into a VHS-format cassette, so old worries about tape size and kind are eliminated. However, large academic collections of 16-mm films still exist, as do many filmstrips and varying formats of videotape programs, that may yield helpful information for research papers. As with other nonprint materials, they are usually cataloged with the general collection holdings and/or in a separate group of audiovisual holdings. You will find what may be useful by checking through subjects. Knowing a particular title will help you discover if it is available to you by checking title listings. And films are also sometimes cataloged by director.

In a **preliminary citation card** for a film or filmstrip, the aspect you will emphasize in your paper should come first. Thus, if you are writing about the director Vincente Minnelli, his name would come first on a citation card for the film *An American in Paris*. However, if you were writing about movie musicals, the title would come first. Or Gene Kelly's name might be first on the citation card if you were writing about him or other film choreographers and dancers. Figure 28 gives you such examples.

Preliminary citation cards do not distinguish among fiction or cartoon or documentary films, although titles, running times, and production or distribution information almost always show those differences. Follow the general conventions on page 90 about noting production information for nonprint sources, and use the examples on page 218 as models.

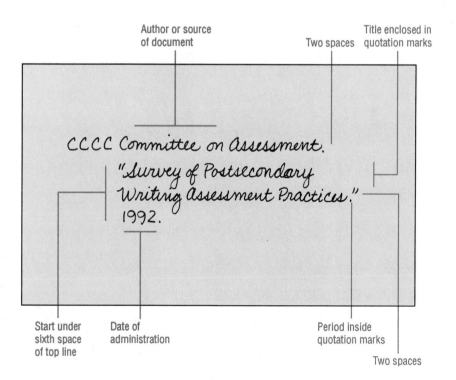

Author or source of document   Two spaces   Title enclosed in quotation marks

CCCC Committee on Assessment. "Survey of Postsecondary Writing Assessment Practices." 1992.

Start under sixth space of top line   Date of administration   Period inside quotation marks   Two spaces

Fig. 27. Preliminary citation card for a questionnaire.

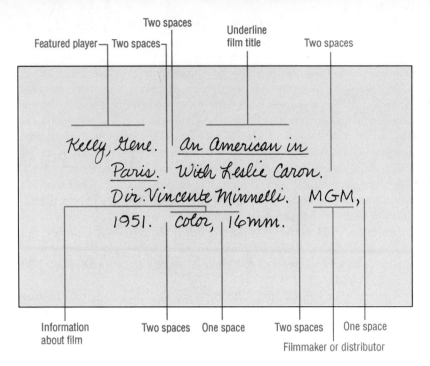

Fig. 28. **A**. Preliminary citation card for a film. (Add names of producer and director, and other information after viewing film when it becomes available. Begin entry with the person you plan to feature.)

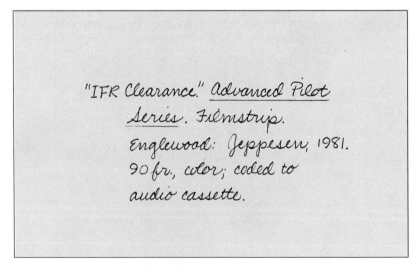

Fig. 28. **B**. Preliminary citation card for a filmstrip. Cite either particular strip in a series you will use or the entire series, showing only the quantity of frames and audiocassettes.

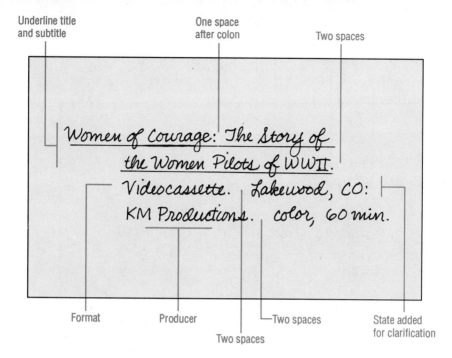

Fig. 29. **A**. Preliminary citation card for a videotape. (Add names of author and director, date, color or B&W after viewing video.)

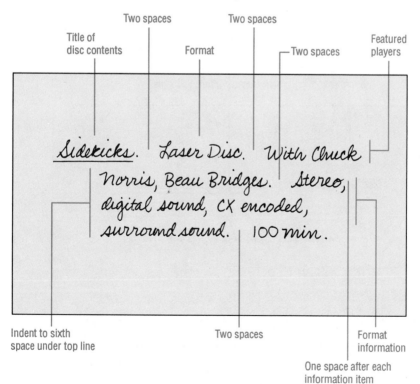

Fig. 29. **B**. Preliminary citation card for a laser disc. (Director, producer, and other information is added after viewing disc.)

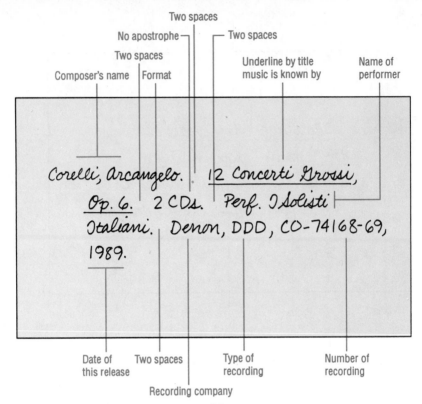

Fig. 30. A. Preliminary citation card for a CD.

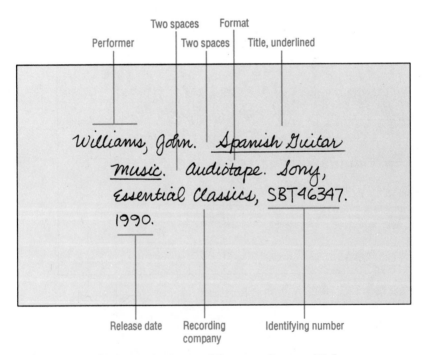

Fig. 30. *B.* Preliminary citation card for an audiotape. (Make necessary accommodations for tapes of spoken word, such as of books and lectures.)

Videocassettes, Laser Discs, and Interactive Video

New technology makes new demands on the researcher, both in finding appropriate material and in citing its use. Instead of ordering new films on reels, videotapes have already replaced them at most libraries and media centers; laser videodiscs are popular in homes, though they were once considered exotic and forward-looking in media centers. The laser disc in conjunction with a computer enables the user to move from one to the other, thus creating interactive video in which the user is an active participant rather than a passive viewer.

These technological innovations are cataloged in the same way as other nonprint sources: in the general catalog of a library's holdings and/or in those of an academic media center or in a departmental library. As of this writing, interactive video is pretty much limited to the collections of academic institutions, but that may change before long. However, depending on the subject you are researching, you may find videocassettes or laser discs in your own or another person's private collection or at a local video rental shop as well as through a library.

The **preliminary citation card** (see Figure 29) for any of these visual media will include the usual three units of author, title, and production (publication) information. Because so many of these tapes and discs are performances that lend themselves particularly to this medium, you may also have to treat such citations partly as films, showing the names of performers as well as of authors and directors.

CDs, Audiotapes, Other Audios

Both music and the spoken word are easily and inexpensively recorded now, particularly on audiotapes. Home-recorded CDs, the industry tells us at this writing, are imminent, though the digital quality of studio recordings, especially of music, will not be easy to emulate. The enormous growth of the audio recording industry means that you have increased sources of information for particular kinds of research work. Music surely comes most immediately to mind.

What you are looking for as source material depends on the subject you propose to write about, of course. Therefore, the general catalog of a library may contain entries of these audio materials. However, in larger academic institutions, individual departments may have their own specialized libraries too. Therefore, if you were looking for information about anything connected with music, probably the most productive place to look is the music department library.

A **preliminary citation card** for any audio recording—play, poetry reading, music, book, and so on—is exemplified in Figure 30. Should you happen upon a vinyl record, and a machine to play it on, you can follow this format also. Feature as "author" the most outstanding quality of the work, in terms of your research paper, whether that be the title of an opera or a music album. The performers must be noted, and often the producer is important enough to be featured. Always give the identifying number of the album or tape and the date of recording or performance, whichever is more important for your purposes. (See other examples of audio recordings on pages 217, 219–20.)

Recording Information

ORDERING TASKS

At last you're ready to take down some information you can actually use in your paper from all the potential sources you identified by searching out materials. Assemble your preliminary citation cards in groups according to where you will have to look for the actual books, periodicals, videos, and so on; then head for the sources.

Using the categories of the Search Strategy in the order you originally followed is a convenient way of approaching the materials, and you can thus use your time most effectively. That is, begin by reading relevant entries in encyclopedias and other general reference works. Then assemble other print sources and work with them. Most people find it easier to take notes from print than from nonprint sources, so if you follow this order, by the time you get to films, interviews, and other nonprint materials, you will be more adept at taking notes. Of course, if nonprint items are primary source material for your paper, you may want to start with them.

PLAGIARISM—AND HOW NOT TO COMMIT IT

Often the source you work from has stated an idea so well you can't imagine saying the same thing any other way. It's tempting to record those words on a note card. But if you do, **remember the quotation marks** and keep an accurate record of the source and page number on which the quote appeared so you can give proper credit in your research paper. Otherwise, you will be guilty of plagiarism.

Perhaps you get so involved in writing note cards that you forget to indicate whether wording on your card is a paraphrase or a combination of a paraphrase and a quotation. Again, if you fail to credit the source or use prescribed punctuation on your note card, you probably won't be able to give proper credit when you write the paper—and you will have committed plagiarism. Actions such as these may be slipups, but they're still plagiarism.

Of Words and Ideas—and Plagiarism

Plagiarism is using someone else's words or ideas without giving proper credit to the person who devised them. It is wrong to plagiarize, whether you do it deliberately or thoughtlessly. Both print materials (including maps, charts, and graphs) and nonprint materials (including films and still photos) are protected by copyright, and to present such materials as your own is to break the law as well as to act unethically.

The most blatant kind of plagiarism is submitting another person's paper as your own. Whether a friend lets you borrow a paper—or even part of one—to help you out or you buy one from a term paper ("research") service, letting a reader think that you did work you didn't really do is cheating yourself and others.

A more subtle kind of plagiarism is to let your reader think that certain words, phrases, or ideas are your own when they are, in fact, the property of other people you failed to acknowledge. Paraphrases and summaries, as well as individual groups of words—facts, opinions, ideas—may be plagiarized. Just varying a word here and there or changing singulars to plurals won't protect you from the label of "plagiarist." Even presenting common knowledge (see page 106) in somebody else's words, without credit, is plagiarism.

Plagiarism is most likely to occur at two stages during the research paper process:

1. When you take notes and fail to credit each source fully and carefully on each note card.

2. When you write the paper and fail to observe the conventions of documentation in acknowledging the sources of words, ideas, or illustrations. (Chapter 8, pages 186–201 will show you how to acknowledge sources in the text.)

Examples of how to make proper acknowledgments on note cards—and what *not* to do—follow in this chapter on pages 120–26.

How *NOT* to Plagiarize

Preventing plagiarism, like many other aspects of the research paper process, depends on attention to detail. Follow the next four simple rules, and you will never need to worry about plagiarism.

1. **Use quotation marks around all words and phrases from any research source, *and also* cite the source**, both on note cards and in the text of your paper. Quotations require *both* kinds of acknowledgment; one alone won't do.

2. **Credit the source of any ideas**, including summaries and paraphrases, by documenting them when you take notes and when you write your paper. The style shown in this book, which is recommended by the MLA (Modern Language Association), suggests that you dispense with superscripts and footnotes in favor of **parenthetical documentation** in the text. Thus, you credit each source immediately, and can't overlook one because you were busy writing out a thought. Two other widely used styles, those by the University of

Chicago Press and by the American Psychological Association (APA), also recommend parenthetical documentation; so, once learned, you can apply this method to writing in varied disciplines.

3. **Be sure every source you document in your paper is also in the Works Cited at the end of the text**. That is, acknowledging something that is not original must appear *both* in the written part, the text, of your research paper and in the Works Cited list at the end.

4. **Give an adequate introduction or otherwise clearly delineate borrowed words and ideas**. Always give enough information for your audience to tell clearly what is your original work and what isn't. Examples of how to do so when you write your paper are on pages 165–75.

To see the documentation forms by which you credit materials that you don't originate, see pages 187–93 of Chapter 8, "Documenting Your Paper." Examples of how to give adequate introductions to quotations, paraphrases, and borrowed ideas as you write are in Chapter 7, "Writing Your Paper," pages 165–70, and in the Sample Research Papers in Chapters 10 and 11, pages 230–46 and 257–71.

Notes That Plagiarize

It's easy to plagiarize when you see something that is well written—and almost every resource you use, whether in print or audible, is written well. Here, for example, is a paragraph from page 158 of *Environmental Science: Sustaining the Earth*, 3rd ed., by G. Tyler Miller, Jr. (Belmont: Wadsworth, 1991):

> For example, biodegradable plastics are an expensive sham. They take many decades to biodegrade in today's oxygen-deficient, packed landfills. Their use also encourages the continuing production of throwaway plastics made from chemicals derived from oil. Instead, the emphasis should be on recycling plastics. Better yet we should not be using plastics for many products that could be produced in reusable bottles or other containers or that could have much less packaging of any type.

PLAGIARIZED NOTE CARD #1

Biodegradable plastics are an expensive fake. They take many decades to break down in today's landfills that are oxygen deficient and packed closely.

COMMENT #1

Substituting "fake" for "sham" and "break down" for "biodegrade" is not original; the wording is still plagiarized. Nor does moving the word "landfills" from the end of the sentence to the middle and adding the word "closely" change the wording enough for this "note card" to be anything but plagiarism.

PLAGIARIZED NOTE CARD #2

Calling a plastic biodegradable is not a true statement because it takes many decades for it to break down in the oxygen-deficient, packed landfill of today.

COMMENT #2

One change here is that plurals ("plastics," "they") have been changed to singulars ("plastic," "it"), but that is not enough to rescue the passage from plagiarism. Nor does making one sentence of two, changing "biodegrade" to "break down," and moving "today" from the middle to the end of the sentence. The "note" is still almost identical to the original.

As you may already have inferred, it is harder to keep from plagiarizing a short passage than a longer one, from plagiarizing a few sentences than many. There is always the danger, if you work with a limited number of words in the original source, that you will be tempted to make your note adhere too closely to what another person has written because you don't have the range and flexibility to put more information into your own words.

Notes That *Don't* Plagiarize

Consider the same paragraph just used as illustration, but this time followed by acceptable wording on a note card:

For example, biodegradable plastics are an expensive sham. They take many decades to biodegrade in today's oxygen-deficient, packed landfills. Their use also encourages the continuing production of throwaway plastics made from chemicals derived from oil. Instead, the emphasis should be on recycling plastics. Better yet we should not be using plastics for many products that could be produced in reusable bottles or other containers or that could have much less packaging of any type.

ACCEPTABLE NOTE CARD #1

Plastics made from oil-derived chemicals never break down enough when they are disposed of to prevent polluting the environment, despite claims that they do. Instead, using minimal packaging, reusable containers, or, at the least, recyclable plastics will provide better protection for the environment.

COMMENT #1

The concept of the paragraph, which is that certain materials are less harmful to the environment than others, is stated but without using the same wording as Miller does in the original. Therefore, this "note card" does *not* plagiarize.

Here is another passage to illustrate how you can write note cards without plagiarizing. This illustration is from page 204 of *Marriages and Families: Making Choices and Facing Change*, 4th ed., by Mary Ann Lamanna and Agnes Riedmann (Belmont: Wadsworth, 1991):

Although individuals may be single for many reasons, they cannot remain happy for long without support from people they are close to and who care about them. This support is necessary for feeling positive about and generally satisfied with being single. Feeling satisfied with being single, of course, probably also depends on whether one is voluntarily single. At the same time, though, persons who find themselves involuntarily single may feel better about their status as they choose to develop supportive networks.

ACCEPTABLE NOTE CARD #2

In order to be satisfied and happy with themselves, unmarried people, whether in that situation deliberately or not, need to develop networks of support.

COMMENT #2

This sentence gives an adequate summary of the paragraph, which emphasizes the need for support for singles to maintain personal well being.

ACCEPTABLE NOTE CARD #3

People who are single "cannot remain happy for long without support from people they are close to and who care about them" (204). Therefore, whether single by choice or not, such persons will feel better about themselves if they develop networks for this support.

COMMENT #3

This note is a combination of a quotation, properly cited, and a summary that does not plagiarize from the original work. The actual note card would contain, in the top right corner, both the authors' names and the page location indicating the source of the entire paragraph.

ACCEPTABLE NOTE CARD #4

Lamanna and Riedmann say singles "cannot remain happy for long without support from people they are close to and who care about them" (204). Therefore, networks are important supportive elements to those who are single through choice or not.

COMMENT #4

This note also includes a quotation, introduced by citing the authors, and a summary. It does not plagiarize because it does not repeat the wording of the original source, except for the quotation.

COMMON KNOWLEDGE

Information that is well known or basic to a study is called "common knowledge" and does not require documentation. You identify the common knowledge for your own research paper either because you already knew such information or you find it repeated in a number of sources, therefore leading you to conclude that "everybody who knows anything about the subject knows *that*."

You may want to write a note card about this information, but you don't need to cite any sources because it could have come from any number of them.

EXAMPLES

- Dates of a well-known person's life
- Chemical formula of a familiar substance
- Location of a famous battle

Even if the information is new to you, finding it in several sources means it's common knowledge.

Certain *value judgments* may also be considered common knowledge and may not require documentation. For instance, so many critics have said that Shakespeare's *Henry IV, Part I* is a better play than his *Henry VI, Part II* that you may consider this judgment a matter of common knowledge.

Of course, if you want to quote a particular person's rendering of common knowledge you must give credit to that individual.

If you're not sure whether or not particular information is common knowledge, a safe rule to follow is "When in doubt, give credit."

READING TO TAKE NOTES

Effective readers use different methods for their varied purposes of reading. You might read a light fiction book very quickly, but you probably read new material for a course quite slowly in order to learn it. Similarly, you should acquire the habit of reading resources in different ways, depending on your purpose.

Previewing

When you *look for an overview and want to get a feel for your subject,* you are previewing. Don't try to take notes as soon as you open a book or turn to a magazine article. Instead, begin by becoming familiar with the subject you are going to read about—that is, by previewing a selection. Then you will have some idea about what to focus on so you can take notes most effectively.

- **If you are working with an article, read all the subheads before you read the entire text**.

- **Read over the table of contents of each book before you start to work with it**. If you know you are going to work with just part of a book, identify the section by checking the table of contents or the index to find the precise pages you will need.

- **Look at prefaces, forewords, glossaries, indexes, and appendices** before examining the content of a book. In short, know the structure of the work in which you are going to look for information.

- **Pay attention to chapter titles, headings, and subheadings before reading selections so you will know what is coming**.

- **Discover the organization of what you are about to read**. The chapter titles and headings are one way to see organization in a long work. In a shorter one, look for subheadings that help you follow a train of thought or a line of reasoning. You will be able to anticipate knowledge by understanding the structure an author has used in a work.

- **Look at beginnings and endings, at introductions and conclusions of whole works and units within them**.

Take time to preview your source material and you will save time when it comes to taking notes. You will be better able to define your subject field and be developing the skill of effective reading. You will also spot what is essential to your note-taking needs and, after previewing, be able to spend your time efficiently.

Skimming

In previewing, you are looking ahead; in skimming, you are looking quickly through a work to identify what will probably be valuable for you to read more slowly and carefully, and to spot what you might want to include in your research paper. Skimming is a quick way of reading that serves two purposes:

1. To get at the main idea of a selection and see it as a whole without undue attention to its details, which may distract

2. To tell if there is enough relevant information in the source to read more closely. If there isn't, you've saved yourself time.

Skimming is particularly important when you have an entire book to go through and need to find the specific information from it that will be useful. Use the table of contents and/or the index to locate the information by pages; then skim them to decide whether or not the contents warrant additional or closer reading.

Journal and magazine articles should also be skimmed to locate what, if any, part of a piece you need to read more closely. Longer newspaper articles usually have subheadings to guide your skim reading.

Scanning

Scanning is a more focused way of looking for material, but still without reading in specific detail. In scanning, you *look for specific information quickly.* Therefore, in order to scan effectively, you must know in advance what you are looking for. Be alert for *key words*, names, dates, or other specifics that indicate you have found information to take notes on. Rather than stopping to read everything on a page slowly and carefully, scan until you come to information that indicates you should pay close attention. You will already have an idea—from skimming—whether what you're looking for is in that particular source.

EVALUATING SOURCE MATERIALS

By virtue of being in a library, your sources of information have already been evaluated in several ways. They would not have been published in the first place without being scrutinized and deemed worthy of being printed. Second, they have been evaluated by librarians before purchase, usually on the basis of published reviews. Most important, if you are working in a school library, recommendations for acquisition have been made additionally by faculty or other qualified persons.

However, not all information you find will be equally useful or relevant to you. Therefore, you yourself will need to make evaluations at two stages of recording information for your research paper:

1. Before you read something

2. While you are reading it

The more closely you evaluate material, the more refined you make your judgment and thus the more you hone your independent-thinking abilities.

The following are some questions you can use as guides to evaluating materials. (You can also use them to help you make annotations on your citation cards, as explained on pages 226–27.)

Before You Read

1. Which authors seem outstanding in the field?

If some names recur as you read and listen, it's a safe assumption that those people are probably experts in the field and thus are reliable sources of information.

A useful guide to an author's credentials is his or her standing in the field. A meteorologist at the National Hurricane Center is likely to be a reliable resource on hurricanes, and an article on retail merchandising by a department store executive will undoubtedly be authoritative. The name of Donald Keene keeps showing up in material about Japanese literature in translation, so you may infer that this person must be an expert in the field (and you'd be right).

Where can you find out about an author? Journals usually identify authors by stating an academic affiliation and previous publications. You can also learn about the work of some authors from a biographical reference book such as *Who's Who in America, Contemporary Authors, Biography and Genealogy Master Index*, or similar sources.

2. What is the date of publication?

While all that is new is not necessarily better, more recent materials are likely to summarize or be based on earlier works. Some will also lead you to works previously published. Read materials in the order of their publication to help see a development of ideas.

Some scientific and technical fields, such as computer technology, change so quickly that finding recent materials may be a prime consideration for your research study. Or a research subject may depend on reaction to a book or an idea first proposed in a learned journal at the time it was published or to an event when it took place.

Remember, too, that the time lag between writing and publication is often a matter of years, especially for books and journal articles.

3. How credible does a source seem?

Five elements ought to be considered here, depending on whether your resource is print or nonprint.

a. **Publisher's reputation**

Ask your instructor or a librarian about the publisher, if the name is unfamiliar to you. Authors sometimes contract with book publishers to bring out their own works, and teachers and librarians can usually tell you the names of some of these "vanity presses." Such books are not necessarily unreliable. But the quality of work is often better if a reputable company has put out money to publish the book; there is a difference between paying to have one's own work put into print and having somebody else think enough of it to lay out the money.

Also, some publishers have known biases that might be reflected in the work they put out, so it's helpful to be aware of such leaning. For instance, an article in a magazine published by a particular religious denomination will probably reflect the theological attitudes of that denomination.

Magazines for Libraries and the *Classified List of Periodicals for the College Library* are two reference sources that librarians use to determine the bias, authority, and credibility for specific periodicals; you could consult them for the same information.

b.   Book's critical reception

Most books that are published are reviewed somewhere by people concerned with their particular subjects. Professional, academic and special-interest publications, as well as those for the general public, either review or note the appearance of books. *Book Review Digest* is a publication often consulted to find reviews. Be aware, though, that the responses you read may influence your own.

c.   Author's documentation

The support that an author offers in a text is another measure of a print source's credibility. If at least some of that documentation is from primary sources, it is likely to be more credible than if most of it had passed through many hands (or sources).

d.   Completeness of material

If you are working with a book, examine the introduction, preface, index, and bibliography. They show further evidence of the author's scholarship and, therefore, of credibility of a source.

e.   Source's personal qualifications

Nonprint information, especially in interviews and questionnaires, ought to be particularly scrutinized. Make sure the person (or persons) you consult is qualified to give the information you are looking for. Someone with a hobby or special interest may be fully as informed for your purposes as one in a vocation. For instance, a knowledgeable jazz record collector may know as much (or more) about the music as someone who regularly writes jazz reviews for a magazine. On the other hand, you may get opinions about the need for a piece of state legislation from interviewing shoppers at a mall, but if you talked with legislators who voted for *and* against the proposed law, you are more likely to get informed opinions and, therefore, credibility.

When You Read

1. What does the language of a source tell you?

Language reveals something of the beliefs and attitudes of the writer, and if you are properly attuned you may be able to learn more from your source than is immediately apparent.

The audience addressed by a speaker or writer, whether lay or specialized, is also a clue to the kind of material you consult. Understanding the way words are used will thus give you valuable clues about how the audience is viewed, whether in a condescending way, as informed equals, as those who ought to be impressed, and so on.

Language that is obviously slanted might affect your use of material—or the use you want to make of it. Discovering bias in a work doesn't mean that you must distrust the source or not use it; it simply means that you should be aware of the bias when using the source or making judgments about it. Here, for instance, is the last paragraph of a *Time* cover story about Attorney General Janet Reno (12 July 1993: 27) by Nancy Gibbs. The ending of an article is a strong position because it is the last thing readers are likely to remember. Therefore, the author's choice of information and wording is a good clue to the laudatory bias of the entire article.

EXAMPLE

And Reno, say those who know her best, believes in plenty. 'Southern liberals are that way because they believe,' says her sister. 'You weren't a liberal because it was a fad or because you were supposed to. You *weren't* supposed to. So you did it from profound conviction.' The real irony here is that Reno may be the New Democrat that Clinton both avoids and aspires to be. Her heart is big but her solutions are sound; she cares more for results than for labels, for ideas over ideology. If the White House is worried about taking the country in a new direction, perhaps it should send Reno on ahead as a scout. If she fails, she'll say so. And if she continues to get it right, she may be the one to lead the revolution.

2. Which sources seem to give you the most information for your purposes?

Some reference materials will tell you more than others about the subject you're researching. Also, some are especially provocative and lead you to think about issues and ideas you might otherwise not have considered. Others are valuable because they suggest additional sources you might decide to consult.

3. What facts or statements keep reappearing in your reading?

Information repeated in several sources is probably important in your study. (It may also be "common knowledge" and thus not need documentation, as explained on pages 106–07.) Once you have a sense of recurring facts from your preview reading of several sources, you can also tell if something that seems standard is omitted, thus indicating that the source is either untrustworthy or biased in a way you need to keep in mind.

QUALITIES OF GOOD NOTES

A research paper is only as good as the notes it is based on. Several weeks or even months may elapse between the time you write notes and the time you use them to write your research paper. Social events, other studies, family problems, all sorts of distractions will intervene. Therefore, you should be especially careful to take notes you can read and work from easily. Deciphering garbled notes or redoing them will waste your time and effort.

Perhaps the most important quality of a good note is that you **limit it to one idea on a note card**. Just this once, forget about saving trees, and use a little more paper. Don't try to cram lots of words onto a single note card. Don't put sequential ideas from a book or article on a single note card, because then you are bound to that one order. Also, what one source shows in close sequence may not be the precise order in which you want to use the information. The whole point of putting notes on cards is to have them in a format you can switch around to set in the order in which you want to use the information you gather. You can do so most easily if your notes are legible, accurate, and complete.

Legibility

1. Take notes on 4- × 6-inch cards.

Unless you are taking notes on a computer database, using this size card will give you enough space to write most notes on. Also, the cards are easy to arrange and rearrange as you work. Even if you've never before taken notes on cards, do so now; it will pay off.

2. Take notes that will last.

Write in ink, unless you are typing or using a computer. Pencil writing may smudge or become difficult to read after much handling.

3. Write on only one side of a card.

Better to see everything on a card at one glance than to flip back and forth looking for wording. Use the reverse side only to finish a statement or complete a quotation. Should you need additional cards for a particularly long note, identify each card in the series by number and author and staple them together in order.

4. Use whatever abbreviations you find convenient.

However, make certain they are abbreviations or symbols you are accustomed to using (as in class or lecture notes) and that they make sense to you. Be consistent so they will continue to make sense to you.

Accuracy

1. Read, see, or listen to your research materials carefully.

That may sound like elementary advice, but distortions and misrepresentations result when material is misread. One word mistakenly substituted for another in reading or listening can change the whole meaning of a passage—and possibly of an entire portion of your paper. Imprecise notes are detrimental to your work.

2. Record precisely.

Emphasize only what the source of information emphasized; don't *ever* second-guess or misrepresent an author's words. Be particularly careful to *check wording and spelling*, especially when you work with materials that are unfamiliar or highly technical.

3. Distinguish among fact, inference, and opinion.

- A *fact* is a statement that can be verified by evidence from the senses: something a person can see, hear, taste, touch, or smell.

- An *inference* is an educated guess based on at least one fact, but usually on several facts.

- An *opinion* expresses a belief held by an individual, but is not observable or verifiable.

Distinguishing among these three is crucial to critical thinking and judgment. You should distinguish among them when you take notes, in case you need to call upon that information when you write your paper. For example, certainly you wouldn't want to be so lax as to present mistakenly an author's inference as a fact. The surest way to make these differentiations—unless the content of that card makes the differences obvious—is to write out at the lower left corner of a note card whether what is recorded on it is a fact, an inference, or an opinion. (Some people find it convenient to use merely the letters *F, I,* or *O* in the lower left corner.)

Be sure to indicate if statements on note cards are *your own* opinion, belief, or inference rather than that of a source you consulted. You wouldn't want to mislead readers by allowing them to confuse your thought with that of another person. Writing "personal comment" at the bottom of a note card (as explained on page 125) is one way of doing this.

4. Use conventional mechanics of spelling, capitalization, and punctuation.

You are duty bound to copy such mechanics when you record a quotation. However, for the sake of accuracy when you draft your research paper later, follow convention on all your note cards.

Be sure you record quotations, titles, and foreign words accurately in notes so you can do the same in writing the text. Use ellipses to omit portions of quotations, and square brackets to enclose comments on the material. These and other customs are explained on pages 114–20.

Completeness

Think how frustrating it is to discover, while you are writing a paper late at night, that you neglected to write down important information. Or consider the wasted time if you need to look at a source again to clarify some point you didn't bother with initially.

Therefore, write down everything you think you might need and later discard any excess note cards rather than find that you must rush back to the library—or, even worse, that you can't get in touch with a person again. Consider that a periodical or book you want again might later be in use and not available to you. (If you do need to find something, the call number or library location on the preliminary citation card will be invaluable.) The following three characteristics of complete notes are shown on the sample cards in Figures 31 through 35 in this chapter.

1. Identify the source of what appears on each card.

The **top right-hand corner** is a convenient place to note source information, because you can see it easily. Write the **author's last name** alone if you consulted only one work by that person; otherwise, use both the author and the title.

Identify other materials by the **title or a shortened form of it**. For instance, Deborah Tannen's book titled *You Just Don't Understand: Women and Men in Conversation* can be identified as <u>Understand</u> on a note card (with the underlining showing that it is a book). **Dates of periodicals** will also be helpful for quick identification.

2. Note page numbers, tape footage, CD or laser disc band number.

The **top right-hand corner** is also the most convenient place for recording this information. Then you can easily write documentation from that note in the text of your research paper. Be sure to record *all* page numbers from which you got specific information, even if you are summarizing a long passage. Remember that both words *and* ideas need to be acknowledged in your paper in order to avoid plagiarism.

3. Identify as specifically as possible the subject of each note card in the top left-hand corner.

The purpose of writing a single idea on each card is so you can order them in any way you choose. Writing the *subject or key idea* on that card (often called a "slug," after the printing term that identifies content of a story) simplifies the later work of organizing these note cards. Instead of having to read through each one for contents, you will be able to tell at a glance what each card contains and thus arrange them more readily. *Never* write the subject of your research as a slug; all the cards you write will be on that subject, so such wording is useless because no separation of ideas will be possible.

CONVENTIONS OF WRITING NOTES

Readers expect to see certain customs followed when they read quotations, punctuation, italics, and spelling in a research paper. The easiest way to be sure your audience isn't disappointed or surprised is to follow those customs or conventions from the start of your work—the notes you take. Pay particular attention to the usual conventions of spelling (and give special care to unfamiliar words) and punctuation. The following list gives you the conventions that apply to some special problems, and their solutions, that you may encounter in taking notes.

1. Quotations

All wording taken completely from a written or spoken source *must be acknowledged in two ways:*

- by enclosing the words in quotation marks

  and
- by crediting the source.

The only way to prevent plagiarism, either deliberate or inadvertent (see pages 100–06) is by making the proper acknowledgment on your note card when you write it.

Use conventional punctuation for quotations, both within your notes and in the written text of your paper. (In the final text, quotations within a sentence are separated from your own words by a comma unless the quotation is the main portion of the sentence.)

EXAMPLE IN NOTES

> *Cannon interview*
>
> *"Like tools in a toolbox, we pull out*
> *whatever tool is appropriate for the job."*

EXAMPLE IN TEXT OF PAPER

```
"Like tools in a toolbox," Cannon said, "we pull out
whatever tool is appropriate for the job."
```

a. **Quotations at page breaks**
    If you use *a quotation that goes from one page to another*, note on your card where one page ends and another begins so you can be accurate in documenting the passage. A virgule, or diagonal line (/), is conventional for the purpose.

EXAMPLE

> *Kruger 41-42*
>
> *"Women who say they have experienced*
> *discrimination are much more likely to mentor*
> *other/women than women who have not*
> *(77% to 55%), and to take on the role of*
> *advocate for women in the organization*
> *(62% to 43%)."*

COMMENT

The virgule on the note card shows where there is a page break in the original source of this quotation. The author is shown on the top right corner of this note card. Page numbers there show that "other" is the last word on page 41 of this magazine article and "women" is the first word on page 42.

b. Quotations within quotations

A quotation within the source you are quoting will be signaled by double quote marks. However, you need to show that fact in your notes (and in the text of your research paper) by using single quote marks within the double ones.

EXAMPLE ON NOTE CARD

Brezina 48

"We will have to learn 'what a long-term,

continuous, and ultimately boring activity'

caring for the environment will be."

Quotations from Margaret Mead's

testimony in favor of EEA before

House and Senate subcommittees

COMMENT

This entire quotation appears in a book by Dennis Brezina. However, in this passage, he repeats the words of Margaret Mead, signified by double quote marks in his book and by single quote marks on this note card.

c. Poetry quotations

For passages of two or three lines in the text, use virgules (diagonal lines that appear on typewriter and computer keyboards) with a space on each side to indicate the end of one poetic line and the beginning of another. The whole passage will be within quotation marks. Retain the capitalization and punctuation of the original poem, of course.

EXAMPLE

"Busy old fool, unruly sun, / Why dost thou thus, / Through windows, and through curtains, call on us?"

If the line you are quoting begins at a point other than the left margin of the poem, imitate the spacing or use ellipses (see below about words omitted).

EXAMPLE

> *". . . Yesterday,*
>
> *We had the daily cleaning. And tomorrow*
>
> *morning,*
>
> *We shall have what to do after firing. . . ."*

Poetry that has unusual spacing must be reproduced as accurately as possible from the original so that you can copy that spacing in the research paper itself.

EXAMPLE

> *"Sweet Peace, where dost thou dwell? I*
>
> *humbly crave,*
>
> *Let me once know.*
>
> *I sought thee in a secret cave,*
>
> *And asked, if Peace were there."*

If the poetry you want to quote will take *four or more lines* when you write it in the final text of your research paper, you must *follow the typography of the poem* you are quoting. Therefore, copy the poetry onto your note card *exactly* as it appears on the printed page that is your source. Long lines across a page may require you to make such accommodations as recording them on paper rather than on a card. A passage that long will not be enclosed in quotation marks. However, if there are quotation marks within the original, change them to single quote marks for both your note and the text of the paper.

d.   Italics within quotations

Any word or words italicized within a quotation should be underlined in your notes. This custom stems from the fact that printers seeing underlined words will automatically set them in italic type. In the text of your research paper, use the underlining if you are typing; but you may use italics if they are available on a word processing program you use.

2. Words omitted from a quotation

You may decide to omit a word, a phrase, a sentence, or even a paragraph, from a passage you are quoting, so long as such omission retains the sense of the original wording or idea. You must indicate that something is left out by substituting an **ellipsis: three periods with a space before and after each one**. If the omitted wording is at the end of the quotation, use four periods: three for the ellipsis and one to mark the end of the sentence.

EXAMPLE

"Ecotactics" 15

". . . corporate and government polluters crave secrecy and deny citizens access to the records of that which is harming their health and safety."

3. Interpolations or commentaries

An interpolation is an interrupter that you supply as commentary to the text of a quotation or to your own wording as you write. **Enclose an interpolation in square brackets** both in your notes and in the text of your research paper. Most computer keyboards and some typewriter keyboards have the square brackets on them. If yours doesn't, draw the brackets in by hand both on the notes and on the paper itself. There are three reasons you may want to make an interpolation.

a.   To relate a pronoun to its antecedent noun that doesn't appear in the quoted passage but without which the quotation wouldn't make much sense

EXAMPLE

> *McBride 14*
>
> *Earth First!'s ". . . militant presence will make it easier for guys like you [a Sierra Club member] to deal with the bureaucrats in smoke-filled rooms."*

b. To show that something is copied accurately, even though it's wrong

The word *sic*, meaning "so" or "thus," in square brackets is evidence that you are aware something in a quotation is wrong, such as spelling or punctuation, but that you have, indeed, copied it down accurately. If you fail to make this interpolation at the time you write out the note card, you may mistakenly believe you've made a mistake when, in fact, the error is that of another person. Sometimes printing errors do occur, but you must not correct them, just copy down what you see and indicate to your own audience that you recognize the error.

EXAMPLE

> *"Many resent [sic] right to know cases come to mind."*

c. To express a personal comment

Your comment can clarify an idea or wording drawn from some other source, or it can merely be a remark that comes to mind when you are writing the notes. Include your comment by putting it in square brackets in your notes. You can then either use or choose to omit that comment in writing the paper.

EXAMPLE

> *Activists read "circumstances and findings of all the relevant court decisions on all levels . . . to date, meaning today!" [emphasis added]*

4. Foreign words and phrases

Non-English words or phrases should be underlined in your notes and in your paper, even though they do not appear that way in the source you are quoting. They may, in fact, be printed in italics and you may also use italics—the equivalent of underlining in printing—in the research paper (or if you are taking notes on a computer that has italic fonts).

5. Titles within quotations and sources

Follow the conventions of writing titles, even though the source you are working from uses a different method. For example, if book titles are in quotation marks or boldface type in your source material, show them as underlined or italicized, unless they are part of a quotation. Then you are bound to reproduce them from the original source, but can follow any with an explanation in square brackets.

Put **quotation marks** around the titles of short stories, poems, essays, chapters in books, newspaper or magazine articles, songs, lectures or speeches, and individual episodes of radio and television series shows. Exceptions are sections of sacred writings, such as the names of books in the Bible.

Underline titles of books, plays, pamphlets, long poems, periodicals, films (including laser discs), computer software, CDs or record sets, radio or television programs or series, paintings or sculptures, even spacecraft. Exceptions are the titles of sacred writings, such as the Bible, the Koran, or the Talmud. Since underlining means italicizing to printers, you may italicize such titles when you write them in your research paper, if your word processing program has such capacity.

KINDS OF NOTES

You can take any of the four basic kinds of notes: **summary, paraphrase, direct quotation,** or **personal comment**. A **combination** of two of more of these is another possibility. The choice of which kind of note to take is a matter of personal preference and what you think you might use in your research paper.

You have already read that **each single note card should be limited to just one idea**. You also know that you should use corners of the card for several identifying kinds of material. Three have already been given, but now it's time to add another, to be sure that when you start writing from the note cards you'll know what kind of note you've taken. Therefore, put these notations on all your note cards in order to be assured that you can later document whatever is necessary in your paper:

- *Top left corner:* slug line identifying specific subject on the card

- *Top right corner:* author and/or title and page number(s) of material on the card

- *Botton left corner:* show what is fact, inference, or opinion on note or quote

- *Bottom right corner:* kind of note on that card. (Though punctuation identifies a quotation, you can't hurt yourself by repeating that fact.)

The paragraph that follows is from an article used by Barbara Howell, the student whose research paper appears on pages 230–46, in preparing her paper. It will serve as the basis for illustrations in this section of the various kinds of notes you can take for your own work. Note that the paragraph appears on two different pages in the original (the split is evidenced by the virgule) and that the words "mini-conference" are within single quotation marks here because on this page the entire paragraph is a quotation (signified by the block indentation).

EXAMPLE

Original Passage:

The elements of political strategy are compromise, bargaining, timing, and trade-offs. These are legitimate procedures in the passing of legislation and not necessary evils of the political system as they often are perceived by critics of the legislative branch. Compromise, for example, is a means of resolving conflicting interests. Along with/bargaining, it was used in the 'mini-conference' held after the Environmental Education Act had been passed by both houses, in which elements of both bills were woven into a final product. A trade-off was involved in forcing the Executive Branch to create an administrative office, with the implicit danger of provoking continuing hostility to the program and causing it to receive a lower funding level. Timing was involved when the congressional sponsors took advantage of the pressures created by the few days remaining before the elections to whip the bill through. There was a sense of urgency in Congress, with the congressmen wanting to get home for the final campaigning, which resulted in a flurry of legislative activity.

Brezina, Dennis. *Congress in Action: The Environmental Education Act.* New York: Free, 1974: 13–14.

Summary Notes

A summary is a statement in your own words of the main ideas of a passage. It tells *only what the author has said* and may *not include your own interpretation or comment* on the meaning. (Save those for the personal comment note cards.) Because **a summary is limited to main ideas**, it will be shorter than the original. However, follow the organization or order of the original source when you write a summary. See Figure 31 below for an example.

Summary notes are particularly useful, and widely used, because they pack a lot of content into a little space. A page in the original may become a paragraph in your notes; a paragraph may become a sentence or a few words. Use summary notes to record

- An overall idea

or

- A large amount of information succinctly

Begin to write a summary note by separating what is most important in a passage from what is less important. Making that distinction is a reading skill, but it's also one closely related to writing, for every time you compose a main idea (or thesis) and develop it, you are using the same skills.

Writing a summary note in complete sentences is a good idea because of the practice that doing so affords. Also, you shouldn't feel held to using the exact wording of a summary you've put onto a note card; you can always change any wording that isn't a direct quotation subsequently in a draft of your research paper.

---

how EEA passed   *Brezina 13-14*

The EEA was finally passed—and hurriedly—because its advocates used the strategies common to politics; they made compromises and struck bargains, and were able to make timing work for them by letting congresspeople get home quickly in return for passing the bill.

summary

Fig. 31. Summary note card.

COMMENT

Note how this summary uses the four key words of this paragraph—"compromise, bargaining, timing, and trade-offs [in return]"—in the same order they appear in the original. Yet, because this is a summary, only the results of each technique are mentioned. Note, too, that the gender-fair word "congressperson" is substituted for the stereotypical "congressmen" of the original paragraph, a leeway permitted in a summary.

Paraphrase Notes

A paraphrase is a phrase-by-phrase statement in your own words of the original passage. Because it follows the original so closely, it has the same organization and is also approximately the same length. *Do not interpret* material in paraphrasing; just restate it.

When you prepare to paraphrase, you examine each phrase and thought carefully, then write each in your own words. Be aware that one pitfall of paraphrasing is the temptation to use wording from the original. However, a paraphrase is a *complete rewriting*, not just a game of rearranging words.

Paraphrase note cards are particularly useful for any of the following:

- Translating technical passages or other specialized information into lay language or other language that is appropriate to your audience and helpful to your own understanding

- Exploring the meaning of poetry by "expanding" poetic expression into prose

- Making sure you understand exactly what an author said by putting it in your own words

Paraphrased notes are often preferable to summaries because they are more detailed and specific. They are often preferable to quotations because the text is in your own words rather than in someone else's, thus ensuring that the wording of your paper will be original and in your own writing style.

There isn't much to gain by paraphrasing some passages rather than summarizing them. However, a paraphrase can always be turned into a summary when you write your paper, although the opposite isn't true.

Figure 32 shows a paraphrase note card for the paragraph by Brezina you saw on page 121.

Fig. 32.   Paraphrase on a note card.

C O M M E N T

The four elements of political strategy of the first sentence are quoted here because they are identical to the original. They are then illustrated in order, just as Brezina does in the original paragraph. Notice that the wording closely follows the original but does not inadvertently borrow from it. "Washington" and "national elections" are added for clarification because the passage is about a bill passed by the U.S. Congress.

Direct Quotation Notes

A direct quotation copies exactly what your source said or wrote and is therefore the easiest kind of note card to write. Taking direct quotation notes requires absolute fidelity to the written word (down to every comma or misspelling in print) or to the spoken word.

Resist using direct quotation notes unless there is good reason, because the more note cards with quotations you have, the more tempting it is to overuse quotations in your research paper. Then, instead of being an original piece of writing, the paper easily becomes a cut-and-paste collection of other people's words (and their styles of writing); your own sense of person can't come through.

On the other hand, one advantage of having note cards containing quotations is that you can use the information for either a summary or a paraphrase if you decide not to use the quotation in writing your research paper.

Take direct quotation notes if any of the following holds true:

- The style of your source is so perfect, so suitable, or so vivid that it seems beyond changing.

- The material is so significant or controversial that wording must be exact.

- The source is so authoritative that you want to be sure not to violate the precision of the wording.

- The wording of the source needs to be transmitted with absolute accuracy.

In writing a quotation note, be sure to follow carefully the conventions that will ensure that you are giving proper attribution when you include the quotation in your research paper. Figure 33 shows what a note card based on the paragraph on page 121 might look like.

C O M M E N T

Note that quotation marks enclose the two sentences, thus marking, along with the bottom right notation, what kind of note this is. The ellipsis after the first word shows that some wording (in this case, the "for example" of the original, which is not needed here for sense) is omitted. The virgule in the second sentence shows the page change from 13 to 14, as noted in the top right corner. And enclosing "mini-conference" in *single* quotation marks shows that it was within double quotation marks in the original passage.

political strategies of EEA   *Brezina 13-14*

  *"Compromise . . . is a means of resolving conflicting interests.
Along with / bargaining, it was used in the 'mini-conference' held
after the Environmental Education Act had been passed by both
houses, in which elements of both bills were woven into a final
product."*

                                                              quotation

Fig. 33. Quotation on a note card.

Personal Comment Notes

Your own comments on your research subject are important to the research paper. Writing them on note cards while you are taking notes from other sources is best because:

- They catch your own insights quickly and preserve them in writing for future use.
- They help you make the synthesis between what you discover about your subject and your own ideas—the basis of a research paper.

Record all these thoughts, opinions, even fleeting notions rather than leaving them to memory or to random scraps of paper. As Figure 34 shows, you obviously can't put a source in the top right corner, but the "personal comment" at the lower right accounts for that lack on your card when you go back to work with it. This example is a comment on the same Brezina paragraph used for other illustrations in this chapter.

universality of "political strategy"

  *Examples of political maneuvering Brezina uses to tell how
the EEA was passed could apply to many occasions or events
besides just getting a congressional bill through.*

                                                      personal comment

Fig. 34.   Personal comment note card.

Combination Notes

You can **combine summary, paraphrase, quotation, or personal comment notes in any way that is workable for you**. Just be sure you note the source at the top right, so you can give accurate attribution in the text of the research paper, and record in the lower right *what form of note is on the card*, so you can maintain such accuracy. Figure 35 is an example of such a combination from the paragraph on page 121 being used as illustration for other kinds of notes.

EEA quick passage   *Brezina 14*

Brezina believes that proper timing, a necessary characteristic of political strategy, was one element leading to quick passage of the EEA. "There was a sense of urgency in Congress, with the congressmen [sic] wanting to get home for the final campaigning [in a national election year], which resulted in a flurry of legislative activity."

                     summary and quote

Fig. 35. Combination summary and quotation note card.

COMMENT

The first set of brackets in the quotation signifies that the wording of the original paragraph, which was published in 1974, would be considered sexist language today but is, here, a precise quotation of the original. The second set of brackets shows how this symbol is used for a clarifying interpolation. If this note card is used in the text of the research paper, either or both interpolations may be omitted, for the quotation would still remain an accurate one.

NUMBER OF NOTE CARDS

Nobody can tell you how many note cards you will need for a particular research paper. If you take effective notes, you will need fewer cards. If you already know something about the subject, you will need fewer cards than if everything is brand-new to you. Some students find that thirty note cards suffice for a 2,500-word research paper; others need three times as many. The *quality* of notes counts, not the quantity.

If you are in doubt about whether or not to record information, better write it down. Should you later discover that you have more information than you need, set aside some of the note cards and don't use them (but don't discard them until you've received a grade on your research paper). No rule says you have to use every card you write on! But it's better to have too many note cards than not enough and having to track down additional resources at the last minute.

A NOTE ABOUT PHOTOCOPYING

You can't write a paper from photocopies! No matter how much you underline or otherwise mark up your photocopies, they are no substitute for actually taking notes on cards! Only on cards do you have information readily at hand in flexible and movable form. Only on cards can you have information in summary or paraphrase form, thus shortcutting continual textual reading.

Take advantage of the convenience of photocopying: you can bring home individual sheets of relevant material, often from books or microforms that you would otherwise have to work from only in a library. But use the material with discretion, and work *from* it rather than with the copy itself.

IF YOU USE A COMPUTER . . .

If you are familiar with microcomputers, if you have one readily available, or if you are accustomed to working on one, you will probably use it in preparing your research paper. Most students who use computers seem to rely on word processing for writing and revising the paper. There are spell checkers, of course, to help with that aspect of writing. There are grammar checking programs and outlining capabilities for many word processing programs.

Notebook computers are more readily available than ever before, and their compact size makes carrying them into libraries to take notes convenient, especially from books that can't be checked out.

A database program is one way to take notes on a computer. Instead of using a note card, you can store the same information as a record on a database program, many of which allow you to choose a format of your own. Later, you can call up and print out those units of information you want.

If you set up a database program to take notes, use the same categories of information (called "fields" in a database) you would put on a note card:

Slug line or key word

Author

Title

Call number of book or location of periodical

Page numbers

Text of note

Type of note (that is, paraphrase, summary, and so on)

The difference between where you put this basic information on a database program entry and on a note card is dictated by the difference in the way you write in each of these media.

Leave plenty of room for your text. And remember to **limit yourself to just one idea per screen or citation**, just as you would if you were taking notes on 4- × 6-inch file cards.

If you don't know how to set up a database—or prefer not to—you can achieve the same effect by setting up what is called a "template" on the computer through a word processing program. That is, use the categories shown for the database suggested, but write them out on a word processing program and repeat the format a number of times. Save them all to the data disc and then simply fill in the spaces when you take notes. A complete printout will give you these notes, and you can cut them apart to organize your information.

In all other aspects, adhere to the same customs and recommendations about writing note cards that you have been reading about in this chapter, including the conventions of writing notes, being complete and accurate, taking various kinds of notes, and, certainly, avoiding plagiarism.

Organizing Ideas

RECONSIDERATION TIME

Ordinarily, 90 percent of an iceberg is under water and remains unseen; only people who know something about icebergs can fully comprehend and appreciate their immense size just by seeing the part above water. A research paper is very much like an iceberg because what you can see isn't the whole story. Only somebody who is familiar with the entire process of selecting a topic, locating and assembling and recording information, selecting what is most useful, and organizing the whole into a coherent work can best appreciate the research paper. What takes only fifteen minutes to read in its final form is the result of many hours of painstaking work.

The part of the process you are about to start is probably one of the most challenging:

- Looking hard at material you've gathered
- Evaluating the notes you've taken
- Organizing the notes you select

At this stage you show your critical judgment when you are willing to discard anything you judge as irrelevant or repetitive. No matter how difficult it is to delete material you've spent time finding and recording, it's better to keep the flow and focus of your paper than to try cramming in the content of every single note card.

When you organize ideas, think again about *the audience* for this research paper you're writing.

- What background or basic information does the audience probably have about this subject? (There is no need to repeat it when you write.)
- What will the reader(s) be likely to want to know about this subject? (Such knowledge will serve as a guide to what the content of your paper should be.)

In order to organize ideas effectively, consider again some *decisions you have already made*:

- Are you satisfied with the approach you selected? (If not, can you vary it and still fulfill the assignment?)

- Will the materials you gathered and your thinking support the approach you selected (or were assigned)?
- Do you need/want to consult any other resources? (Do so now.)

PUTTING THE PARTS TOGETHER

Until now, you have been working with parts of your research paper—with individual sources and separate note cards. But now you are ready to organize the ideas you've collected and make a transition from working with the parts to seeing them as elements in the whole unit: the research paper.

1. Consider each note card on its own merits.

As you read through the note cards, begin thinking about the main point you want to make in your paper. See whether what you've written on a particular card relates directly to that main point and what you think you want to put into the paper. If the card content doesn't fit well, put the card aside rather than try to cram in extraneous material. (Keep all the note cards; you may decide you want some of the information as you are writing.)

2. Group the note cards according to slug lines or key words in the top left corner.

If you've done a good job of choosing these identifying words, you have a ready-made way of grouping ideas and one step of organization is done.

If you have too many cards with the same key words or find that some don't really express the idea of a note as well as you thought when you wrote them, try "renaming" the note card. Look again at cards you can't at least pair up and rename them in order to make groups.

If you've taken notes on a computer database, now is the time to sort the notes by key words. You should also make a printout, or hard copy, of the information so you can see exactly what you have to work with.

3. Make personal comment note cards.

In learning about your subject, and in thinking about it now, you surely must have encountered ideas you want to question or comment on. If you haven't already noted them, do so now.

You are now an informed source on your subject, so your comments are worth considering; and writing them on note cards now will ensure that you don't overlook them in the haste of writing. Besides, incorporating your own views is an important part of the synthesis that separates a research paper from a simple report.

4. Look for a central idea in all that you've learned through research.

Remember that you now know enough to be able to take a stand about your subject and support it. Decide what you want to emphasize about your subject, what you want to build your work around as you review your notes. That central idea will become the thesis statement for your paper.

5. Alphabetize the preliminary citation cards.

You will need to use these cards when you start writing the initial draft of your paper. When you write in-text citations, you may need to get some information from the preliminary citation cards. Certainly, you will also need these cards to make the Works Cited listing at the end of your paper. Therefore, putting these cards in alphabetical order according to author's last name or according to first words in titles of anonymous works will make it easy to consult them for both purposes.

Also, now is a good time to be sure you've consulted all the sources you can. If you were instructed to use both primary and secondary sources, both books and periodicals, some nonprint media, and articles from scholarly journals as well as from the popular press, then make sure you have fulfilled all those qualifications.

WHAT A THESIS STATEMENT *IS*

A *thesis statement* is a specific declaration that summarizes the point of view you will take in your paper. It is the touchstone of your paper—the starting place that synthesizes your discoveries about your subject and your evaluation of them. **The thesis statement must be in sentence form.** It is usually one sentence, though it may be several if you plan to write a particularly long paper or your subject is especially complex. The more succinct and specific you make your thesis statement (while keeping it complete), the easier it is to use as the basis for an outline, which is the next step in organizing ideas and should be completed before you actually begin writing your paper.

People arrive at thesis statements in different ways. For some, the statement comes first—an immediate, overall, global view of the work and a sense of the principal thrust of the paper. For others, the statement evolves only after grouping individual ideas into units (according to the slug lines on note cards), then looking at the units to see how they fit together in a general way. One helpful way of working is to list specifics you want to include in your research paper, then finding the unifying idea(s) underlying them all. Whichever method you use, the goal is to develop a thesis statement that you can work from in organizing the ideas within your paper.

Here are the characteristics of a successful (that is, a workable) thesis statement:

1. The thesis statement is limited so it can give direction to the paper.

Earlier you decided on an approach to your subject: to examine or analyze it, evaluate it, compare and contrast it to something, establish a relationship, or argue a point of view. If your research and study lead you to change some earlier ideas or choose a different approach, provided it will still meet an assignment, now is the time to make that change. The thesis statement sets limits on the scope of what you will cover in the paper, so it should reflect the contents accurately.

UNLIMITED   Several factors extend human life.

LIMITED   Technological developments that prolong human life are not necessarily desirable for all patients and their families.

2. The thesis statement is specific.

Anyone reading the thesis statement should know what the paper is about. Vague words won't do.

VAGUE   Child care is a big issue for working parents.

SPECIFIC   Vouchers, on-site nursery schools, flexible work hours and days, co-ops, and after-school programs are among employers' innovative solutions to the problem of needed child care for working parents.

3. The thesis statement is a way to unify ideas within the paper.

That's why it is *written first*, before you begin to write the paper. Usually, it is also written before you begin an outline—so it becomes a "peg" upon which to put the specifics of the outline. If you stick to the thesis statement when you compose the outline and write the paper, you will keep yourself from straying to extraneous ideas, no matter how individually interesting they may be to you.

4. The thesis statement is an aid to coherence for your paper.

A good thesis statement holds together diverse aspects of the paper. When you write the outline, check everything you plan to put into it against the thesis statement and omit anything that doesn't relate directly to it.

WHAT A THESIS STATEMENT *IS NOT*

Sometimes it is easier to understand an idea when you can see what it isn't, rather than only what it is. Accordingly, the four following statements tell and illustrate what a thesis statement *is not*.

1. A promise or statement of purpose is not a thesis statement.

If you promise to say or show something in your paper, go ahead and do it. But phrase the thesis statement to show that you have fulfilled your expectations, not simply that you *have* expectations.

PROMISE (Not a Thesis Statement)

In this paper I am going to show that pro football salaries are not too high.

THESIS STATEMENT

> Because the money that goes for pro football salaries
> puts money into the economy by supporting many people and
> businesses, players' high salaries are justified.

2. A topic or subject by itself cannot serve as a thesis statement.

The topic or subject tells only what the paper is about rather than what you have to say about the matter.

SUBJECT (Not a Thesis Statement)   **Fitness craze**

Capitalizing the first letter of each word, or even adding a few words, won't make a thesis statement, although it might eventually make a *title* for a paper.

TITLE (Not a Thesis Statement)

The Fitness Craze in the United States

Adding a predicate to a subject, however, might yield a thesis statement.

THESIS STATEMENT

> The fitness craze in the United States has resulted in
> a population more aware of the role of exercise and good
> eating habits in lengthening people's lives and in making
> them more productive.

3. Words added to a title but *not* forming a complete sentence cannot be a thesis statement.

NOT A THESIS STATEMENT

The potential of music for education

That's unsatisfactory wording because although it suggests the contents of the paper, it doesn't express an attitude toward either music or education. Moreover, it isn't a sentence (a requirement for a thesis statement) and is therefore not a complete thought.

THESIS STATEMENT

> Because young people absorb the words of the music they
> listen to most often, popular songs should be used more
> often and more fully as methods of education.

Now you can see clearly what the paper is about and the approach it will exemplify (argumentive). The paper will be easier to write because the thesis statement serves as a framework that only requires development to express what the author wants to convey to readers.

4. A question cannot serve as a thesis statement.

This is obvious, because a question isn't a statement at all! A question can only mean that an answer will follow.

QUESTION (Not a Thesis Statement)

What will Maya Angelou's place in literature be?

WEAK THESIS STATEMENT

Maya Angelou will have a secure place in several genres of literature.

This statement is weak because it is vague—and a thesis statement must be specific. A reader would want to know what is meant by "secure place" and what the "several genres" are. It isn't a statement that would help a writer organize information to include in the paper; therefore, it's not a useful thesis statement.

IMPROVED THESIS STATEMENT

Maya Angelou is an accessible writer whose prose, poetry, and film scripts will long be read because they deal with human conditions, not just with the problems of African Americans.

Such specific wording for a thesis statement gives the paper direction and provides for unity and coherence. You could easily develop an outline from a thesis statement such as this, which presents substantial information in logical order.

HOW A THESIS STATEMENT EVOLVES

Think about the central idea for your paper while you gather note cards, sort through them, and look at the contents carefully. If you haven't already decided on a main emphasis, you need to make that decision in order to develop a thesis statement.

Write out a statement you think will serve as a controlling idea or thesis for your paper. A thesis statement in your head won't serve the same purpose as one on paper; it's too fleeting, too elusive. You need to put it in writing so you can see in front of you what you're working with, can tinker with it, rephrase it, or further limit or enlarge its scope.

However, don't try to keep stretching a prospective thesis statement to make it accommodate every phrase or idea that comes to you. Trying to put every single thing you've learned about your subject into one research paper will surely weaken the work. You have to be willing to discard ideas just as you must discard note cards when they don't fit a structure.

Barbara Howell, the student whose MLA format research paper is the sample in Chapter 10, was assigned to write a persuasive research paper, so she knew that her thesis had to express a position she could defend and convince her audience (classmates) to accept. Already a committed environmentalist when she began to search out information for this paper, Ms. Howell developed ideas for her thesis as she worked. Here is her record of the various tries at forming a suitable thesis statement and her evaluations of each.

FIRST TRY

Effective and lasting objectives of the environmental movement are realized through a combination of direct action, education, and legislation.

COMMENT

All three components are certainly important. But "direct action" leaves open the door to the confrontational and violent actions of some groups. That's not what I intend to advocate.

SECOND TRY

Nonviolent activists will be able to promote effective and lasting safeguards for the environmental movement.

COMMENT

Again—true. But this leaves out the legislative aspect of environmental activism, and without laws none of the actions taken can be lasting or have any enforcement. At least this is a persuasive statement, so it will result in the kind of research paper assigned.

THIRD TRY

The lasting solutions to Earth's environmental ills are achieved through nonviolent and legal means.

COMMENT

This is pretty close to what I want to say, but I think it would be better with something about effective solutions being included. I do want to get back to including something about activists solving these ills.

FOURTH TRY

The most effective and lasting solutions to environmental problems are realized when activists employ legal, nonviolent tactics.

COMMENT

Education is important, but will have to be left out in favor of the chief point, which is nonviolence, and the specific kind of action, which is legal action. I'll go with this one.

HOW AN OUTLINE EVOLVES

A thesis statement leads the way to an outline, a pattern to follow when you write the paper. If you've already grouped note cards according to similar ideas by checking the key words or slug lines at the top left corner of each card before composing the thesis statement, you have completed the first step toward writing an outline. If the note cards are not yet grouped, you must do that now.

A good way to work is to put the written thesis statement in front of you so you can keep looking at it and stay on track. Then arrange the groups of note cards in an order you think will help guide your audience to the same understanding or belief about your material that you have already reached. (Some kinds of order are suggested in the next section.) Only after deciding on an order will you be ready to start structuring information into a form you can develop into an outline.

The content of some subjects dictates the best way to organize the content of a research paper. Often a thesis statement points the way toward organization. However, if you think in terms of what you want to include in each section of the paper, according to the note cards you've sorted, you are not working backwards, just differently. The outline then begins to be sketched out from slug lines or key words, and they, in turn, lead to the thesis statement.

Here are some possibilities based on two sample thesis statements shown earlier in this chapter.

THESIS STATEMENT

    Technological developments that prolong human life are

    not necessarily desirable for all patients and their

    families.

The subject of this research paper will be technological developments—but only those that prolong human life. The operable part of the statement is in the predicate: "are not necessarily desirable." The thesis, therefore, points to an *argumentive paper using comparison and contrast* (desirable vs. not desirable) on the subject.

An obvious way to begin working toward an outline for such a paper is first to mention or explain some technological developments and then to list both desirable and undesirable results of prolonging human life through them, in this manner:

Technological Developments

Drugs

"Breathing" machines

Desirable	Not Desirable
1. Patient remains alive	1. Poor to bad quality of life
2. Assuages family guilt	2. For family, not patient
	3. Extremely high cost
	4. Patient may not know of medical and family efforts

Later, these notes will form the basis of an outline from which the argumentive research paper can be written using the organizational pattern of comparison and contrast.

THESIS STATEMENT

    Vouchers, on-site nursery schools, flexible work hours

    and days, co-ops, and after-school programs are among

```
employers' innovative solutions to the problem of needed
child care for working parents.
```

Here a problem is stated: the need for working parents to have satisfactory child care. The statement also presents some "innovative solutions." Following that inherent structure of solution to a problem, an author might well decide there's no sense in proposing solutions to a problem the audience is unaware of. Therefore, the preliminary organizational listing for such a research paper might reverse the two components, becoming a *problem to solution* order, and look like this:

Problem

Working parents need child care that is:

> Safe
>
> Affordable
>
> Reliable

Solution—By Employers

Vouchers

Nursery schools at workplace

Flexible work time

Co-op arrangements

After-school programs

The order of listing various solutions by employers is highly changeable and can be either most likely to least likely or vice versa or any other order at all.

Note that the thesis statement limits solutions to this problem to those that can be offered by employers. Thus, even though parents may have some solutions, such as care by relatives, that aspect of child care has no place in this particular planning for an outline to write from.

WAYS OF ORGANIZING CONTENT

The limited examples just presented show how a carefully written thesis statement may lead to ideas about organization, an intermediary step before starting to design a formal outline. Whether or not you feel a "necessity" for organizational form stemming from your thesis statement, consider the following six ways of organizing ideas:

- Time
- Known to unknown *or* simple to complex
- Comparison and contrast
- General to particular *or* particular to general
- Problem to solution *or* question to answer
- Cause to effect *or* effect to cause

If you have taken a composition course, then this list, and the information that follows, will look familiar. They are ways of organizing material for *any* kind of nonfiction writing, from answering an essay exam question to writing a magazine article. Choose the method that will most easily and clearly help you convey to the audience your approach to your subject and the content of your thesis statement.

Time

Many subjects clearly lend themselves to presentation in chronological order. Some examples are a paper that examines the critical receptions of a novel over a period of time, one that shows background leading to an historical event, or a paper showing a manufacturer how to phase in new production methods to keep up with increasing orders.

Known to Unknown or Simple to Complex

One of these methods leads readers from what is familiar to what might not yet be known or understood. The other begins with what is simple or easy to comprehend and takes readers to more difficult content. For example, a paper on the effects of prolonged space trips might begin by discussing the more familiar (and easier to understand) concepts of time that we already know and then go on to the more complex notions of time as perceived on space trips. Or a research paper on theater of the absurd might be developed by briefly reviewing the more traditional and familiar theatrical types before going on to explain the absurd.

Comparison and Contrast

Both comparison and contrast show relationships among things, ideas, or people. But *comparison focuses on similarity*, while *contrast concentrates on dissimilarity*. The latter, however, is more effective if shared characteristics are first established. So, although the methods may be used separately, they are usually combined in a research paper. You might use comparison and contrast to organize information if you were presenting the platforms of candidates for elective office, the relative merits of three different sites for a new sports complex, or an analysis of different publications addressed to members of the same profession.

Point-by-point comparison and contrast is one effective method of organizing a paper. That is, you deal with one aspect of the topic at a time, showing comparison and contrast before moving on to another element of similarity and difference. This method is used often, because the reader can readily see the relationships you point out.

EXAMPLE

You are comparing and contrasting Idea A to Idea B and have four

elements of relationship. Present the information in this *point-by-point*

order:

Compare Point 1 of Idea A to Point 1 of Idea B.

Contrast Point 1 of Idea A to Point 1 of Idea B.

Compare Point 2 of Idea A to Point 2 of Idea B.

Contrast Point 2 of Idea A to Point 2 of Idea B.

(*and so on*)

Item-by-item order is another way of organizing a comparison-and-contrast paper. In it, you present all the material about one subject before moving on to all the material about another subject.

EXAMPLE

You are comparing and contrasting Idea A to Idea B in four respects.

Present the information in this *item-by-item order:*

Explain Points 1, 2, 3, 4 of Idea A.

Show how Points 1, 2, 3, 4 are the same in Idea B.

Show how Points 1, 2, 3, 4 are different in Idea B.

One drawback some readers find in coping with item-by-item organization is that by the time they finish reading extensive information about one element, they forget what came at the beginning and therefore may have some difficulty following the comparison and contrast the author is establishing.

General to Particular or Particular to General

When you begin by writing some fairly broad ideas or statements and then arrange the remaining information as a series of specific points, you are following the general-to-particular arrangement of the content for your research paper. Or you might organize your paper on the opposite basis: first present a series of specific pieces of information that you then put together into a general conclusion or statement.

Of course, there will be specific and supporting points within any good piece of writing, but they aren't the same as the structural or organizational framework now being discussed. For example, a research paper on the short stories of James Agee (or any other writer) might begin with the broad issues he examined and then move to the instances of those issues in particular short stories. Or, the entire organization of the paper could be reversed, with the examination of the stories coming first.

Problem to Solution or Question to Answer

If your research has been about how a problem was solved—or how to go about finding a solution to something— you might use the problem-to-solution organization for your paper. That is, you would begin by stating the problem that exists (or existed) and then make suggestions for its solution (or show how it was solved).

Many business and technical papers are written to seek solutions, so this kind of organization is often used for material written outside of school situations. A variation on the problem-to-solution organization is the familiar format for scientific papers that proceeds from formulating a hypothesis to evaluating proposals and then to solving a problem.

Sometimes a question is posed (although not as the thesis statement!) and a paper is developed around an answer to it. The question is, in effect, the problem to be solved. For example, a paper might begin by posing the question of how the federal government has coped with illegal aliens, and be organized by showing various answers that have been proposed as well as tried.

Cause to Effect or Effect to Cause

Both these methods of organization are built around the notion of causality, so you have to establish and maintain that idea throughout the paper. You could begin by writing about an event (cause) and then show its result (effect). Or you could specify a situation (effect) and then trace its causes. Some topics that lend themselves to either of these two forms of organization are how reorganizing the administration in a county office (cause) would bring about more effective service to people and more efficient use of employees' time (effect), or how revised wetland use laws (effect) resulted from land grabs and misuse of resources (cause).

RELATING ORGANIZATION TO OVERALL APPROACH

In Chapter 3 (page 48) you read about five possible approaches to the subject you decide to research: examine or analyze, evaluate or criticize, compare and contrast, establish relationships, and argue or persuade. You were also urged to select one of these approaches before you began searching for information and recording it. That global approach is not the same as the organization with which you will present the content; and though it may suggest the organizing principle, you should consider a variety of possibilities.

EXAMPLES

Approach: Examine or Analyze

Possible Subjects	*Possible Organizing Methods*
national park system	time
black holes in space	known to unknown
learned dependence of elderly	problem to solution or effect to cause

Approach: Establish Relationships

Possible Subjects	*Possible Organizing Methods*
diet and health	cause to effect
TV violence and children	general to particular

Approach: Argue or Persuade

Possible Subjects   *Possible Organizing Methods*
hazardous waste disposal   problem to solution
homosexuals in military   question to answer

Courses or books about composition will show how to go about presenting the content within each of the organizing methods. In general, the emphasis will be on supporting statements or contentions with details—and in a research paper, many of the details will come from the notes you have already taken and the sources you have consulted (and which will be documented according to the techniques you will read about in Chapter 8).

VISUAL ORDERING—-CLUSTERING AND MAPPING

Writing is a linear creation: you start at one place and proceed in order to another and another. Some people, either through habit or because of the way they think, find that working with something more visual—with diagrams rather than only with words—is easier, more agreeable, or preferable for them. The result is an ordering of ideas, but one arrived at in a slightly different way from either listing or outlining (information on both of which follow). Called **clustering** or **mapping** (although the terms have slightly different meanings, the words are often used interchangeably), these visual ways of ordering ideas depend on using key words in a way that shows their relationships to each other.

Clustering generally begins with one word in the center of a circle on a page. As ideas occur, words expressing them are added to the page, each enclosed in its own circle, and lines are drawn to connect one to others; the goal is to show relationships among ideas. The technique is similar to one used to catch stream-of-consciousness thinking that generates ideas to write about. However, using clustering to organize information already found and thought about is likely to be more organized as you write down the words and ideas that will be used in a research paper. On the next page, is an example of clustering done by the author of the student sample research paper on pages 230–46.

Mapping is a bit less free-wheeling and tends to have more order imposed on it from the start. It is a visual representation (thus, a "map") of the author's way of leading the reader through the content of a research paper. For example, a map to show order of ideas may be developed as a tree trunk and branches. Or the map may be a drawing of other recognizable things such as the maze on page 143 or people, which the author labels so as to show their interrelationships.

There are no rules or conventions to follow when you cluster or map. Indeed, the result may be something so idiosyncratic that only you, the author, can make sense of it and use it as the organizational basis for writing. Or you may decide to use the cluster or map as the basis for a formal outline, particularly if the latter is required as part of the research paper assignment.

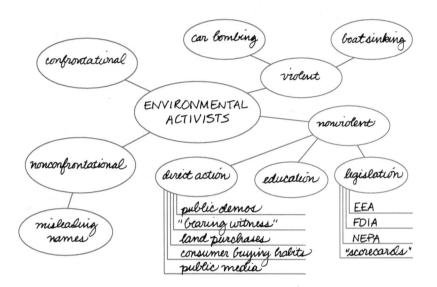

Clustering by the author of the sample research in Chapter 10.

OUTLINES

An outline is **an orderly plan, in writing, showing the division of ideas and their arrangement in relation to one another**. Its function is to show which ideas are of major importance and which are subordinate to the several major points your research paper will make.

The outline is developed *after you have decided on the thesis statement*, because its purpose is to amplify the many ideas inherent in the thesis statement and to show how they relate to one another. It is *usually written after you decide on a way of organizing* your material, because then you have a guide on how to proceed. You may find, however, that one organization doesn't work and you need to try another.

An outline is *always written before the text of a paper*. Making an outline after a paper is written, just to fulfill an assignment, is foolish and useless!

Even though you may have an order of presentation in mind when you write the thesis statement, the outline is important because it:

- Keeps ideas firmly in mind, even if writing the paper takes a long time

- Lets you rearrange ideas and try out new arrangements without difficulty (and sometimes even while writing the paper)

- Shows you how parts and transitions fit together

- Exposes strengths and weaknesses of the research paper in time to make adjustments before (or even during) writing

Don't be surprised if your outline isn't "perfect" the first time you put it down on paper. Few processes in writing are! Make changes as you go along; even make

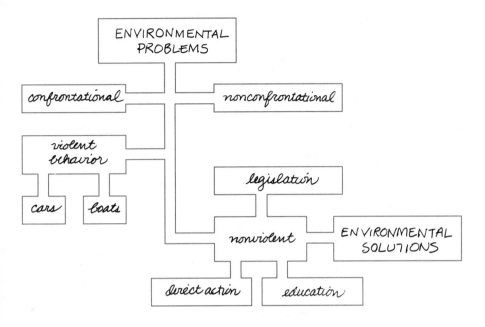

The maze as a map of the sample research paper in Chapter 10.

several different outlines as the many ideas of your research come into focus and you envision the proportion of the final paper. The whole point of an outline is to work out the structure of your paper. Then, when you write the paper, you need only follow the plan—the outline—you've made.

If you don't find the main ideas readily, prompt yourself with a bit of role-playing: pretend to be your audience, and ask questions based on the thesis statement. Jot down the questions and then consider that the responses may well be the main ideas that ought to be developed in your paper. (If your actual audience, such as classmates, is available, let them ask you questions based on the thesis statement.)

The outline you develop becomes the sketch for your research paper. As with a painting, subsequent details of the work emerge from that sketch. The outline shows key ideas and emphases and where various levels of development fit in.

There is no way of telling how long an outline should be in relation to the finished paper. Since it is only a guide, it shouldn't be so minutely detailed that it becomes a paper in itself. On the other hand, it shouldn't be so brief or vague that anybody reading it would have to guess about what you meant.

Content of Outlines

The most important part of an outline is what you put into it—the words that carry your ideas and help you organize what you plan to say in your research paper. Here are some guides for making the content of your outline meaningful and therefore helpful to you in writing.

1. Every word in the outline should say something about the content of your paper.

For that reason, "Introduction," "Body," and "Conclusion" are words that *don't* belong in an outline. They only describe the parts of *any* piece of writing—which has to have a beginning, a middle, and an end—but give no information about the subject or what you plan to say about it. Instead of such "empty words," always use content-giving words in an outline.

Similarly, "who" or "why" phrases (as in "Who responds to the ads" or "Why magazines are used") are not helpful in an outline. Rather than such vague phrasing, use language and information that tells exactly what your final paper will contain.

EXAMPLE

THESIS   Environmental damage from inadequate disposal of hazardous waste materials continues in many states.

"EMPTY" WORDING

```
I.   Introduction
II.  Problems about hazardous waste
     A.  Where it is
     B.  Who does it
```

CONTENT-GIVING WORDING

```
I.   Sources of hazardous wastes
II.  Current disposal methods
     A.  Landfills
     B.  Incinerators
     C.  Storage
         1.  Deep-well injection
         2.  Containers
```

2. The information for each subheading must be directly related to, and subordinate to, the heading under which it appears.

The outline shows relationships among ideas, so the entire content is a matter of showing visually how each thought relates to every other one. That is, although some content will be of equal importance to other content, what is supportive and subordinate must be so designated.

Note, also, that because the entire content of the outline (and of the research paper) is related to and subordinate to both the title and the thesis statement, *neither one can appear as an individual item* within the outline itself.

If you have only one thing to say about any part of the outline (and you know you can't divide something into just one part), instead of trying to make artificial subdivisions, revise the wording or rethink the idea.

EXAMPLE

THESIS   Arthur Miller used elements of a
sophisticated mistress in one story and a childlike wife
in another to develop the character of Roslyn Taber in his
cinema-novel The Misfits.

WRONG OUTLINE

I. "The Misfits" was published in 1957.

   A. The story concerned three cowboys on a mustang
      hunt.

      1. Roslyn meets them.

   B. Roslyn is an eastern sophisticate.

. . .

IMPROVED OUTLINE

I. Roslyn appears in "The Misfits," published in 1957.

   A. She is an eastern sophisticate.

   B. She meets three cowboys going on a mustang hunt.

. . .

COMMENT

The second outline is improved, because the single item was combined
with another. However, since the thesis statement indicates that this research
paper is going to focus on Roslyn, a character in the novel, the focus of the
outline ought to be on her.

BEST OUTLINE

  I. Roslyn is an eastern sophisticate in "The Misfits"
     (1957).

   A. She enjoys new sights and experiences.

   B. She feels sorry for hurt animals.

 II. Roslyn is a charming . . .

COMMENT

Reference to the three cowboys and their mustang hunt is omitted because the paper is about Roslyn, not about them. Whatever needs to be said
of the men will be worked into the content of the paper as the author writes
from the outline.

3. Make relationships clear by using the same symbol (that is, roman numerals, capital letters, and so on) for ideas of equal importance.

Because the outline divides ideas, the symbols must show how the content of
the research paper will be divided or subdivided into groups of thoughts related
to one another.

EXAMPLE

THESIS   Ernest Hemingway's writing evolved from his own life.

WRONG OUTLINE CONTENT

   I. Early journalistic career

  II. Participation in WW I

 III. The Sun Also Rises

     A. Other successful early novels

     B. A Farewell to Arms

  IV. Sympathy with Loyalists

     A. For Whom the Bell Tolls

     B. Participation in Spanish Civil War

COMMENT

The phrases after each roman numeral give three different kinds of information: periods in Hemingway's life, a book he wrote, and an attitude he had. Not only do Sections III and IV differ from the others, but they also are not of equal importance in the outline. In light of the thesis of this proposed paper, Hemingway's beliefs should be emphasized, not a particular book that can be used to illustrate a belief.

The following version is improved, because the content shows that the paper will follow from the thesis statement:

PROPER OUTLINE CONTENT

   I. Early journalistic career

  II. Participation in WW I

 III. Expatriate novelist years

     A. The Sun Also Rises

     B. A Farewell to Arms

  IV. Participation in Spanish Civil War

. . .

COMMENT

The revised outline shows that all of the symbols represent ideas of equal importance. The roman numerals show key periods in Hemingway's life, and the capital letters show books written during one of those periods. The third book title, appearing in the original outline, is omitted because it would have had to stand alone—impossible within the conventions of outline form. However, the author of a paper written to this particular outline could easily say something about *For Whom the Bell Tolls* in Section IV, even without noting it in the outline.

4. Only principal points appear in an outline.

Illustrations, amplifications, and development of the main points are added in the actual writing. You will be reminded of these matters when you rearrange your note cards to coincide with the structure of the content you have decided on. Thus, you should concentrate on putting principal ideas, rather than their support, in the outline.

Forms of Outlines

Outlines follow very specific forms. The two principal ones are **topic outlines** and **sentence outlines**. *Paragraph outlines* and *decimal outlines* are each used occasionally for particular purposes or disciplines.

Topic Outline

In a topic outline, you write your ideas in a *word, a phrase, or a dependent clause* after one of the traditional symbols. There is no punctuation after any words in a topic outline, because there are no complete sentences. However, do try to use a parallel and consistent grammatical structure throughout the topic outline.

EXAMPLE

    I. Issues of censorship

        A. Intellectual freedom

        B. Values taught

    II. Censorship in past

Sentence Outline

The sentence outline presents *statements as grammatically complete sentences*, with a period at the end of each. (Questions are *never* used in an outline.) Sentence outlines are widely used, because they force you to think through ideas completely in order to write them in full sentences.

EXAMPLE

    I. The issues of school library censorship stem from two
        principal sources.

        A. Some people feel that schools must foster the
            intellectual freedom of students.

        B. Some people feel schools have the obligation to
            impart values to students.

    . . .

Paragraph Outline

A paragraph outline has the same symbols as topic and sentence outlines, as shown in the next section (on conventions), but each symbol is followed by several sentences that make a paragraph. Such outlines are generally used for extended material (certainly more than 3,000 words) and for complex material. Otherwise, writing the outline would be tantamount to writing the whole paper.

Because of the amount of writing involved, paragraph outlines are not as quick to make as topic or sentence outlines. Also, there is a danger that students who aren't careful in constructing a paragraph outline will end up writing a whole paper, merely putting outline symbols in front of each paragraph. The result is not a plan but an executed work, though not really a paper either.

Decimal Outline

The decimal outline uses a different symbol system from those just illustrated. Each main item in this kind of outline is assigned an arabic numeral, and the support for it carries the same numeral followed by a decimal point and numerals to indicate further subdivisions. Thus, a decimal outline looks like this:

```
1.
    1.1
        1.1.1
        1.1.2
        1.1.3
    1.2
        1.2.1
        1.2.2
2.
    . . .
```

Either phrases or sentences follow each numerical designation throughout. This kind of outline is used more frequently in business and scientific writing than in other academic or professional work.

Conventions of Outlines

The most general convention of outlining is to use a **consistent form**. Decide in advance whether you will use a topic outline or a sentence outline, and then *stick to it throughout*. If you start with a topic outline, you may not write sentences within it. If you start with a sentence outline, you must write sentences all the way through.

1. Numbers and letters are used alternately.

These are the symbols you use to show relationships in all outlines except the decimal form. Basic to outlining is that *ideas of equal importance in the overall concept of the paper will have the same kind of symbol.*

- Roman numerals show the major divisions of the paper, so each major idea you propose to write about will be noted next to a roman numeral.
- Capital letters indicate the first subdivision.
- Arabic letters show divisions of the content indicated by the capital letters.
- Lowercase letters are used to subdivide information further.

Even finer subdivision is possible, but seldom necessary for school research papers. However, should you want a finer subdivision, follow the numeral-letter sequence, first using arabic numerals within parentheses, then small letters within parentheses.

2. Symbols in an outline must always appear at least in pairs.

That is, if you have an *A*, you must have a *B*; if you have an *I*, you must also have a *II*. The reason for this convention is obvious: an outline shows the *division of ideas* you will include in your paper; and since *you can't divide anything into just one part, you must have at least two parts of everything divided.* If you can't find two subdivisions for a unit, try combining the ideas of that single symbol with the one above it.

Two more notes about symbols in an outline:

- You may have *more* than two subdivisions for any item.
- There is no need to make an equal number of subdivisions, even under similar symbols. Your material and what you have to say about it should be your only guides.

EXAMPLE

```
I.
    A.
        1.
        2.
        3.
            a.
            b.
    B.
    C.
II.
    A.
    B.
        1.
            a.
            b.
            c.
        2.
```

3. Every symbol in an outline is followed by a period.

The period acts as a separation between the symbols that establish the relationships and the wording itself. Put two typewriter spaces after a period and before the words begin.

4. Capitalize the first letter of the first word after every symbol.

You would normally do that at the beginning of a sentence (and thus in a sentence outline), but an outline convention is to capitalize the first word even in a topic outline. Thereafter, capital letters are used for words only in the normal fashion: titles, names, places, and so on.

5. Grammatically complete sentences require normal sentence punctuation.

There may be commas, colons, and semicolons, as well as periods, in sentence outlines. Obviously, there will be no question marks, and exclamation marks should be avoided.

6. All symbols of the same kind should be in a vertical line.

Doing so will emphasize the relationships among ideas and make reading the outline easy. Lining-up will take a little juggling on a typewriter or computer because the roman numerals will take one, two, or three spaces, but you should try to compensate and set up an easy-to-read format, as illustrated throughout this book.

One way to line up symbols is to type the first roman numeral two spaces (three columns) in from the left margin, which should be one inch from the edge of the paper. Roman numerals of two digits can then be indented one space and those with three digits begun at the left margin. To keep successive columns of symbols even, indent each five spaces, or a multiple of five spaces, from the left margin. Thus, all capital letters will occur in the same column, all Arabic numerals in the same column (you probably won't be using more than a single digit), and so on.

7. Begin succeeding lines of writing under the start of the first word after a symbol.

That is, if a statement requires more than one line, begin the second and subsequent lines under the first wording of the previous line. This format prevents interference with the vertical alignment of the symbols of the outline and thus keeps relationships among ideas visible, so adhere to this custom whether you type or write in longhand. The format of your outline should look like this:

```
A.  This is an especially long statement and requires
    three lines, so the subsequent lines begin under the
    first word after the symbol.
```

8. Type an outline in double spacing.

That is, keep the spacing in an outline the same as in the rest of your research paper.

Revising Outlines

Don't be satisfied with your first outline, even if you think it's pretty good. The next version will be even better. Test the outline constantly as you work, by thinking through each idea in relation to the others you want to express. Move ideas around and try them out in different relationships until you feel comfortable with the structure and content of what you will be writing. It's easy enough to make adjustments from one outline draft to another. When you think you've finally formulated a satisfactory outline, put it away and forget about it for a few days (another good reason not to let writing a research paper go until the last minute!).

When you take the outline out again, test it by putting yourself in the position of the audience. Could whoever will read the paper follow your ideas and understand your viewpoint on the basis of the outline? If the audience will be someone from whom you expect no familiarity with the subject, try out your outline on a friend or relative for whom the subject is new; if your "stand-in" audience can get a sense of what the final paper will be like, you may have completed a satisfactory outline.

Here is an example of two drafts of a topic outline developed by a student. On the left is an early (though not the very first) version; on the right is her final version.

THESIS   Animals can fulfill the social, physical, and emotional needs of elderly people whom society has neglected.

Early Version

I. Early man-animal relations
II. Current statistics
    A. Elderly population
        1. Nursing home costs
    B. Animals as pets
III. Benefits of animal relationships
    A. Mental
    B. Social
    C. Physical
IV. Research studies
V. Support
    A. Organizations
    B. Government legislation

Final Version

I. Precedents
II. Benefits
    A. Companionship
        1. Physical
        2. Communication
    B. Decreased isolation
    C. Medical
        1. Blood pressure
        2. Heart disease
    D. Reduced depression
    E. Better self-perception
        1. Esteem
        2. Autonomy
III. Arguments for use
    A. Individual
    B. Professional
    C. Governmental

COMMENT

Notice that the student cleared up some of the difficulties evident in the early version: problems of division of ideas (as in IIA-1), of focus (statistics and research studies ought to support ideas, not be considered principal points by themselves), and of emphasis (the three elements cited in the thesis are initially buried within the outline as divisions of III). You can see from the proportions of the final outline that section II will be the emphasis of the paper. Also, note that although the thesis statement cites three benefits, the student has not limited herself to just three subdivisions but has augmented them according to what she wanted to include in her final writing.

COMPUTER AIDS TO OUTLINING

If you are comfortable enough to do word processing on a microcomputer, you may also want to make an outline on the computer. One possibility is to use the computer as you would pen and paper, though you would have the advantage the computer gives of easily making changes and moving words around. On the other hand, many computer screens display only a limited number of lines of text at one time. If you work best by having everything visible simultaneously, you may be comfortable using the computer for your outline only if you can immediately print a hard copy after working on-screen.

Another possibility is to use one of the commercially available "idea processor" programs, sometimes built into a word processing program, designed to format your "loose" ideas into an outline or an approximation of one, sometimes without symbols but with indentations. Doubtless, other variations will continue to come onto the market because so many people outside of academics need to work with organizing information and thus with outlines.

A FINAL CHECK

As soon as you have a satisfactory outline, **put your note cards into working order by keying each with the outline symbol its content will be used to support**. The top left corner where you have written a slug line or key word is a good place to put this notation. That is, you might write *I. A. 2.* on one card to indicate it contains information about the second item listed under Roman numeral *I* and capital letter *A* of the outline, and write *I. A. 3.* on another group of cards. Write these symbols in a color of ink different from what you wrote the note with (for instance, use red or green for them), and you'll be able to locate groups of symbols easily. Moreover, if the cards should become scrambled, having outline symbols on them will enable you to put them back into working order quickly.

At this point, unless your instructor objects, show your outline to at least one other person. That "other" may be your instructor, especially if she or he is following along the research paper process with you. Or the "other" may be a classmate. Ask whoever reads your outline to give it a really critical—which means evaluative—reading. The least helpful remark you can get is "Yes, it's good." (If anybody tells you that, ask why and get some details.) Have your helper make sure that all of the following are true:

- The outline shows a progression of ideas that supports your thesis statement.
- Major and subordinate ideas are so designated by units and symbols.

- Subordinate units are reasonably balanced throughout the outline (such as not having eight units under one heading and only two under its parallel heading).

Ask your helper to tell you what he or she expects to find in your research paper. If the response doesn't coincide with what you plan to write, ascertain areas of disagreement and adjust either the outline or your proposed writing. Because your research paper is being written for an audience, let your helper serve as an audience for you at this stage of the process.

Writing Your Paper

WHAT "DRAFTING" MEANS

What some people call "writing" a paper is called "drafting" by others. The latter term is preferred by many people because they feel that a draft of a paper doesn't have the finality that a completed paper does. That is, all the time you are working at writing various versions of your research paper you are actually drafting (or writing drafts) of it.

Drafting—or writing—doesn't come easily to most people, and you may be one for whom words don't flow readily onto paper. Don't expect your writing habits to change suddenly and dramatically, even if you've done your preparatory work well. And don't expect that just because you've done that necessary preparatory work you can quickly write out a paper, then merely "fix up" spelling and punctuation before turning it in. Writing just doesn't work that way.

But *do* expect that all your serious and concentrated preparation *will* pay off when you take pen to paper or sit before the typewriter or computer keyboard. And *do* expect to produce a good piece of work because you have a plan to work from and the material with which to fill it in and see your research paper take shape.

Writing is a complex activity that involves constant thinking through of ideas and searching for the best wording and phrasing, all the while putting words on paper. New thoughts will occur as you write, and as you go you should certainly fill in with common knowledge and with your own thinking rather than relying solely on notes from other sources.

People write drafts in all sorts of ways. Some say they can only work on notebook paper when they sit in the library; some swear by late-night sessions at the computer. Some prefer to write slowly and carefully from the beginning, making changes and corrections as they go along. Others find the best way to write, especially for a first or "zero" draft, is to put everything down on paper as quickly as possible and then later to make extensive revisions. For many writers, drafting means moving ahead slowly, backing up to rephrase something, rushing ahead with ideas, then getting stalled. Drafting does take a long time, but it's certainly worth doing well. And it's definitely smart to hold off checking the mechanics of spelling and punctuation until you've finished what you think will be the last draft.

Time is always a problem for busy students, and last-minute writing is seldom good. So, a useful method is to set aside chunks of time during which to draft your research paper. Work on it as much as you feel you can, in sessions as long as you can manage without interruption. If you don't have time to work through certain passages as you go, write yourself a note or use some symbol to indicate you will pay special attention to that part in another draft.

Many people find that drafting on a computer is less inhibiting than composing in longhand or on a typewriter. It's also easier to make changes as you compose and to make subsequent changes when you revise. You will probably also want to follow the lead of many authors who compose on the computer but need to see a hard copy of the work in order to make final revisions and be completely satisfied with what they've produced!

If you're going to use word processing to write your paper, be completely familiar with the program *before* you begin writing. Trying to figure out how a computer program operates at the same time you're figuring out how best to present the materials you've found just doesn't work.

WRITING STYLE

Remember that your primary objective is to communicate clearly to your audience, so work at clarity and keep your audience in mind. The way you write a research paper is not very different from the way you would write any other discourse. As in any good piece of writing, you should *vary sentence structures and sentence length*. Writing, insofar as possible, in the *active voice rather than the passive voice* will help readers keep moving along.

Especially in a research paper, you should write as specifically as possible and certainly *avoid unsubstantiated generalizations*. Also, beware of catchall words. For instance, "young" may mean any age from six months to twenty (or more) years, depending on the age and orientation of the audience; but "five years old" is precise.

Consistency in the way you write is particularly important in a research paper, because you are working from notes, including quotations, that may sound like a far different person from yourself. By and large, refer to a composition textbook or handbook for particulars about writing style and conventions.

However, writing a research paper does mean you are expected to adhere to a number of stylistic customs.

1. Usually, write in the third person.

That is, the words "I," "we," and "you" will not normally appear in the text, except as they occur in quoted material. A sense of distance between you and your material is customary in a research paper. Besides, the focus has to remain on *what you have to say* rather than on you, the person who is saying it. Writing in the first person (I) focuses attention on the author, and writing in the second person (you) draws the attention of the audience to itself. Therefore, using the third person directs the reader's entire attention to what you have to say.

2. Write straightforwardly.

The style of a research paper should be neither artificially formal nor as loose and relaxed as a personal letter. Many instructors feel that contractions are out of place in this style of writing. For example, the preferred phrasing is "Writers do not usually . . ." rather than "Writers don't usually . . ." Check with your instructor if in doubt about her or his preferences.

3. Always refer to individuals by their full name (given and surnames) or by surname alone.

Never refer to a person by first (or given) name alone. Thus, "Steinem says . . ." or "Gloria Steinem says . . ." is the form to use—*not* "Gloria says . . ." Follow this custom in writing even if you've interviewed a person with whom you are on a first-name basis or if you've read enough of (or about) a person's work to feel you know the individual well. You may, however, use a title with a person's name as identification, as in Dr. Jane Smith, President Truman, Dame Sutherland, and so on.

4. Guard against wording that shows bias regarding a person's age, gender, race, political attitude, religious beliefs, sexual orientation, or national origin.

Unless such information—laudatory as well as derogatory—is necessary to what you are writing, strive for balance and nondiscriminatory language. If any such language appears in a passage you are quoting, you may want to acknowledge your awareness of such bias in the original by writing "[sic]," as appropriate.

Changes in job designations have helped eliminate some biases; for example, the jobs of police officers and flight attendants include both men and women. Writers and their readers are increasingly sensitive to the fact that "he" and "his" are masculine pronouns and thus inappropriate as pronouns referring to groups that include both sexes. Wording is usually recast—as yours should be.

Unless an individual's religion is an issue or has some bearing on what you are writing, you may safely omit such a reference even though a source you worked from might have mentioned the matter. The same is true for biases about national origin and other common biases listed above.

In sum, fairness should be evident in your writing, whatever the subject.

STARTING YOUR PAPER

As in all aspects of writing, people work in different ways: slowly, stop and start, straight through. Some are ready to begin the draft of a paper as soon as they sit down; they may already have thought out much of the wording and have only to commit it to paper. Some simply can't get those first words started, even though they are thoroughly familiar with their subject matter. An outline helps, but the actual act of writing is difficult for many.

You may like to start writing at the beginning. But if you have trouble getting started or if writing the opening of a paper intimidates you, *don't waste time worrying over it.* (Know that you're not alone, either; many people have trouble writing openings.) Instead, begin with another part of your outline, perhaps with a part that seems easier to write. Then *return* to the opening. No rule says you have to write material in the same order your audience is going to read it!

Good Openings

Some research papers open with an expansion of the thesis statement, with the main ideas of the paper developed into the first paragraph. But that isn't necessarily the way you should begin *your* paper. Here are nine different kinds of starts you might use to begin your research paper, each illustrated by a sample beginning. Consider these as idea starters rather than as what you should imitate slavishly. The best opening for your *own* research paper is the one that comes most naturally to you on the basis of what you've decided to say about your chosen subject.

1. **Clarify the subject** you are going to write about.

    The legality and desirability of abortion continues as a
    controversial issue in our time. However, along with that
    now comes another, and related, controversial issue: fetal
    tissue research. While opponents of fetal tissue research
    fear a corrupt and unethical industry will be created in
    order to obtain fetuses, experts believe that fetal tissue
    research is approaching the new frontier in medical
    technology from which will come many benefits used to help
    people.

    (*from* "Fetal Tissue Research" by Elejandro Interian)

    This paragraph indicates that the paper will focus on the ethics of fetal tissue research rather than on other aspects of the issue. However, it also prepares readers for a paper that will examine the beliefs of both opponents and proponents of such research.

2. **State your position** on the subject you have chosen.

    An earlier view of family structure in this country was
    that of the husband as the partner with earning power and
    the wife as homemaker. Now there is a different family
    structure: the dual-income family, in which both husband
    and wife hold income-producing jobs. In spite of the many
    difficulties and economic costs experienced by dual-income
    families, the psychological, intellectual, and monetary
    benefits obtained provide them with a far better lifestyle
    than that of single-income families.

    (*from* "Dual Income Families" by Clifford Rigaud)

There is no question, on the basis of this paragraph, that the student who began his research paper this way will devote the rest of it to making his case for the dual-income family. It states a line of reasoning that will lead the reader through a research paper that proves his point.

3. **Relate your topic to something current or well known.**

> In the 1990s two of every three new workers will be women. By the year 2000 experts project that 80% of women from twenty-five through fifty-four years of age will be employed, comprising nearly half (47%) of the paid labor force (Yalow 49). With such a large number of women in the workforce, many of them mothers, employers need to take into account some of these women's needs. Some employers have already done so. They have started by acknowledging that, besides having to work, many have family responsibilities. To ease the burden, especially that of child care, employers have started assisting their employees by offering a variety of benefits. They, in turn, have received tangible corporate payoffs.
>
> *(from* "Positive Impact of Employer Sponsored Child Care" by Lissette Feijoo)

That a large part of the workforce in this country consists of women who also have child-care responsibilities is certainly well known. Statistics at the beginning of this paragraph serve to emphasize that familiar statement. However, because such information is proportionately less than half the paragraph, the paragraph amply illustrates a research paper beginning with what is current and well known.

4. **Challenge some generally held assumption about your topic.**

> If you worked hard until you were 65 years old, you could look forward to spending your last few years comfortably retired on a company pension plus government help from Social Security. No more getting up early and spending the day away from the home you worked hard to buy and maintain for your wife and family. Now there was time to fish or read or talk politics with cronies in the courthouse square. That was the "ideal," the picture sold to the public through the media and word of mouth: a dominantly male, small-town, imaginary kind of life. Today we know better. Retirees may be any age; they are as often female as male; with companies increasingly cutting off or misusing pension funds, they may not have incomes

that were counted on; they often have ever-mounting and
overwhelming medical bills; and many choose to lead
active, involved lives--even to the point of starting <u>new</u>
careers.

(from "Redefining Retirement" by Gene Dana)

This paragraph starts by sketching a "traditional" view of retirement, especially as promulgated until relatively recently in various media and among large segments of the working public. It concludes, however, by pointing out present realities that are at odds with that view and points the way to elements that will follow in the research paper.

5. **Show something paradoxical** about your subject or about the material you will present.

When asked if they believe in ghosts, a surprising
number of people will say that they do; and when asked
why, they will say that too many ghostly figures have been
reported for it not to be true. According to the results
of a nationwide telephone poll of 1,236 U.S. adults
conducted at random in June 1990, one in four believe in
ghosts, one in ten say they have either seen or felt the
presence of a ghost, and one in six claims to have spoken
with the ghost of a deceased person ("Believe It or Not").
Obviously, enough people believe in ghosts to warrant
search for proof of their existence. As yet, however,
there is no conclusive evidence for that, and the majority
of ghost reports seem to have natural explanations: strong
belief, dream, or hallucination.

(from "Ghosts and Popular Beliefs" by Rachel Loubeau)

The student who began her research paper this way is certainly going to deal, in the rest of it, with the paradox of belief in ghosts and the natural explanations that should remove such beliefs.

6. **Use a brief quotation** if you can find one that is applicable or provocative or that makes a general statement about your subject.

A look at the 1990 U.S. Census figures is enough to set
the stage for an examination of the changing lifestyles of
members of the 500 tribes and bands of Native Americans in
this country. As Hodgkinson wrote:

> Of the 1.9 million, about 637,000 are living
> on reservations or Trust Lands. However,
> 46,000 live in the New York/Long Island/New

Jersey/Connecticut Combined Metro Area (CMA);
87,000 in the Los Angeles CMA; 15,000 in the
Chicago CMA; and 40,000 in the San Francisco
CMA; just to name the largest. A minimum of
252,000 Native Americans lived in cities in
1990. (1)

(*from* "Changing Lifestyles Among Native Americans"
by Jason Robertson)

7. **State some striking facts or statistics** you discovered about your topic.

A 1991 estimate (Yanowki 1231) is that at least 5% of
young women in the United States between the ages of 15
and 25 are sufferers of bulimia, an eating disorder in
which a person alternately binges and purges to lose or
maintain weight in order to be socially accepted. It is
a disorder sufficiently widespread that it has become the
subject of television investigative reports and plays.
There is also evidence that as the disorder becomes more
widely known and therefore more readily identified, the
percentage of women afflicted may prove to be greater than
when this estimate was made.

(*from* "Bulimia and Society: Unrealized Expectations"
by Christi West)

The student who opened her research paper with this paragraph tried unsuccessfully to find out approximately how many women between the stated ages were in the United States at the time the estimate was made, reasoning that an actual number in millions would be more striking than the statistics she was able to find and use. Nevertheless, this opening was startling to her classmates, many of whom were either unaware of the disorder or of its extent.

8. **Place your topic in time** by giving some historical or chronological information.

For centuries homosexuals have served honorably in
the military. In the 1940s, the U.S. military started
discharging any personnel believed to be a homosexual.
The person in question did not have to engage in any overt
homosexual activity; just being identified as a homosexual
was grounds for dismissal. More than 50 years have passed,
and the military's practice of discharging personnel on
the sole basis of sexual preference is still being

```
exercised. Homosexuals feel that now is their time to
come out of the closet and serve in the military openly.
```

(*from* "Homosexuals in the Military" by Maria Caraballo)

Written at a time when the matter of homosexuals being permitted to serve in the armed forces was in the news, this opening paragraph of a research paper quickly sketches a chronology leading to a national controversy everyone in the audience (a classroom) was well aware of. The audience, however, was almost entirely unaware of the background of the current news, so this beginning to one student's research paper set it in perspective.

9. **Give a brief description or background résumé of some person or event of significance to your topic.**

```
Lady Murasaki Shikibu was born about A.D. 978 and died
about 1030. She had the enviable position of being a
member of the Fujiwara clan and a member of a family that
produced mikados, statesmen, and at least one celebrated
Japanese poet. Because she was of the nobility, she had
the time and the education to write. Her book Genji
Monogatari, known in English as The Tale of Genji, is now
the West's chief source of information about court life in
11th century Japan.
```

(*from* "Amorality in 11th Century Japanese Life" by Margaret Haag)

Since *The Tale of Genji* provides one of the chief sources of information for this research paper, the author opened by establishing the identity of the author of that book. Readers who were unfamiliar with Lady Murasaki are thus informed and will accept the veracity of the information in the research paper that comes largely from her writings.

Bad Openings

Just as there are good openings for your research paper—first paragraphs that draw the reader into your work—so there are also poor openings that detract from the quality of your paper. Six ways you *should not* begin a research paper follow.

1. **Don't repeat the title.** It has already been read, usually right before beginning the text of the paper, so repeating it in the first paragraph is an obvious attempt to fill space and stall for time.

2. **Don't tell what you propose to do in the paper.** Simply *do it!* Such a statement may be customary in some styles of business and technical reports, but it's unsuitable for research papers written for class. Any writing that says "In this paper I am going to . . ." is not only juvenile, but it also puts off readers and makes them impatient. Besides, it shows lack of imagination and subtlety.

3. **Don't feel compelled to repeat the thesis statement completely in the opening of the paper**. Although you may certainly use the wording of the thesis statement, remember that you wrote it mainly as a *guide to your own preparatory work* and as a way of focusing your paper. Besides, your thesis statement may disclose more information than you want the audience to know at the outset.

   You could, however, begin by stating an idea inherent in the thesis statement. Or you could vary the wording of the thesis statement in order to use its ideas in the opening of your paper.

4. **Don't ask a question.** You might get an unexpected answer.

5. **Don't give a dictionary definition**. You may certainly refer to a dictionary as you would to any other source of information. But beginning with a definition you didn't write—especially since most definitions in dictionaries are not particularly well written for the purposes of research papers—suggests that what follows the opening will be just as dull and lifeless as the definition.

   Instead, you can probably define any necessary terms more effectively in your own words. If you really feel you must quote from a dictionary, try holding off until later in your research paper.

6. **Don't write a cute or folksy opening**. Such wording often falls flat and ruins the whole effect of your paper. Besides, a research paper is usually considered a serious work of scholarship and there is no room in it for cuteness or excessive informality.

WRITING THE BODY OF YOUR PAPER

You explain and support your thesis in the body of your paper. Obviously, you will acknowledge the sources you consulted as you write. But remember that you are doing *original writing* about your subject, *not* just stringing together a series of quotations and paraphrases.

All the skills you learned in writing courses through many years of school should be applied to this task! Take time to put into practice all you know about explaining and supporting ideas fully. Clarify information that may be new to your audience, and give needed background or illustrations to your readers. Names and terms that may now be familiar to you through your research may need to be defined or identified for your audience.

All the qualities of good writing that should be part of your paper can be found in any book on composition or rhetoric. Take time to consult one or more such books as you're working—either those you use (or used) in classes or those available in any library.

The next four sections are reminders of some qualities of good writing that you should be particularly aware of in writing your research paper. If they sound familiar, it's because you've probably read the same information in your composition textbooks.

Unity and Coherence

A **unified** research paper is one that deals with a single subject and has a central idea it sticks to about that subject. If you have chosen a subject carefully and prepared a good outline—which you basically stick to as you write—you may be certain that your paper is unified. Don't get carried away with ideas that strike you while you are working, for digressions detract from the unity of a research paper.

A **coherent** research paper is one that hangs together well, that not only holds the attention of readers but also helps them move from one point to another. A well-structured outline from which you write a carefully organized paper helps tie everything in it together.

The following are elements of writing that make for unity and coherence.

- **Transitional words** ("therefore," "however," "because," and others) **and phrases** ("in the second place," "at the same time," "as a result," and others) are signals to a reader that you are moving from one thought to another and that you are establishing a relationship between them. Use transitions between sentences to move one idea to another and between paragraphs to tie them together.

- **Pronouns** (such as "he," "she," "they," "them," and "those") tie ideas together because they substitute for nouns, thus integrating the writing. Remember, however, that the noun that each pronoun replaces (that is, its referent or antecedent) must appear just before the pronoun, not several lines before it and certainly not after it. Clear and unequivocal pronouns help writing attain coherence.

- **Repetition** of important words and phrases acts as an interlocking device. Repetition *doesn't* mean simply beginning a sentence with the words that ended the previous one; that's boring and is usually unnecessary. Repetition is usually the same wording, though it may also be synonymous.

EXAMPLE

BORING REPETITION

```
Gradually, more people are taking up the cause of
nonviolence to protect the environment. Protecting the
environment by nonviolence has worked in several states.
```

COMMENT

Note that the underlined wording and the italicized wording are so close it's almost like reading the same thing twice.

REPETITION FOR COHERENCE

```
Gradually, more people are taking up the cause of
nonviolence to protect the environment. They believe
that confrontational tactics do more harm than good in
convincing others to save our surroundings.
```

COMMENT

"Confrontational tactics" is the opposite of "nonviolence," but the sentence goes on to point out how the former is not good. "Surroundings" in the second sentence is a synonym for "environment" in the first.

- **Consistent point of view** means that the attitude or stance you take toward your subject remains the same throughout. Jumping from being one who figuratively sits back and contemplates the overall view of a situation to one who vigorously supports a course of action in relation to that situation is to be inconsistent in point of view. The writing that results tends to be fragmented rather than coherent.

- **Integration of information** so that quotations, summaries, and other information drawn from sources are joined within the text to make the writing flow. If these elements are merely plopped down, one after another on a page, the result is choppy and disjointed. But if they are carefully introduced and integrated, the entire research paper holds together and sounds as if one person—you—wrote it. A separate section of this chapter, beginning on page 165, is about integrating sources.

Adequate Support

Writing that simply tosses out ideas has little believability, no matter how worthwhile or intriguing the thoughts may be. On the other hand, were those same ideas supported adequately, they would demand credence and even acceptance by readers.

Support for various statements in your research paper can take many forms, details of which are in most composition books. For instance, you might offer examples or statistics. Actually, the *documentation* you offer throughout your paper will be the major support for what you write. (See pages 166–71 about how to integrate documentation as you write the paper, and Chapter 8, pages 187–91, about forms of documentation.) Using *authoritative sources* is part of such documentation.

Emphasis

When you speak to somebody, you can emphasize what you believe is important by repeating words, by stressing particular ideas with your voice, or by pausing before making an important statement. Only repetition is available to you when you write, and even then it doesn't work the same way as in speaking.

To emphasize ideas in writing, you can do any of the following:

- Use proportion to give more space to more important ideas.

- Repeat words and ideas that are important.

- Position what you want to emphasize where it will be seen readily, such as at the beginnings or ends of paragraphs.

- Use visual devices, such as underlinings, special layouts (as in this bulleted listing), or subheads for units.

Concreteness and Specificity

Good writing tells the audience exactly what you want to convey, leaving nothing to chance or to guesswork. Therefore, wording ought to be concrete rather than abstract, and specific rather than general.

Concrete words name what you can ascertain through the senses: what you see, hear, smell, touch, and taste. "A blue two-story house with red shutters" is concrete, because the words tell what you can see. **Abstract words,** on the other hand, name feelings, beliefs, or ideas. "Beauty," "happiness," "honor," "intellectual freedom," and "the American way" are examples of abstractions, because they may signify different concepts to those who read or hear such words. Although you can't do much advanced or sophisticated writing without using abstractions, concrete words are of great help in conveying your own thoughts (even abstractions) directly to your audience.

Specific words limit meaning in another way; they narrow the concept expressed by a **general word.** "Animal" is a general word, because it signifies a wide range of living creatures, from whales to amoebas. "Whale" is more specific than animal, but even *it* can be made more specific: "baleen whales" describes a particular group, and "humpback whale" differentiates between that species and other kinds of baleen whales. In writing your research paper, the more specific the wording you use, the more accurately you convey your thoughts to readers.

INTEGRATING RESOURCE INFORMATION

The chief characteristic of research writing is that it not only acknowledges the sources of ideas used in the paper but also does so in specific forms. But those sources are the backup for what *you* have to say; they support and explain what you offer. Documenting them isn't an end in itself, and you must be careful not to let the resources become the dominant element in your research paper.

Here are three simple examples of how the author and a page number, adequate documentation for most purposes, can be used to acknowledge a quotation. Note how that information in each of the three is sufficiently integrated with the text that it doesn't interfere with smooth reading.

EXAMPLE 1

```
The writing is graphic enough for nonpilots as well
as pilots to follow. For example,"I throttled down,
allowing just enough revs to prevent the ship from
stalling at the slow speed required to land in so
small a space" (Markham 48).
```

COMMENT

Documentation is in parentheses and follows what needs to be acknowledged, which, in this case, is a quotation.

EXAMPLE 2

Then Markham wrote, "I throttled down, allowing just
enough revs to prevent the ship from stalling at the
slow speed required to land in so small a space" (48).

COMMENT

If the author's name is part of a sentence leading into or concluding material that must be acknowledged, only the page number is noted in the parentheses.

EXAMPLE 3

On page 48, Markham says, "I throttled down, allowing just
enough revs to prevent the ship from stalling at the slow
speed required to land in so small a space."

COMMENT

If the text includes both author and page source, the acknowledgment is complete and no other documentation is required.

When you acknowledge sources right in the text at the point where you use them, you are using **parenthetical documentation**. This form will be used in the research paper you are preparing because it is the standard for the MLA (Modern Language Association) that is the basis of this book and is similar to that employed in several academic disciplines. (See Chapter 11 for conventions of other documentation systems.) You will find the conventions of parenthetical documentation and some examples of how to use them explained on pages 187–91 in Chapter 8. Each parenthetical documentation in your text is supported by a complete citation, such as you have written on the preliminary citation cards, in the Works Cited at the end of your paper.

To keep the focus of your writing on your own ideas instead of on the documentation, you should integrate the two *smoothly* so as not to disrupt the flow of writing in your paper or call attention to differences in style and tone between what you write and what your reference sources wrote. Therefore, the mark of a well-integrated resource item is that it doesn't call attention to itself!

Here are six ways you can integrate documented information into the text of your research paper.

1. **Use wording that shows what follows is not your own**. That is, if you indicate at the beginning of a passage that you are about to present material that will be documented, you prevent misunderstanding or confusion on the part of the reader. Careful readers are often frustrated to come upon a passage they ascribe to the author of the research paper, only to find later in the paragraph that it was actually a summary, a paraphrase, or an idea the author had carefully credited. (Quotations are evident by their punctuation, so the problem is less acute.)

EXAMPLES

HELPFUL LEAD-IN

The Sierra Club's <u>Grass Roots Primer</u> (249-50) relates a success story from Middletown, New Jersey, in which the Nature Conservancy helped a small citizen's committee preserve undeveloped land. [The rest of the paragraph and a listing that follows tell how the Nature Conservancy helped.]

COMMENT

Consider how misleading the paragraph and list would have been if the student writing this research paper had first detailed the participation of the Nature Conservancy, leaving readers to wonder about how she got information from New Jersey, and only at the end of a long passage acknowledged that the information came from the Sierra Club publication.

HELPFUL LEAD-IN

Nader's "Curriculum" (148-52) provides many suggestions on using the media effectively.

COMMENT

The reader is now assured that what follows will be suggestions made by the publication, not by the author of the research paper.

2. **Vary the wording of introductory phrases**. Easy as it is to write that a person "says" or "writes" something you use in your research paper, good writing style demands that you be more imaginative and less repetitive in introducing such material. A dictionary or thesaurus may be helpful in solving this problem.

POSSIBILITIES

Professor Jason Roberts *states*
asserts
believes
thinks
insists
contends
confirms
declares
emphasizes
adds
affirms
points out

This sort of varied wording may be used to introduce indirect as well as direct quotations or any other material you are documenting.

3. **Document information anywhere in a sentence or in a paragraph**. Looking at a paper with documenting parentheses at the end of paragraph

after paragraph gives most readers the impression that the author has done little more than paste together pieces of information, one after another, without much thought of the relationship of other peoples' ideas to the author's own. End-of-paragraph documentation is particularly disturbing to readers if the endings of paragraphs are quotations. Therefore, as you write, try to vary the location of documentation in both sentences and paragraphs. Your goal should be to avoid a cut-and-paste look!

EXAMPLES

Documentation at the beginning of a sentence and a paragraph

```
Another article ("New Group") informs readers of the
existence of the Superfund Action Coalition that has been
formed . . .
```

Documentation in the middle of a sentence and the middle of a paragraph

```
. . . Even Greenpeace's Quaker tactic of "bearing witness"
(Christrup 13) to environmental atrocities repeatedly puts
activists in the line of fire between whales and whalers,
seals and hunters, Earth and nuclear devices.
```

Documentation at the end of a sentence and middle of paragraph

```
. . . Oakland police had disregarded previous reports
of death threats and tried to prove the group members
had planted the bomb themselves (Rauber 24-30). This
illustrates . . .
```

4. **Make documented material fit grammatically into your own sentences**. Do this in any of three different ways:

   a.   Delete words from a quotation and use ellipses to show you have done so.

   EXAMPLE

   ```
   According to Sive (527), the prepared activist is
   one who has read "all the constitutional provisions,
   federal and state statutes, ordinances, agency
   regulations, etc. that pertain to [their] case, . . .
   circumstances and findings of all the relevant court
   decisions on all levels . . . to date, meaning today!"
   ```

   b.   Use square brackets to clarify or provide information that would otherwise not fit in the context of your own writing. See the preceding example and the one that follows.

   EXAMPLE

   ```
   (2) It served as a repository for and kept an
   accounting of the funds [they] collected.
   ```

c. Use only the most relevant part of a passage you document; no rule says you have to use every single word you put on a note card.

EXAMPLE

NOTE CARD

high-sounding group names   D'Esposito 2-3
"The Endangered Species Act Coordinating
Council" and "The Foundation for Environmental
and Economic Progress" sound like environmental
groups. "But, in fact, they are lobbyists representing
timber barons, open-pit mining companies, fishing
interests, pesticide manufacturers, and large land
developers out to portray the Endangered Species
Act as hostile to the economy and a thief of jobs."

USE IN RESEARCH PAPER

"The Foundation for Environmental and Economic Progress"
and "The Endangered Species Act Coordinating Council" are
two such groups with the real goal of undermining the
Endangered Species Act.

5. **Instead of documenting every line in a paragraph, group the citations for a single passage**. To document every line suggests you have little to say for yourself. As writing, excessive documentation is unnecessary and awkward. Instead, combine ideas and use one citation for several sources.

EXAMPLE

Undaunted by this tragic loss, Greenpeace sued the French
government, eventually winning eight million dollars, and
on April 8, 1992, France announced a moratorium on nuclear
testing for at least one year (Christrup 18; Greenpeace 1;
Nader "Curriculum" 109; Riding).

6. **Use paraphrases and summaries, not just quotations**, to support what you say. Certainly you will want to use quotations in your research paper. But as you come to a note containing a quotation, consider if you might convey

the same idea by paraphrasing or summarizing it in the text of your research paper.

EXAMPLES

NOTE CARD QUOTATION   [Ellipsis shows that not all of the law is quoted here, though it is on the note card.]

Sec. 2 (b) of EEA (Public Law 91-516): "It is the purpose of this Act to encourage and support the development of new and improved curricula to encourage understanding of policies, and support of activities designed to enhance environmental quality and maintain ecological balance . . . to provide for community education programs on preserving and enhancing environmental quality and maintaining ecological balance; and to provide for the preparation and distribution of materials by mass media in dealing with the environment and ecology."

IN THE RESEARCH PAPER

Among this act's goals are to foster environmental awareness in every citizen through the funding and developing of new curricula for students, and training programs for teachers, government employees, and society in general.

COMMENT

The part of the Environmental Education Act quoted in the note is long (it is abbreviated on this page) and, although clear, is necessarily written in legalese. In writing the research paper that is the sample in Chapter 10, Barbara Howell decided that including such a long quotation—and it's all a single sentence—would impede the movement of ideas through her work; she therefore chose to summarize in the paper what she believes are the most relevant goals.

Nobody can tell you how much documentation to include in your paper. Certainly you need to give the sources of content in the paper you didn't already know or of what is not common knowledge. Therefore, the more information you discovered, the more you will have to document; sources on your notes will be a guide. Your concern at this point, especially in the initial drafts, is how to work into the body of your research paper the various quotations, summaries, paraphrases and personal comments you want to include—and how to do so smoothly.

RECORDING AND PUNCTUATING QUOTATIONS

Although you will probably choose to use quotations sparingly in your research paper to avoid any suggestion that you relied on other writers and speakers more than on yourself, certainly you will want to use quotations in the body of your research paper. Your note cards should show the spelling, punctuation, and capitalization used in the original source. When you include that information in the text of your paper, follow the usual rules of punctuation and a few conventions that are found in writing handbooks and textbooks (several of which are repeated here for your convenience).

- If the end of a quotation is also the end of your own sentence, put the period inside the concluding quote marks.

- Use a comma to signify the end of the quoted sentence that is not the end of a text sentence; but if the quotation ends with a question mark or an exclamation mark, use that mark, even in the midst of a text sentence. Put a period as you normally would at the end of the entire sentence you write, which includes the quotation.

- A question mark or an exclamation mark that ends a quotation (or that you use in your own writing) goes inside the concluding quote marks, even though your own sentence continues to its conclusion and may have a period at its end.

- Direct quotations are either part of a sentence or are separated from introductory wording by a comma, depending on the construction of the sentence. Only occasionally does a colon introduce a short quotation.

- Use a capital letter to begin a fully quoted sentence, even if it does not also begin your own sentence of text.

- Retain any special punctuation or other markings of the original passage when you reproduce it as a quotation in your paper.

In addition to signaling that you are using the words of another person, not your own, quotation marks are used to acknowledge that *familiar words are used in a special sense.*

As in all writing, a quotation within another quotation (that is, when the source you quote contains a quotation) is indicated by single, instead of double, quotation marks. Any comma ending the quotation appears before either of those quote marks.

Short Prose Passages

A "short" prose quotation of either fiction or nonfiction is one that occupies *four or fewer lines of text* in your research paper. Write it as part of the regular text of the paper, using the same spacing but observing the conventions of punctuating quotations just noted.

EXAMPLE

```
Mead went on to say, "A short-term perspective won't
protect the environment. We will have every polluter
back polluting cheerfully in five years unless we build
structures that last."
```

Parenthetical documentation is put as close as possible to the passage, either in the lead-in wording (which is the case in the preceding example, which appears in the sample research paper on page 240) or outside the ending quotation marks. The main guide is that documentation shouldn't interfere with the flow of the text.

Longer Prose Passages

Quotations of *five or more lines of text* in your research paper are considered "longer" and are signaled to the audience in a different way. There is usually introductory wording; it often, but not necessarily, ends with a colon. The entire quoted passage is then *indented ten spaces from the left margin.* Do not use quotation marks, and do not change the double spacing of your typewriter or word processing program.

EXAMPLE

```
As Nader points out in "Ecotactics,"

        . . . corporate and government polluters crave
    secrecy and deny citizens access to the records
    of that which is harming their health and
    safety.
            State and federal agencies keep
    undisclosed data on how much different companies
    pollute. Thus has industrial lethality been made
    a trade secret by a government that presumes to
    be democratic. (15)
```

COMMENT

The first part of this long quotation comes from the middle of a paragraph, so there is no left-side paragraph indentation, only the ellipsis to show that some of the quotation is omitted. However, the paragraph indentation after the initial quoted sentence shows that a paragraph began at that point in the original. The author and source of the quotation is in the lead-in to this quotation.

Put the actual page reference for a long quotation *in parentheses two spaces after the period* ending the quotation.

Short Passages of Poetry

Any portion of poetry, *from part of a line through three lines*, may be quoted as part of the text of your research paper; the lines are usually included as part of a sentence. Record such a short passage of poetry as you did on your note cards: that is, retain the capitalization of the original, and use a virgule (slash mark) with one space before and one after it to show how the poetry lines were set in their original form.

EXAMPLE

In Sonnet 116, Shakespeare announces, "Let me not to the marriage of true minds / Admit impediments. Love is not love / Which alters when it alteration find."

Longer Passages of Poetry

Quotations of *four or more lines* of poetry should appear in the text of your research paper the same way they do in the original poem, and each line should begin ten spaces in from the left margin of the text. However, if you can't get a complete verse line on a single line of type that's indented ten spaces, or if doing so would make the quoted poetry look unbalanced, you may begin each line closer to the left margin.

EXAMPLE

The daughters of the Seraphim led round their sunny flocks,
All but the youngest: she in paleness sought the secret
    air,
To fade away like morning beauty from her mortal day.
Down by the river of Adona her soft voice is heard,
And thus her gentle lamentation falls like morning dew:

"O life of this our spring! why fades the lotus of the
    water?
Why fade these children of the spring, born but to smile
    and fall? . . ." (William Blake "The Book of Thel")

The text of quoted poetry continues to be double-spaced. Its source is acknowledged two spaces after the last period of the poetry, just as for prose.

Since accurate quotation of poetry requires you to reproduce the original typography and formatting, you may need to ignore customary indentation if the poem you are reproducing has an unusual format. Then, copy the poem exactly as it appears in the original source, as in this example of "Easter Wings" by George Herbert.

EXAMPLE

```
          Lord, Who createdst man in wealth and store,
              Though foolishly he lost the same,
                  Decaying more and more,
                      Till he became
                          More poore:
                          With thee
                      O let me rise,
                  As larks harmoniously,
              And sing this day Thy victories:
          Then shall the fall further the flight in me.
```

Identify the author and title of a long poetry quotation as part of the text, as shown in the introduction to the preceding example, or at the beginning of the poem, this way:

```
                    Easter Wings
                  by George Herbert
```

Drama

Since dramatic quotations will be in either prose or poetry, follow the form recommended for the genre of drama you will be quoting from. That is, up to three lines of dialogue or stage direction may be incorporated into the text, but longer passages (four or more lines) should be indented ten spaces from the left. Be sure to include the name of the character speaking, either in the introduction to the dialogue or just as it appears in the source you used. If you quote a passage that contains more than one speaker, be particularly careful that each one is indicated.

EXAMPLES

Short Quotation

```
Romeo begins what is popularly called the balcony scene by
saying, "He jests at scars that never felt a wound."
```

Longer Quotation

```
    Here is a key interchange between Romeo and Juliet in
what is popularly called the balcony scene:
          ROM.  O, wilt thou leave me so unsatisfied?
          JUL.  What satisfaction canst thou have tonight?
          ROM.  Th' exchange of thy love's faithful vow
                for mine.
```

<pre>
JUL. I gave thee mine before thou didst request
      it;
      And yet I would it were to give again.
</pre>

COMMENT NOTES

The parenthetical documentation you use to cite sources of information are usually all you need in the text of your research paper. However, you may find that you want to add to or qualify something that can't be accomplished without distracting from the text. Rather than break into the thoughts being expressed in the paper, make such comments—sparingly—in **endnotes** that, in the MLA style, appear at the conclusion of the research paper. (In APA style they are called "Footnotes," although they, too, are put on a separate page at the end of the text rather than at the bottom or foot of a page. See Chapter 11.)

Comment notes are used for any of the following:

- Brief elaboration, qualification, or addition to what is in the text
- A necessary evaluative comment on a source
- Identifying a series of sources which, if shown in parenthetical documentation, would interrupt the text of the paper

Signal comment notes by *numbering them successively throughout the paper* with superscript arabic numerals, such as this,[1] at the place where they are most relevant and after punctuation markings, except dashes. Use the same arabic numerals at the beginning of the note; then give the information.

E X A M P L E

<pre>
[1] No periods or other marks are used with the
superscript numeral and no space is used before it.
However, one space always follows the numeral, both in the
text and on the note page.
</pre>

Start endnotes on a separate page headed "Notes" (centered one inch down from the top of the page) at the conclusion of the research paper and before the Works Cited page. Double-space after the heading and throughout the notes on the page. Begin each note by indenting the superscript numeral five spaces from the left margin; leave a space after it and then start the words of the note, writing as far as necessary toward the right. Second and succeeding lines of each note begin at the left margin of the page.

You can see endnotes used for comment on the text of the sample research paper on page 244.

ENDING THE PAPER

Stop writing when you finish what you have to say. When you come to the end of your outline and note cards, conclude gracefully but not abruptly. Don't pad at the end, and don't try to write a sudden one-sentence "summary" of the whole paper. In particular, *don't introduce or even suggest any new ideas in the last paragraph or so of your paper!*

The following are some suggestions about how to end a research paper. The ending you decide on may be a combination of these, or may not fit into such specific categories, but you should let the ending stem from your text, not try to change it to fit a formula.

1.   **If you have written an argumentive or persuasive paper, remind the audience of what you want them to do or think in response to your presentation.**

   EXAMPLE

   Society continues to dictate that the ultra-thin body is
   the ideal for women. The intense pressures on young women
   to achieve this false, Madison Avenue image lead many
   into the desperate downward spiral of bulimia. For society
   to drastically change its ideals of the "proper" body
   appearance is unrealistic. However, to combat this,
   people should be encouraged to be more accepting of the
   differences in weight and physical appearance among
   individuals. Even more immediately attainable is the
   realistic and very desirable goal of providing affordable
   treatment for bulimia.

   (*from* "Bulimia and Society: Unrealized Expectations" by Christi West)

   Two points this author has made in her research paper—individual acceptance and affordable treatment—conclude the work as a reminder of the direction that this entire persuasive paper has taken. Because they are the last words readers see, they are the most likely to be remembered. Moreover, because Ms. West stressed the success of treatment that is so expensive as to be beyond the reach of many bulimics, she concludes with the point she considered most significant in the paper.

2.   **Use a brief quotation that summarizes the ideas or attitudes you have expressed throughout the paper.**

   EXAMPLE

   In a 1938 speech before the National Education
   Association, President Franklin Delano Roosevelt said:
   > Freedom to learn is the first necessity of
   > guaranteeing that man himself shall be self-
   > reliant enough to be free. . . . If in other
   > lands the press and books and literature of all
   > kinds are censored, we must redouble our efforts
   > here to keep it free. . . . The ultimate victory

> of tomorrow is through democracy with education.
>
> (qtd. in "Censorship and Libraries" exhibit)
>
> (*from* "School Libraries and Book Banning" by Carol Matz)

Use a quotation only if it bears out the points you've made within your research paper and does so in a style you think especially suitable to the subject. In this case, Ms. Matz felt the quotation was particularly suitable because of the authority carried by a president's words.

3. **Make some statement about your thesis instead of merely repeating it.**

EXAMPLE

> We have seen the Roslyn of the original story, whom the
> men wanted too much to please, become the charming but
> somewhat cloying girl of a later Miller story. When she
> was transformed into a major character in The Misfits,
> Roslyn grew in complexity and lost the simple definition of
> innocence or sophistication that each of her "ancestors"
> had. In these three works, Miller has provided us with an
> excellent view of the development of a dramatic character
> from first sketches to boldly colored completeness.
>
> (*from* "Roslyn: Evolution of a Literary Character" by Judith Anndy)

The thesis of this research paper was: "Arthur Miller used elements of a sophisticated mistress in one story and a childlike wife in another to develop the appealing but not fully explained character of Roslyn Taber in *The Misfits*." While the concluding paragraph alludes to that statement, it also includes other material that was presented in the paper.

4. **Return to some initial generalization and show how you have proved, disproved, or enlarged upon it.**

EXAMPLE

> Don Quixote, then, was not simply a mad old man. Rather,
> he was a person of deep humanity whose misadventures
> stemmed mainly from attempts to help the oppressed.
> Furthermore, what seemed to be his foolish dreams are
> really the hopes of the sanest and least foolish people
> everywhere; what seemed to be his useless persistence is
> really idealism; what seemed to be his inability to cope
> with his time is really the doubt and tension that every
> human lives with. The character Cervantes created cannot
> be called "man" unless each of us is willing to accept
> that label also. For he is a composite of us all--and each
> of us has within the self a bit of Don Quixote.
>
> (*from* "The Madman Who Was Most Sane" by Ida Kaufman)

This concluding paragraph begins with a generalization that has pervaded the text of the research paper. The specifics that support the generalization are summaries of those that have been offered throughout the text as proof. So to end this paper, the author merely drew together the various strands already developed.

5. **Link what you have written either to something known or to what seems a future possibility.**

   EXAMPLE

   Nonviolent action, education, legislation: these are
   tools readily available to everyone who cares about the
   environment. They can be used by people of all ages, in
   all places, and do not cost anything except time and
   personal commitment. Yet these are the very tools that can
   build a sustainable society for both the immediate and the
   long-range future.

   (*from* "Nonviolent Tools for Environmental Activists" by Barbara Howell)

   This research paper has examined the three activities at the beginning of the paragraph, so the information is now known to the reader. The last sentence suggests a resulting possibility.

6. **State a conclusion you have reached about your subject.**

   EXAMPLE

   The polygraph has been called "inherently intrusive . . .
   [and the testing] invades privacy and degrades human
   dignity" (Pear). Added to that, results are often
   inaccurate and operators unreliable. The evidence <u>against</u>
   using the polygraph to screen employees in private
   businesses seems overwhelming. Relatively few people are
   dishonest. To seek them out with a lie detector does not
   justify the honest people being subjected to the
   intimidation and heartbreak of polygraph testing.

   (*from* "Polygraph Tests and Employment Practices" by Ronnie B. Londner)

   As a result of her research and writing the text of the paper, this author concluded that polygraph tests for employment should be abolished and so states this conclusion as the final paragraph.

Bad Endings

The ending is the last thing your audience sees, and so it will leave a strong impression, despite anything else you may have written in your paper. To keep that impression good and maintain the impact of a well-written paper, avoid these bad endings.

1. **Don't bring up a new idea.** The end of a paper is the time to finish everything, not to make a fresh start.

2. **Don't stop abruptly or simply trail off.** Your paper needs a specific ending and deserves one that brings your ideas to completion.

3. **Don't ask a question.** You might get an answer you didn't count on!

4. **Don't make any statement or suggestion that needs extensive clarification.** The time to make explanations has passed.

5. **Don't fumble.** Stop when you have nothing more to say.

6. **Don't tell explicitly what you have done in the paper.** Give your audience credit for having *understood* what you did in the paper. Also, don't be so unimaginative as to write anything like "In this paper it has been shown that . . ." The audience realizes what you have shown.

7. **Don't make a change in your style.** Keep your writing style at the end the same as it was at the beginning.

REVISING YOUR PAPER

Good writers—students, businesspeople, hobbyists, attorneys, and everyone who makes a living by writing—make changes in wording and presentation of ideas as they write. That is one kind of revision, of tinkering with a piece of writing until it says exactly what you want it to say.

Another kind of revision comes after the first draft or first complete writing of the paper. Then you may add, delete, or rearrange words and ideas. Even if you were working from a satisfactory outline, you may find that when the whole research paper is written out, there are parts that would fit better in one place than in another.

Revision is another chance to look at what you've written and change it, to make it convey your intentions to your audience more precisely. In fact, writing is a matter of multiple drafts and is often described as a "messy process" because of constant revision.

You don't have to be a professional writer to be dissatisfied with a first draft. In fact, such writers not only rewrite extensively themselves, they follow advice from their editors. You can emulate that working arrangement by conferring with classmates, either during class time set aside by the instructor or by getting together outside of class to exchange papers. If you do work with peers, be sure to give praise for writing that is good as well as to note portions that could be clarified or otherwise improved. As you become an increasingly proficient writer, you will develop your own critical facilities so you know what can profit from revision, especially in idea presentation, word choice, sentence structure, and accuracy.

Revising is easiest when you approach a work as if seeing it for the first time—admittedly a difficult job if you've been working for weeks on a research paper. However, you *will* find it helpful to put the first draft away for several days or a week, if you have time, before looking at it with an eye toward making changes.

Attend to the niceties of mechanics—that is, correcting spelling, punctuation, capitalization, and paragraphing—at the last reading before typing your paper or getting ready to print a hard copy from a computer disc. Use a dictionary and refer to a composition handbook if you need to as a way of sticking to the conventions of Edited American English that your audience will surely expect to find in your research paper.

Word Choice and Sentence Structure

Often people engrossed in writing down their ideas can't find just the right word at the moment they need it. Instead of stopping and losing a train of thought, they use a second-best word. A better way of finding the right word is to mark the passage, as you write, with a symbol to show that you know you need to improve some wording or restate the passage. If you've selected a second-best word or marked some wording for revision, now is the time to check back and find wording you believe should be changed or improved. Take time in revision to select the best words for every idea in your paper.

Remember, as you reread your writing, that although *you* may know what you mean, your reader might not. Look for precision in wording when you revise. And don't let sentences get away from you; revision gives you the chance to tighten them.

DRAFT SENTENCE

The decision was not only about the rights of the students in this particular case to wear armbands, but it was also really about all other ways that students express themselves in schools in today's society.

INTENTION   The decision was about one case but it had far-reaching consequences.

REVISED SENTENCE

The decision didn't relate only to the wearing of armbands; it was really about all forms of expression in the schools.

Wording, remember, must make the content of your research paper accessible to the audience. During your research, you may learn a considerable amount of jargon—the words and phrases characteristic of a particular field and used by people knowledgeable in it. Unless you are absolutely sure that your audience understands this special "language," wording ought to be "translated" so the audience can readily understand what you are writing about.

EXAMPLE OF JARGON

Soon Dorothy Liebes's trademark became her skip dent warps of textured and metallic yarns with unusual weft materials.

REVISION

```
Soon Dorothy Liebes's trademark became the fabrics she
designed of unevenly spaced textured and metallic yarns
crossed by unusual threads or even by thin strips of wood
or metal.
```

Here are some other techniques you can use to attain good writing through revision:

- Use a variety of sentence structures.
- Combine a series of short, simple sentences into one, more complex sentence.
- Use transitional words and phrases (such as "in addition," "therefore," "equally important," and "nevertheless") to connect ideas smoothly within and between sentences and paragraphs.
- Make sure modifiers are near the words they modify.
- Be sure antecedents of pronouns are clear.

These and many other aids to good writing are developed in composition and rhetoric books; consult them.

Mechanics

People expect to find the spelling, punctuation, capitalization, sentence structure, and paragraphing of the English language to follow the conventions of what they usually read. You owe it to the audience of your research paper to meet those expectations. Any change from the expected is an interference to the audience, an annoyance to readers. Therefore, help your audience by following the conventions of Edited American English, and present a paper that exemplifies such customs. A check of these conventions is ordinarily the last step in revising your paper.

If you have questions or doubts, a good place to check on the following matters of mechanics is an English handbook or other standard guide.

- Use conventional punctuation.
- Make capitalization accurate.
- Keep verb tenses consistent in accord with what you write.
- Be sure subjects and verbs agree in number.
- Limit abbreviations to accurate ones used only where permissible.
- Adhere to spelling conventions, and check every word whose spelling you're not absolutely sure about. Customarily, keep a dictionary handy, and use it when you revise.

In short, do everything you can to be sure your audience focuses on what you have to say rather than on distracting errors of mechanics that could easily have been cleared up by careful editing.

REVISING ON A COMPUTER

If you draft your research paper on a computer using a word processing program, you may revise somewhat differently from those who write with pen on paper or with a typewriter. People who compose on computers usually do more revising as they write than they have done in other media. And although various versions of a piece can be saved as printouts, few people bother doing so.

What is almost necessary for people who use computers is to print out a hard copy of the final version that is saved on disc and to use that for final revision. Editing on that printed copy has several advantages.

- You can see all at once what was written, and in larger "chunks" than you may be able to see on a computer screen.

- You can turn back and forth to various pages, even put several side by side to check continuity and prevent repetition.

- You get a better picture of what your final research paper will look like than you can from seeing it on a monitor.

- Seeing your work in a different format (that is, hard copy vs. on-screen) makes you aware of elements, especially mechanics, that you might overlook because of familiarity or expectation.

Block moves of words are so easy on a computer that you should take advantage of this technology, which allows you to move to different places a few words to a few paragraphs, as a way of finding the best location for some elements of what you write. Especially, if some phrasing doesn't seem to read well, try it in another place; or try revising it or even eliminating it completely. If you have a hard copy of the passage before moving, you can make a comparison. Or you can use the capabilities of some word processing programs to examine different versions of a passage side by side on the monitor screen.

Use the **search** capacity of most word processing programs if you want to make some consistent change not considered during the writing of your research paper. For example, if you've been writing "on-line" with the hyphen and decide that "online" is more consistent with general use, the computer can make the correction of every instance in far less time than it would take you to search out two examples of what you want to change.

One of the most widely used—and most appreciated—editing aids available to those who work on a computer is a **spell checker**, a program that will test your spelling against the conventionally spelled words in its dictionary. Many computer writers ask for a spelling check of single words every time they're in doubt while writing; others prefer to wait until a work is finished and then check all the spelling at once. No computer will make corrections for you, but most spell checkers will give you choices and make suggestions of how to spell a word it highlights. What *no* computer program can do, however, is to know whether a word fits into a given context (at least not on home computers, as this is written). For example, "red" will be accepted because it's a word in the program dictionary, even though it makes no sense in a sentence such as "I red the book." The watchword for using spell checkers, therefore, is to use it as a prompt but not to rely on it blindly.

Many word processing programs have a **thesaurus** built in, so writers can readily search for synonyms. Use it as a revision aid if you have one available. The caution that needs to be observed, however, is the same as in using a print thesaurus you can hold in your hand: don't substitute one word for another without understanding exactly what each word "means" and how each is customarily used. And certainly don't go searching for "big words" in an effort to sound intelligent or mature or sophisticated!

There are also programs that **analyze writing style**. They will perform such functions as spotting passive verbs (and encourage you to change them to active ones), tell you about sentence length and word choice, and give you other information usually helpful in revising the wording and sentence structure of what you have written. One drawback of such programs, however, is that the choices a program recommends are not always those that will improve your own writing. For instance, all passive constructions are not necessarily "bad"; one may be exactly what you mean in a particular spot. You may often need to check a writing handbook or composition text for confirmation of your own—or the program's—choices. Or, as one evaluator of some style analyzers has pointed out, if a writer knows all he or she needs to know to accept or reject the recommendations of such programs, the writer doesn't need the programs.

SELECTING A TITLE

If you haven't already chosen a title for your research paper, you ought to do so by the time you finish writing the paper. Your research paper will be known by its title, so choose one carefully.

A title that **gives readers information** about the contents of the paper is preferable to one that is vague or general.

VAGUE   A Look at William Dean Howells

IMPROVED   The Concept of Work in the Novels of William Dean Howells

Titles don't need to be stuffy or dull, but they should generally give readers some idea at the outset of what the research paper will contain.

Usually, choose a title that is a phrase rather than a complete sentence. The thinking behind such an admonition probably has its genesis in the recognition that book and article titles are not complete sentences; thus, research paper titles, too, should not be sentences. Besides, a sentence gives so much information away that a reader will look for support of the title rather than allow support for the thesis statement to direct the reading.

LESS DESIRABLE   A Wide Array of Activist Tools Makes Violence Unnecessary

IMPROVED   Nonviolent Tools for Environmental Activists

As in other aspects of writing, sometimes you get notions about what *to do* by knowing what you shouldn't do. So here are a few kinds of titles to **avoid**:

1. **Cute or coy titles seldom work well.** That's not to say you can't ever use a pun or clever words if they catch the spirit of the paper they name and if they are easily understood by the audience for whom the research paper is written. However, generally choose a straightforward title over other kinds.

    C O Y   Look Who's Pushing the Puffs

    I M P R O V E D   Changing Language in Printed Cigarette Ads

2. **Don't use a question in place of a title.** No matter how provocative you think a question will be, it could easily work against you if a prospective reader responds negatively to it. Better to let the title answer the question you thought of posing.

    Q U E S T I O N   Should Private Clubs Be Able to Limit Membership?

    I M P R O V E D   The Case Against Sexual Discrimination in Private Clubs

3. **Never use a thesis statement as a title**. It's bound to be too long and tell too much. Besides, it will be a sentence, and a phrase is preferable for a title.

    T H E S I S , N O T T I T L E   Intellectual Freedom Is Threatened When School Libraries Ban Books

    I M P R O V E D   Consequences of Book Banning in School Libraries

4. **Avoid a long, detailed title that gives too much information**. This is particularly important if you think such a title will make your work sound "academic" or "scholarly." It won't! Rather, such a long title is distracting to most readers.

    T O O D E T A I L E D   An Examination of the Setting as Metaphor in the Films of John Ford, with Particular Reference to Fort Apache

    I M P R O V E D   Setting as Metaphor in John Ford's Films

These examples of "improved" research paper titles illustrate several **conventions you should observe**:

- *Do not use any punctuation at the end of a title.*
- *Capitalize the first letter of each word in the title, except conjunctions, articles, and prepositions.*
- *Do not underline a title or enclose it in quotation marks.*

- *Follow conventions for acknowledging titles within your research paper title*. That is, enclose the titles of other works within quotation marks or underline them as you would normally; note the underlined film title, <u>Fort Apache</u>, in the preceding example. (If you use a word processing program that permits italics, use them in place of the underlining.)

Documenting Your Paper

WHERE AND HOW TO MAKE ACKNOWLEDGMENTS

By now you know that you *must acknowledge the sources of all material that is not original* in your research paper. That means you must tell readers where you got

- Direct quotations
- Borrowed ideas, including paraphrases and summaries
- Visual materials, such as maps, charts, diagrams, and pictures

Such acknowledgment is in the form of documentation that establishes your own honesty and scholarly exactness; it also gives support to those ideas and conclusions that are your own. Acknowledgment also enables a reader to identify or to verify your material and, perhaps, to study further some aspect of it.

Only "common knowledge," that is, basic or well-known information that can be ascertained in many sources (such as the dates of a person's life, the chemical formula of a familiar substance, the location of a battle, and so on) as explained on page 106, does not need specific documentation in a research paper. Of course, if you have used someone else's words to present the common knowledge, usual documentation is required. However, sometimes the question of what requires documentation and what doesn't (or what is common knowledge and what isn't) is troublesome. Therefore, a general rule to follow is: *when in doubt, cite the source.* It's better to have too much documentation in your paper than not enough, to be considered overzealous rather than careless.

Acknowledgment means that you must provide documentation in **two places:**

1. Within the text of the research paper
2. In the Works Cited listing at the end of the paper

The first of these is the subject of this chapter; the second is explained in Chapter 9. Basically, if the resource was in print, you must tell *in the text* the exact page (or pages) from which you took the information as well as indicate the author and/or the title of a work. (Author, title, and publication information will be in the Works Cited.) If the source was not in print and you can provide specifics analogous to a page number about locating the material you used (such as the track on a CD), you should do so.

You also know that documentation must be *in a prescribed form*. In the previous chapter, on pages 166–71, you read examples of documentation forms used in the text of a research paper. In this chapter you will find more details of documentation so that you can apply the conventions to suit your own needs. (When you wrote your preliminary citation cards, you already practiced the punctuation and spacing that are the forms for the Works Cited list.)

Plagiarism—that is, presenting another person's material as if it were your own (without documentation)—is less likely if you were cautious about acknowledgment when taking notes than if you were careless in the early part of the research process. But be aware that unless you are alert when writing your paper, you might still commit plagiarism by omitting information from your note cards or by failing to include proper acknowledgment in your first draft.

PARENTHETICAL DOCUMENTATION: MLA (MODERN LANGUAGE ASSOCIATION)

Parenthetical documentation is so called because you **enclose the documentation in parentheses at the appropriate place in the text** and give readers needed information without sending them to look elsewhere in the midst of reading. It is the standard in English and other disciplines in the humanities.

Several qualities of parenthetical documentation make it particularly helpful.

1. Typing is easy, because you put in documentation as you write, without worrying about keeping numbers in order or writing part of the information in one place (the text) and part in another (endnotes).

2. Reading is easy, because the source information is part of the text and doesn't have to be sought elsewhere.

3. Once you learn MLA parenthetical documentation you can readily adapt it to other formats used, albeit with slight differences, in the social sciences and natural sciences.

Conventions of Parenthetical Documentation

As with so many other aspects of the research paper, several customs govern parenthetical documentation.

1. **Do not use the word "page" or any sort of abbreviation for it in documenting your sources**. A number in parenthetical documentation is assumed to be a page number. Citations in drama or classics are easily recognizable and won't be confused with a page number you are citing.

2. **Omit a page number if the source is complete on a single page**, as in some newspaper and magazine articles.

3. **Omit page numbers in citing alphabetically arranged entries in a reference work** such as an encyclopedia if the entry is complete on a single

page. However, use a page number if what you are documenting is within a multiple-page entry.

4. **If two authors with the same last name are among your sources, you will need to use both given name and surname** in the documentation to differentiate between them.

5. **Long titles**, if you need to use them, **may be shortened**, provided they are easily identifiable. For instance, if a title is "Almost 13 Years of Book Protests and Now What?" you may cite it as "13 Years."

6. **Cite act and scene or verse and line of dramatic and classic literary works by using two arabic numerals with a period between them**. Readers will recognize that the first number is that of the larger unit, the act or the verse; it may also refer to the book in certain classical works.

EXAMPLES

```
Tamburlaine, in the play about him, acknowledges his
satisfaction when he crowns himself (2.7).
```

or

```
"Not all the curses which the Furies breathe / Shall make
me leave so rich a prize as this" (Tamburlaine 2.7).
```

or

```
We know a great deal about the battle dress of the early
Greeks by reading a description of Agamemnon (Iliad 11.
15-44).
```

COMMENT

The first two examples refer to Act 2, Scene 7 of the play *Tamburlaine*. The parenthetical documentation for the *Iliad* is to book 11, lines 15 to 44.

Punctuation and Spacing in Parenthetical Documentation

The customs of documentation dictate that punctuation and spacing must conform to the conventions for writing research papers. The following will serve as a guide.

1. **Allow one space before and one after the parentheses that enclose documentation within a sentence**. See examples in this and the previous chapter, particularly.

2. **Documentation at the end of a sentence follows the last word or the closing quotation marks by one space**. The period marking the end of the sentence is put immediately after the closing parentheses. See the next example.

3. **Separate a series of sources by semicolons**. However, use discretion in the number of items you include in one set of parentheses.

EXAMPLE

Several writers have explored some of the many "reasons"
censors give for wanting books removed from school library
shelves (Pell 118; Books Behind Bars; Darling 120).

If you seem to have a particularly long list of sources to note at once, you may find that you can divide a long series of items by grouping them according to content references and locating the groups in different places.

4. **At the end of a long quotation** (five or more lines and indented ten spaces from the left margin), **put the parenthetical documentation two spaces after the period marking the conclusion of the quotation.**

Identifying Sources in Parenthetical Documentation

In Chapter 7 (pages 165–71) you read about integrating resource information smoothly into the text of your research paper as you write it. You also read there that the documentation could occur at the beginning, the middle, or the end of a sentence and saw a number of examples of parenthetical documentation. How you acknowledge a source in your text, as you know, may vary.

1. **Prefer to use an author's last name and a page number.** The reason for this is simple: the Works Cited will alphabetize citations by the last names of authors, when they are available, so any reader can then find the title and publication information for a source readily. Whether you use these two elements within parentheses or incorporate one or both of them in a sentence, you do readers a favor by using the author's name.

    EXAMPLE

    Stunts like the Sierra Club's peanut-shell caper in 1969
    creatively spotlight environmental ills in need of a cure
    (Stallings 90).

2. **If no author of a work is given, cite it by title and page number.** If the source consisted of only one page, use the title alone.

    EXAMPLE

    An increasing number of incumbents are finding themselves
    running against "Green" candidates ("Let's Party" 12).

3. **If you use more than one work by the same author, indicate which title you are citing.**

    EXAMPLE

    Nader's "Curriculum" (148-52) provides many suggestions
    for using the media effectively.

4. **Sources of multiple authorship are documented as they appear in the Works Cited.** That is, use up to three authors' names in the parenthetical

documentation; if there are four or more authors, use the last name of the first person followed by "et al." as well as the page designation.

EXAMPLE

Banned author Kurt Vonnegut referred sardonically to the
first amendment to the Constitution in his testimony
(Carmen, et al. 8).

5. **Use an author's last name and/or the title of a work if you refer to the complete work.** Obviously, then, there will be no page numbers.

EXAMPLE

Ciardi's translation of <u>The Divine Comedy</u> clearly shows
the rhyme scheme Dante used.

6. **When citing two or more locations of information within the same work, separate each by a comma and a space.**

EXAMPLE

Westin points out the trends and how the speed of a
computer is pushing them toward reality (158-62, 166).

7. **If a work you quote from contains a quotation from another work, both sources must be acknowledged.** You may be able to track down the original quotation, but sometimes that isn't necessary or expedient. Indicate that you are quoting the original speaker or writer by giving as much information as is available to you about the originator and then documenting the source from which you obtained the quotation.

EXAMPLE

As John Muir said a hundred years ago, "When we try to
pick out anything by itself we find it hitched to
everything else in the universe" (qtd. in Mitchell 23).

If the original source appears within quotation marks in the source you used, put that wording in single quotation marks within double quote marks or within the block indentation of a longer quotation.

8. **Use an arabic numeral to refer to the volume if the source you used is part of a multiple-volume series.** Use the abbreviation "vol." if referring to an entire volume. If you identify a page also, write the volume number, a colon, leave a space, then write the page number(s).

EXAMPLE

The articles about New York show that he was an inveterate
name-dropper (Huneker, vol. 2).

but

Antonin Dvořák is called "Old Borax," although the source
of the nickname is never explained (Huneker 2: 65-69).

or

```
Huneker calls Antonin Dvorak "Old Borax" (2: 65-69),
although he never explains the source of the nickname.
```

9. **Document nonprint sources as much as possible the way you cite print sources.** Any precise information you can provide to help locate an exact place, such as the side of a laser disc or the number of feet on a video-tape or the movement of a symphony will be appreciated by a reader.

E X A M P L E S

For documenting an act of an opera

```
One would hardly call realistic a song of farewell to an
overcoat (La Boheme 4), yet it fits easily into the opera.
```

For documenting a location on a videotape

```
Trick photography and clever sound splicing enable Domingo
to play both parts in a duet from Il barbiere di Siviglia
(Hommage a Sevilla 10'49).
```

DOCUMENTING VISUALS: ILLUSTRATIONS, MAPS, CHARTS, GRAPHS, AND TABLES

If you use any sort of visual within your research paper—a map, chart, table, graph, diagram, picture, or any similar item—you must document it within the paper and show its full source in the Works Cited. However, since you cannot do so in parentheses as part of a text, you provide a line of acknowledgment *below* the item and as close as possible to the text it illustrates.

Figure is the term by which charts, graphs, photos, figures, and drawings are known. Label each of these "Fig." (always using this abbreviation for the word), and give each a consecutive Arabic numeral throughout your research paper. Begin the documentation at the left margin and *directly below the figure.* Keep that margin and double-space if the label requires more than one line.

In addition to the number of the figure, documentation includes as many items as possible coinciding with those used for written works. That is, it should include the name of the originator (unless you have created the item for your paper and thus do not credit yourself), a title for the work, and where the original is located (unless what appears in your paper is an original).

E X A M P L E

```
Fig. 2. Francisco Goya, Señora Sabasa García, National
Gallery of Art, Washington, D.C.
```

or

```
Fig. 3. How Each Tuition Dollar Is Allocated.
```

If you are not the author or creator of the visual material, you must also acknowledge it by inclusion in the Works Cited. (You do not list yourself there because it is considered part of the entire research paper you produced.)

A **table,** whether in words, numbers, or a combination of the two, is so titled and assigned an arabic numeral showing its order in your paper. That designation should be put *above the caption or title of the item;* both are placed above the title, beginning at the left margin of text. If the table had no title in the source you took it from, or if you originated it, give the table an identifying title using appropriate capital letters, as for other titles.

Provide documentation *beneath the table*, also beginning at the left margin, and double-spacing if you need to write on more than one line. That is, after the word "Source" and a colon, cite the place from which you got the table.

EXAMPLE

Table 5.3

Young Adults Living with One or Both Parents, by Age, United States, 1960, 1970, 1980, 1988

Sex and Year	Percentage Living with Their Parents	
	18-24	25-34
Total		
1960	43	9
1970	47	8
1980	48	9
1988	54	11
Men		
1960	52	11
1970	54	9.5
1980	64	10.5
1988	61	15
Women		
1960	35	7
1970	41	7
1980	43	7
1988	48	8

Source: U.S. Bureau of the Census 1988b, Table A-6. Rptd. in Lamanna and Riedmann, Marriages and Families: Making Choices and Facing Change, 4th ed. (Belmont: Wadsworth, 1991) 185.

Since complete information about the source appears in the Works Cited, an alternate form is to use the same kind of documentation you do for text material. That is, give the source author or authors and page number on which the table appeared.

```
Source: U.S. Bureau of the Census 1988b, Table A-6. Rptd.
in Lamanna and Riedmann 185.
```

USING COMMENT NOTES IN ADDITION TO PARENTHETICAL DOCUMENTATION

Sometimes you have additional or explanatory material to add to the text or you want to make some comment on what you have written in your research paper, but adding to the text would impede the flow of reading. For this reason, as you read in Chapter 7 on page 175, comment notes may be used *in addition to the parenthetical documentation* in your paper. An example of comment notes used in the sample research paper in Chapter 10 is on page 244.

MLA ENDNOTE DOCUMENTATION

Although parenthetical documentation is widely used and preferred, some instructors may ask you to use endnote documentation instead. MLA still recognizes this method of documenting sources, so it appears here in case an instructor prefers that you use it. (Footnotes, which use the same format as endnotes but appear at the bottoms of pages on which there is relevant text, are not often used any more for undergraduate research papers.)

Endnotes are so called because documentation appears at *the end* of the research paper. Text citations and endnotes **work in pairs between the text and the page of documentation;** a *superscript number provides the coordination.* Write the superscript numbers sequentially throughout the paper and immediately after each borrowed idea or quotation in the text; then use the corresponding numbers to give the complete documentation on the endnote page.

Endnotes give four pieces of information about each source you used: *author, title, publication information,* and *the actual pages or pages—or other specific location.* The form to use the first time you acknowledge the source is illustrated on pages 194–200; those for the second and subsequent times you use one of those sources is on pages 200–01.

All the information you need for documenting sources with endnotes is already on your preliminary Works Cited cards; you need only make some adaptations. The chief differences between forms are these:

Information	*In Endnotes*	*In Works Cited*
Format	Paragraph indentation	Hanging indentation
Three units: author, title, publication information	Separated by commas or parentheses	Separated by periods
Author's name	Written in usual order	Surname, then given name
Publication information for books	In parentheses	No parentheses

Information	*In Endnotes*	*In Works Cited*
Page numbers or location in nonprint	Given for each note entry	None given

The **paragraph indentation for endnote format** means that the first line of each note is indented five spaces from the left margin and that succeeding lines each begin at the left margin. Type endnotes **double spaced,** just as for the text of your paper.

Begin a page of endnotes by typing the word "Notes" at the center of a page, one inch down from the top. (Continue, of course, putting your last name and successive page numbers 1/2 inch down and ending at the right margin.) Double-space between the heading and the first line of notes, and continue double-spacing throughout the endnotes.

Note Numbering System

Places **in the text** where you must direct a reader to endnotes are marked with superscript arabic numerals successively throughout the research paper. Put the note numbers at the end of a phrase, clause, or sentence so if the reader turns immediately to the citation, the flow of thought isn't interrupted.

The numerals are put in superscript—that is, typeset 1/2 line above the text line. On a typewriter you can stop typing and turn the roller half a line to put in the superscript. Most computer word processing programs have a signal that controls superscript numbers, but you must use a printer that supports the feature.

Put the note number immediately after the end of a word. *Never* use a period or other mark before or after superscript numerals in the text. If your citation comes at the same point you would ordinarily use punctuation, such as a comma or a period, put the numeral *before* the punctuation.

EXAMPLE

```
This decision, indicates Snyder3, offered the most clear-
cut definition of students' constitutional rights that has
been handed down from the courts.
```

The examples in the next section show how the note number will be **coordinated with the first reference** of the endnotes.

First References in Endnotes: Books

The first time you write an endnote listing, give complete information about the source; in subsequent references show only the author or title and a page number or its equivalent that will help locate something in a nonprint source. Allow one space after the superscript number, then write the author's full name. Put a comma after the name, allow one space, and write the title of the book you used (underlined, of course), then allow another space. Enclose the publication information in parentheses: the place of publication followed by a colon and a space, the name of the publisher in the shortened form as explained on pages 63–65, then a comma, a space, and the date of publication. Close the parentheses and allow one space before writing the exact page or pages from which you obtained the information. End the documentation note with a period.

EXAMPLE

The same customs prevail for documentation endnotes as you used on preliminary Works Cited cards and as you will use for the Works Cited listing with regard to using only the names of cities (not states), using shortened forms of publishers' names, and using abbreviations if you can't find some items of the publication information (see "Conventions of Parenthetical Documentation," pages 187–89).

The following examples show some of the various kinds of first references for books in endnotes. A complete list of the Works Cited forms for these, and other resources, is in Chapter 9, pages 204–20. If what you need isn't shown here, make the necessary adaptations from the Works Cited entries.

Begin each entry with the superscript number to match the one you used in the text for acknowledgment. Notice that all endnotes are double spaced and have paragraph indentation.

BOOK BY TWO OR THREE AUTHORS

[2] Lydia Temoshak and Henry Dreher, The Type C Connection: The Behavioral Links to Cancer and Your Health (New York: Random, 1992) 16.

BOOK BY MORE THAN THREE AUTHORS

[3] Val L. Eichenlaub, et al., The Climatic Atlas of Michigan (Notre Dame: U of Notre Dame P, 1991) 87.

ORGANIZATION OR INSTITUTION AS AUTHOR

[4] National Collegiate Athletic Association, 1992-93 NCAA Manual (Overland Park: NCAA, 1992) 112.

BOOK IN COLLABORATION

[5] H. Norman Schwarzkopf with Peter Petre, It Doesn't Take a Hero: The Autobiography of General H. Norman Schwarzkopf (New York: Bantam, 1992) 239.

BOOK WITH SINGLE EDITOR OR COMPILER OF A COLLECTION

   [6] Peter B. Levy, ed., <u>Documentary History of the Modern Civil Rights Movement</u> (Westport: Greenwood, 1992) 67.

ANTHOLOGY (or COLLECTION) WITH NO EDITOR GIVEN

   [7] <u>Southern Living 1993 Annual Recipes</u> (Birmingham: Oxmoor, 1993) 19-20.

WORK IN AN ANTHOLOGY WITH EDITOR'S NAME GIVEN

   [8] Joseph H. Suina, "And Then I Went to School," <u>The Horizon Reader</u>, eds. Harry Brent and William Lutz (New York: St. Martin's, 1992) 197.

INTRODUCTION OR FOREWORD OR AFTERWORD, OR PREFACE BY OTHER THAN AUTHOR

   [9] Ralph Nader, introduction, <u>Ecotactics: The Sierra Club's Handbook for Environmental Activists</u>, eds. John G. Mitchell and Constance L. Stallings (New York: Simon, 1990) 14.

WORK IN SEVERAL VOLUMES

   [10] Robert Browning, <u>Works of Robert Browning</u>, 10 vols. (New York: AMS, 1992) 5: 167-69.

TRANSLATED BOOK

   [11] Fernando Pessoa, <u>The Book of Disquiet</u>, trans. Alfred MacAdam (New York: Pantheon, 1991) 46.

EDITION OF A BOOK

   [12] Audrey J. Roth, <u>The Research Paper: Process, Form, and Content</u>, 7th ed. (Belmont: Wadsworth, 1994) 220.

REPUBLISHED BOOK

   [13] James L. Ford and Mary K. Ford, eds., <u>Every Day in the Year: A Poetical Epitome of the World's History</u> (1902; Detroit: Omnigraphics, 1992) 267.

First References in Endnotes: Periodicals

The first time you give an endnote reference to a periodical, the form to use is almost exactly like that for a Works Cited entry *except* that commas, each followed by one space, replace periods in the entry and the author's name is given in usual, rather than reverse, order. Also, the *exact page* you used for specific information is given. Observe paragraph indentation and double spacing throughout. This example shows how to record a magazine article by a known author in a publication that is paged by issue:

E X A M P L E

superscript   1 space   comma   date, month, year
↓   ↓   ↓   ↓

[14] Amy Nutt, "The Odessa Odyssey," <u>Sports Illustrated</u> 2 Aug.

1993: 49.   quotes   end quotes

↑
page

The following examples show how to record endnotes for selected kinds of first references for periodicals. If you don't find models here for the kind of endnotes you need, make the necessary adaptations from the examples of periodicals for the Works Cited listing on pages 204–20.

ARTICLE BY KNOWN AUTHOR IN PUBLICATION WITH CONTINUOUS PAGINATION

[15] Margaret Finders, "With Jix," <u>College Composition and Communication</u> 43 (1992): 497-98.

BOOK OR FILM REVIEW IN A MAGAZINE OR JOURNAL

[16] Jack E. White, "Pushed Off the Tightrope," rev. of <u>Volunteer Slavery: My Authentic Negro Experience</u>, by Jill Nelson, <u>Time</u> 26 July 1993: 71.

NEWSPAPER ARTICLE BY KNOWN AUTHOR

[17] Ana Santiago, "Rules Pose Problems for Cuba Travelers," <u>Miami Herald</u> 30 July 1993, final ed.: B1+.

NEWSPAPER EDITORIAL, NO AUTHOR SHOWN

[18] "Teaching Neglected Undergraduates," editorial, <u>Chicago Tribune</u> 28 June 1992, city ed.: A4.

BOOK OR FILM REVIEW IN NEWSPAPER

[19] Jean Patteson, "Tale Links Women Through Generations," rev. of <u>Daughter of the New World</u>, by Susan Richard Shreve, [Ft. Lauderdale] <u>Sun Sentinel</u> 31 May 1992, final ed.: F9.

First References in Endnotes: Other Print Sources

When you record pamphlets, letters, and print sources other than books and periodicals, follow the same general rules and conventions that apply to the formats already explained in this section. That is, double-space the endnotes, in paragraph indentation, with superscript numbers at the beginning of each and commas followed by single spaces separating the units.

The following examples will serve as guidelines for you to record other print sources as references in endnotes. If you need to acknowledge a source not shown here, adapt it from the Works Cited forms on pages 204–20.

DOCUMENT FROM AN INFORMATION SERVICE

[20] Kenneth Allen, "The Information Age: Promise or Dream," ERIC 1992, ED 337196.

PAMPHLET BY KNOWN AUTHOR

[21] Audrey J. Roth, Words for the Wise, (Miami: privately printed, 1992) 12.

PAMPHLET BY UNKNOWN AUTHOR

[22] Air Travel for Your Dog or Cat (Washington: Air Transport Assn., 1991) n.p.

C O M M E N T

The "D.C." after "Washington" is assumed and therefore omitted.

The designation "n.p." signifies that there are no page numbers in this pamphlet. In the interests of scholarship, you cannot simply count pages and supply a number no matter which part of the pamphlet you are acknowledging!

PERSONAL OR UNPUBLISHED LETTER

[23] Sharon Lee, letter to the author, 22 Nov. 1993.

GOVERNMENT PUBLICATIONS

[24] Federal Aviation Administration, U.S. Dept. of Transportation, Human Behavior: The No. 1 Cause of Accidents (Washington, n.d.) 3.

C O M M E N T

Although most government publications are printed by the Government Printing Office (GPO), that designation does not appear on this pamphlet and thus cannot be in your endnote acknowledgment.

There is no publication date printed on this pamphlet, although there are two identifying FAA numbers. However, the "n.d." where a year would ordinarily appear signifies the publication does not show a date.

The following pamphlet is one of a series specified as a publication that is underlined; its stated subject is taken as the title and is enclosed in quotation marks.

²⁵ Federal Aviation Administration, U.S. Dept. of
Transportation, "Pilots' Role in Collision Avoidance,"
Advisory Circular (Washington: 18 Mar. 1983) 6.

First References in Endnotes: Nonprint Sources

You may have found that computer programs, films, paintings, interviews, radio or television programs, CDs, videos, or laser discs extend the range and kind of resources from which you get information for your research paper. When you quote these sources or borrow ideas from them, readers will want to know the important elements of each source, so you feature them in the documentation for each medium.

Record the necessary information by following the models here, which are based on the Works Cited examples on pages 204–20, or by adapting what you already recorded on your own preliminary Works Cited cards. In most cases, that means substituting commas for periods and giving names in conventional order. Endnotes are double spaced and have paragraph indentation, and there is one space after the superscript numeral and after each comma within the note.

PERSONAL OR TELEPHONE INTERVIEW

²⁶ Judith A. Matz, personal interview, 4 Aug. 1993.

²⁷ Alan Roy Dynner, telephone interview, 10 Oct. 1993.

WORKS OF ART

²⁸ Pierre-Auguste Renoir, San Marco, Minneapolis
Institute of Arts, Minneapolis.

²⁹ Hanukah Lamp from Poland, Jewish Museum, New York.

³⁰ Constantin Brancusi, Sleeping Muse, Metropolitan
Museum of Art, New York.

C O M M E N T

The titles of works of art are underlined or put in italics.

LECTURE, SPEECH, ADDRESS

³¹ Margaret J. Geller, "Mapping the Universe," National
Air and Space Museum, Washington, 24 Mar. 1993.

COMPUTER SOFTWARE

³² FAX stf for the Macintosh, computer software, STF
Technologies, 1992.

C O M M E N T

Often computer software is available in different releases. For example, Microsoft *Word* is available in Version 4.0 or Version 5.0. If that is the case for software you are citing, put the version information one space after the comma following the title, and place a comma after the numeral. If an author of the software is featured, begin the citation with that person's name.

RADIO OR TELEVISION PROGRAM

[33] <u>Evening Music with David Garland</u>, WNYC-FM, New York, 15 Apr. 1993.

[34] <u>Chantilly Lace</u>, dir. Linda Yellen, with JoBeth Williams, Talia Shire, and others, Showtime cable, 18 July 1994.

FEATURE LENGTH FILM

[35] <u>Jurassic Park</u>, dir. Steven Spielberg, Steven Spielberg Film, Universal Pictures, 1993.

C O M M E N T

If the version of the feature-length film you viewed was on videotape rather than on reel to reel say, so. It is not necessary to give the timing of a feature-length film or to indicate if it is in black and white or color.

VIDEOTAPE, SHORT FILM, SLIDE PROGRAM, OR FILMSTRIP

[36] <u>Amelia Earhart</u>, Films for the Humanities & Sciences, n.d. PI-1749 (VHS color, 13 min.).

LIVE THEATRICAL OR MUSICAL PERFORMANCE

[37] <u>Festival Jazz Miami</u> with Joao Gilberto, Nester Torres, Mongo Santamaria. Jackie Gleason Theater, Miami Beach, 30 July, 1993.

CD (individual or album), AUDIOTAPE, CASSETTE RECORDING, OR PHONOGRAPH RECORD

[38] L.L. Cool J, "Mr. Good Bar," <u>Mama Said Knock You Out</u>, Def Jam/Columbia CK 46888, 1990.

Subsequent References in Endnotes

Once you have recorded the full information about a source, you can shorten the citation the next time you refer to the work and **give only the author or title and a page number** for printed sources. Author or title and any identifying location, if possible, suffices for nonprint materials.

You may make as many references as needed to a work once the first documentation is made in endnotes; the order of doing so is dictated by the use of the source in the text of your research paper. Simply continue the superscript numerals in order.

The following examples show how a series of first and subsequent references might appear:

¹ Paul Rauber, "No Second Warning," Sierra Jan./Feb. 1991: 24.

² Rauber 24.

³ Mary Robinson Sive, Environmental Legislation: A Sourcebook (New York: Prager, 1976) 138.

⁴ Rauber 28.

If an author is represented by two or more references within the research paper, give both the author's last name and some indication of title in the subsequent reference.

The abbreviations "ibid." (meaning "in the same place"), "op. cit." (meaning "in the work cited"), and "loc. cit." (meaning "in the place cited") are no longer used in research paper documentation.

Preparing the Works Cited List (MLA Form)

WHAT TO INCLUDE

Until a few years ago, people who wrote academic research papers relied almost entirely on written sources. Therefore, the word *bibliography* (meaning a list of information sources in print) was commonly used at the end of a paper to show readers what researched material the paper was based on. But since students, as well as other researchers, began using such nonprint resources as films, audiodiscs, and interactive computer programs, the literal meaning of "bibliography" no longer applies. The customary word is no longer accurate, though using it remains a habit many people still cling to.

Works Cited is a term that fits with the parenthetical documentation you read about in the last chapter. The sources you need to cite within your paper are acknowledged in the text. Now, at the conclusion, you provide *complete documentation about the works you have already referred to.* (Be sure you list *every* source that you drew from; use revision time to check the paper against note cards.)

In the Works Cited you give complete information—author, title, publication information, production details, or whatever else will help a reader locate a source you used. Most of these details will be on your preliminary Works Cited cards; some of them you may have to add as a result of having consulted the resources themselves. For instance, most periodical indexes give only the initials of authors, yet the Works Cited list requires that you give full names. Remember, too, that in the Works Cited you need to show the edition and section of a newspaper in which an article appeared; however, you only use the volume number of a periodical if it is paged continuously throughout a year. There is some leeway in recording nonprint resources, depending on the emphasis in your research paper. For example, for a feature-length film you might list first its director or leading performer or writer or cinematographer or the title, depending on the focus of your research.

Remember that **a Works Cited list may only include materials you actually documented within the text of the paper.** Thus, you *can't* list material you looked at but found irrelevant, repetitive, or insufficient for your purposes.

Conventions to Follow

Some customs you have already read about and incorporated into your preliminary citation cards, such as how to record the title of a film included in the title of a book, or not distinguishing a hardbound from a softbound book. You also know that *hanging indentation* marks the Works Cited listing, so the first line of an entry begins at the left margin and subsequent lines are each indented five spaces from that margin. Here are some other conventions not previously noted. You can see them illustrated on pages 245–46 immediately after the sample research paper in Chapter 10.

1. **Start the list of Works Cited on a new page at the conclusion of the text of your research paper**.

2. **Number the Works Cited page(s) successively following the text of your paper**. That is, if the last page of the text was 16, then the first page of the Works Cited will be 17. Follow the custom of previous pages by putting the numeral after your name and 1/2 inch down from the top right-hand corner of the page.

3. **Center the heading Works Cited** (or Annotated List of Works Cited) **one inch down from the top of the page**.

4. **Double-space between the heading and the first entry—as well as throughout the list**.

5. **List entries alphabetically according to the last name of the author**, or according to that of the first author given if there is more than one person. Do *not* use titles (such as Dr.) or honorofics (such as Sir or O.B.E.), even if they are shown with the author's name in the source you used.

6. **If no author is shown, begin with the title of a work, as part of the alphabetized list** (omitting the articles *A*, *An*, and *The* if one of them is the first word).

7. **If there are several entries by the same author, use the name in the first entry only**. Substitute **three spaced hyphens in place of the name for subsequent works by that person**. (See Ralph Nader listing in the Works Cited of the sample research paper on page 246.) Alphabetize the titles of the person's works to determine the order in which works will be listed.

8. **Do not use page numbers within a book *except*** if your source is a work in an anthology or a collection or is only a specific part of the book, such as an Introduction or Afterword.

9. ***Never* use the word "page" or an abbreviation of it in the Works Cited**.

10. ***Never* number the entries in a list of Works Cited**.

11. **Supply annotations for the Works Cited if requested to do so**. (Read about annotations on pages 226–27 of Chapter 10.)

STANDARD FORMS FOR WORKS CITED

The entries that follow are examples of various books, periodicals, and non-print research sources to serve as guides to your Works Cited listing. The examples are divided into those three sections, and within each is a variety of samples, each section progressing from the simplest and least complex forms to those that may be less likely to be used. Look particularly at the punctuation, spacing, and formatting of the examples that are applicable for your purposes. Use hanging indentation and double spacing for Works Cited entries.

Books

The author, title, and publication facts are those needed by readers of your research paper. The examples that follow are guides to the forms, most of which should already be on your preliminary Works Cited cards. Use a single space after a comma or colon and two spaces after periods.

BOOK BY SINGLE AUTHOR

    Koontz, Dean R. Hideaway. New York: Putnam, 1992.

Note that the period after the middle initial serves as the period ending the author unit.

BOOK BY TWO OR THREE AUTHORS

    Temoshak, Lydia, and Henry Dreher. The Type C Connection:
        The Behavioral Links to Cancer and Your Health. New
        York: Random, 1992.
    Coe, Sebastian, David Teasdale, and David Wickham. More
        Than a Game: Sport in Our Time. New York: BBC-
        Parkwest, 1992.

Only the name of the first author shown on the title page of the book is given in reverse order (that is, last name, a comma, then the first name). The "and" before the name of the second or third author is preceded by a comma, and those names are in the usual order.

BOOK BY MORE THAN THREE AUTHORS

    Eichenlaub, Val L., et al. The Climatic Atlas of
        Michigan. Notre Dame: U of Notre Dame P, 1991.

The Latin abbreviation "et al." (for *et alii* or, in English, "and others") is used instead of writing a string of names. The period after the abbreviated word suffices as the period to end the author unit.

ORGANIZATION OR INSTITUTION AS AUTHOR

    National Collegiate Athletic Association. 1992-93 NCAA
        Manual. Overland Park: NCAA, 1992.

BOOK IN COLLABORATION

> Schwarzkopf, H. Norman, with Peter Petre. It Doesn't Take
>
> a Hero: The Autobiography of General H. Norman
>
> Schwarzkopf. New York: Bantam, 1992.

If the title page shows that the book is by someone "as told to" or "with the collaboration of" another person, use those words rather than the "with" as in this model.

ANONYMOUS BOOK

> Try Us '92: National Minority Business Directory.
>
> Minneapolis: Try Us, 1992.

AUTHOR'S NAME ABSENT FROM BOOK BUT KNOWN FROM ANOTHER SOURCE

> [Dynner, Eugene.] Camera Techniques, 3rd ed. Miami:
>
> Travelogue, 1991.

The square brackets indicate interpolation by the author of the research paper. In this case, the person who prepared the list of Works Cited was able to determine the actual or probable author, although that name wasn't on the title page of the book.

BOOK BY PSEUDONYMOUS AUTHOR BUT REAL NAME SUPPLIED

> Craig, Kit [Kit Reed]. Gone. New York: Little, 1992.

Note that the author's real name is in usual first-name-last-name order and that the period concluding the author unit is after the brackets containing the real name.

BOOK IN WHICH ILLUSTRATOR OR PHOTOGRAPHER IS IMPORTANT

> Woods, Michael, photo. Paris and the Surrealists. Text
>
> by George Mally. New York: Thames, 1991.

Use *photo.* to show that the photographs are primary in a book and are the work of the one person whose name appears on the title page.

> Minor, Wendell, illus. The Seashore Book. Text by
>
> Charlotte Zolotow. New York: HarperCollins, 1992.
>
> **or**
>
> Zolotow, Charlotte. The Seashore Book. Illus. Wendell
>
> Minor. New York: HarperCollins, 1992.

An abbreviation for "illustrator" is used. If the illustrator is featured on the title page of the book, or if your research paper centers on book illustrators or art work (or on this particular person), use the first form. Use the second version if the book is more important in your research than the illustrator.

BOOK CONDENSATION OF A LONGER WORK

> Bradford, Barbara Taylor. <u>The Women in His Life.</u> Cond.
> from <u>The Women in His Life</u>. Pleasantville: Digest,
> vol. 2, 1991.

The word "condensed" is abbreviated as shown. Give the name of the author of the original book first. If the name of the person who wrote the condensation is available, write it after the word "by" following the second time the title appears.

BOOK WITH SINGLE EDITOR OR COMPILER OF A COLLECTION

> Levy, Peter B., ed. <u>Documentary History of the Modern</u>
> <u>Civil Rights Movement</u>. Westport: Greenwood, 1992.

Put a comma after the author's name, and let the period after the abbreviation for "editor" stand as the period concluding the author (that is, editor) unit. The abbreviation *comp.* is used if the word "compiler" or "compiled by" rather than "editor" appears on the title page of the book.

BOOK WITH TWO OR MORE EDITORS OR COMPILERS

> Newton, Lisa H., and Maureen M. Ford, eds. <u>Taking Sides:</u>
> <u>Clashing Views on Controversial Issues in Business</u>
> <u>Ethics and Society</u>. Guilford: Dushkin, 1992.

The plural of "ed." is "eds." Follow the custom of multiple authorship if a book is the work of several editors or compilers.

ANTHOLOGY (or COLLECTION) WITH NO EDITOR GIVEN

> <u>Southern Living 1993 Annual Recipes</u>. Birmingham: Oxmoor,
> 1993.

BOOK EDITED BY OTHER THAN AUTHOR OF CONTENTS

> Melville, Herman. <u>Selected Poems of Herman Melville</u>. Ed.
> Hennig Cohen. New York: Fordham UP, 1991.

or

> Cohen, Hennig, ed. <u>Selected Poems of Herman Melville</u>.
> New York: Fordham UP, 1991.

WORK OF AUTHOR CONTAINED IN COLLECTED WORKS.

> <u>The Droll Stories of Honore de Balzac</u>. Garden City: Blue
> Ribbon, 1946.

The contents of this anthology had to be translated (Balzac wrote in French), but no name of a translator appears in the book.

BOOK BEARING AN IMPRINT OF A PUBLISHER

```
Jolley, Elizabeth.  Cabin Fever: A Novel.  New York:
    Harper T-HarperCollins, 1991.
```

An imprint identifies a group of books a publisher brings out under a name different from its own. Show the imprint before the hyphen and the publishing company after the hyphen.

SEVERAL-VOLUME WORK UNDER GENERAL TITLE BUT WITH EACH VOLUME HAVING SEPARATE TITLE

```
Long, Robert Emmet.  The State of U.S. Education.
    New York: Wilson, 1991.  Vol. 63 of The Reference
    Shelf.
```

BOOK IN SERIES EDITED BY OTHER THAN AUTHOR

```
Wekesser, Carol.  Africa.  Eds. David L. Bender, and Bruno
    Leone.  Opposing Viewpoints Series.  San Diego:
    Greenwood, 1992.
```

WORK IN SEVERAL VOLUMES

```
Browning, Robert.  Works of Robert Browning.  10 vols.
    New York: AMS, 1992.
```

The page number and specific volume used will appear in the parenthetical documentation of the research paper. This entry in the Works Cited shows the total number of volumes in the work; obviously, you need not have used all of them.

TRANSLATED BOOK BY KNOWN AUTHOR

```
Pessoa, Fernando.  The Book of Disquiet.  Trans. Alfred
    MacAdam.  New York: Pantheon, 1991.
```

List the book by author if references in your paper are to that person or work. However, if the translator is the subject of your paper or figures importantly in it, put that person's name first, as in the following example.

```
MacAdam, Alfred, trans.  The Book of Disquiet.  By
    Fernando Pessoa.  New York: Pantheon, 1991.
```

The abbreviation for translator is always *trans.*, but it is capitalized only when it appears before the person's name. "By" precedes the author's name when it appears after the title.

TRANSLATED BOOK WITH AUTHOR'S NAME INCLUDED IN TITLE

The Heart-Stirring Sermon; Stories by Avraham Reisen.

Trans. and ed. Curt Leviant. New York: Penguin, 1992.

EDITION OF A BOOK

Roth, Audrey J. The Research Paper: Process, Form, and

Content, 7th ed. Belmont: Wadsworth, 1994.

Some editions carry designations such as "rev." (revised) or "alt." (alternate); use in the Works Cited whichever wording is on the title page of the book, as in the example below.

Denyer, Ralph. The Guitar Handbook, rev. ed. New York:

Knopf, 1992.

PRIVATELY PRINTED BOOK

Peggy Osterkamp's New Guide to Weaving, Number 1: How to

Wind a Warp and Use a Paddle. Sausalito: Peggy

Osterkamp, 1993.

or

Gray, Herbi. On-Loom Cardweaving. Olympia: Self-

published, 1982.

Some privately printed books are published by their authors, as in this designation. If the book is privately printed by contract with a publishing company (a so-called "vanity press"), write the publication information as you would for any commercially printed work.

REPUBLISHED BOOK OR MODERN REPRINT OF OLDER EDITION

James, George Wharton. Indian Blankets and Their Makers.

1914. New York: Dover, 1974.

The date of the original publication stands by itself after the title. The name of the original publisher, if different from the new one, is not shown.

Portions of Books

If your reference source was only part of a book—a poem in an anthology or an introduction, for example—rather than the complete book, the name of the author of just that section begins the Works Cited entry; to show only the book information would be misleading to anyone trying to locate the source material you used. Also, in addition to the author, title, and publication information, *the page numbers on which this part appears* are added to the citation, beginning two spaces after the copyright date. Do *not* use the word "page" or any abbreviation of it.

POEM IN ANTHOLOGY

> Stafford, William. "Traveling Through the Dark." The
>
> Compact Bedford Introduction to Literature, 3rd ed.
>
> Ed. Michael Meyer. Boston: Bedford, 1994. 505-06.

ARTICLE, CHAPTER, STORY, OR ESSAY IN A COLLECTION EDITED BY OTHER THAN AUTHOR

> Gornick, Vivian. "Mama Went to Work." Calling Home:
>
> Working-Class Women's Writings, An Anthology. Ed.
>
> Janet Zandy. New Brunswick: Rutgers UP, 1990. 149-53.

INTRODUCTION, FOREWORD, AFTERWORD, or PREFACE BY OTHER THAN AUTHOR

> Agee, Philip. Foreword. CIA Off Campus: Building the
>
> Movement Against Agency Recruitment and Research.
>
> By Ami Chen Mills. Boston: South End, 1991.

Use the name of the person who wrote the introduction, etc., if that person is more important than the author of the book itself or is someone who is important in your research paper. Name whichever descriptive heading (of those listed above this example) is used in the book you are recording in the Works Cited.

SIGNED ARTICLE IN REFERENCE BOOK

> Catala, Pierre J. "Analog Microwave Link Design." The
>
> Froehlich/Kent Encyclopedia of Telecommunications.
>
> New York: Dekker, 1991.

Volume and page numbers are omitted from alphabetically arranged reference sources. If an author's initials, but not whole name, appear with an article in a reference book, check for a list of names that the initials stand for; often this list is near the front of a volume.

UNSIGNED ARTICLE IN REFERENCE WORK

> "Tanzania." Encyclopedia of the Third World, 4th ed. New
>
> York: Facts, 1992.

or

> "Mainland China and Hongkong Affairs. Republic of China
>
> Yearbook. 1991-92. 1991. 135-46.

Some reference works are designated only by the year of the edition you used, so that's the only information you can record.

Periodicals

The three units of information recorded for each periodical article are author, title, and publication information—including the page numbers on which the article appears. Your preliminary Works Cited cards will also show a volume number for continuously paginated journals and magazines, an edition of a newspaper, or other information particular to periodicals. The examples that follow are guides to the forms, most of which are probably already on your preliminary Works Cited cards. Since **spacing** after periods, commas, and colons is **important**, use these sample entries as a check on your own work.

The headlines of newspaper articles are considered their "titles." Authorship is shown in a byline, unless you are citing a letter to the editor, which is signed at the end. A wire service, such as AP or UPI, is **never considered an author**.

ARTICLE BY KNOWN AUTHOR IN MAGAZINE OR JOURNAL WITH PAGINATION BY ISSUE

```
Gibbs, Nancy.  "Truth, Justice and the Reno Way."  Time 12
    July 1993: 20-27.
Driscoll, F. Paul.  "Signing Off."  Opera News Aug. 1993:
    33+.
```

If an article is on successive pages in the magazine, use a hyphen to show the inclusive pages. If it is not, a "+" symbol after the first page shows there are other, but not successive, pages to the article.

```
Whitaker, Elaine E.  "A Pedagogy to Address Plagiarism."
    College Composition and Communication 44.4 (1993):
    509-14.
```

Academic and professional journals show publication title, the volume number followed (without spaces) by a period and the issue number, then the year in parentheses.

ARTICLE BY KNOWN AUTHOR IN MAGAZINE OR JOURNAL WITH CONTINUOUS PAGINATION

```
Rust, Val Dean.  "Educational Responses to Reforms in East
    Germany, Czechoslovakia, and Poland."  Phi Delta
    Kappan 73 (1992): 386-89.
```

Because this publication numbers its pages successively throughout a publishing year, the citation shows the volume after the title and the year in parentheses. Note, also, that the hundreds digit in page numbering is not repeated.

MAGAZINE ARTICLE BY UNKNOWN AUTHOR

```
"Problems of Shift Work."  Monthly Labor Review Feb.
    1992: 2.
```

MAGAZINE EDITORIAL

Foell, Earl W. "Shrimps from Elsewhere." Editorial.
World Monitor June 1992: 3.

The editorial is so designated in order to distinguish it from other articles within a publication. This editorial has a title and the author is stated. However, editorials often don't have titles, as in the following example.

Patrick, Jane. Editorial. Handwoven Sept./Oct. 1992: 4.

BOOK, FILM, VIDEO, OR CD REVIEW IN MAGAZINE

Graff, Henry F. "Directly from the People." Rev. of
Truman, by David McCullough. The New Leader 1 June
1992: 7-9.

or

Schickel, Richard. "Love N the Hood." Rev. of Poetic
Justice. Writer-Dir. John Singleton. Time 26 July
1993: 67-68.

The name of the person writing the review comes first in this citation. "Rev." indicates the title of the work being reviewed and the name of the author (or performer or director) follows. If the review neither is titled nor shows authorship, begin with: Rev. of . . .

NEWSPAPER ARTICLE BY KNOWN AUTHOR

Rosenberg, Carol. "Christopher Mediates in Mideast."
Miami Herald 4 Aug. 1993, final ed.: 4A.

Sometimes newspapers move an article from one location to another or make other changes in different editions; thus, show the edition of the paper you used, if possible. Copy the section of the paper as well as the page number as it appears in the newspaper; a letter designating the section may appear either before or after the page number. If the section number or letter is not part of the pagination, write the abbreviation "sec." preceded by a comma and a space; follow it by a space and the section number before the colon that shows the page number.

NEWSPAPER ARTICLE BY UNKNOWN AUTHOR

"We Love You, Raggedy Ann; Turning 75, This Redhead Is
Still a Doll." Orlando Sentinel 28 June 1992, city
ed.: A3.

Follow the same custom of showing the page number as for articles by known authors.

NEWSPAPER EDITORIAL

"Pass It, Sign It, Live by It." Editorial. <u>Miami Herald</u>
4 Aug. 1993, final ed.: 12A.

If the editorial is signed, begin the entry with the author's name.

BOOK OR FILM REVIEW IN A NEWSPAPER

Patteson, Jean. "Tale Links Women Through Genrations."
Rev. of <u>Daughter of the New World</u> by Susan Ricards
Shreve. [Ft. Lauderdale] <u>Sun Sentinel</u>, 31 May 1992,
final ed.: 9F.

or

Cosford, Bill. "Shakespeare Lite Goes Down Easy in
Branagh's 'Much Ado.' " Rev. of <u>Much Ado About
Nothing</u>, dir. Kenneth Branagh. <u>Miami Herald</u> 30 July
1993, Weekend: 6G.

This film review appeared in a special section of the newspaper called "Weekend," so that designation is given in place of either a "final" or "late city" or other edition designation. Note, also, that the title of the film appears in single quotation marks within the double quotation marks of the title of the article.
or

Perkins, Ken Parish. "'Amelia Earhart' Offers Rare
Portrait." Rev. of <u>Amelia Earhart</u>. <u>Dallas Morning
News</u> 26 Oct. 1993: 1C+.

This is a newspaper review of a film that was shown on television. The edition of the paper was unknown, so it cannot appear in the citation.

MUSIC, THEATER, or DANCE REVIEW IN A NEWSPAPER

Ross, Alex. "Prolific Jarvi Offers Quality with Quantity."
<u>Miami Herald</u> 16 Jan. 1994, final ed.: 9I.

ARTICLE IN NEWSPAPER SUPPLEMENT IN MAGAZINE FORM

Matz, Judith. "Who You Gonna Call?" <u>Tropic</u> in <u>Miami
Herald</u> 16 Jan. 1994: 7+.

Other Print Sources

DOCUMENT FROM AN INFORMATION SERVICE

Allen, Kenneth. "The Information Age: Promise or Dream.
White House Conference on Library and Information
Services." ERIC, 1992. ED337196.

The name of the information service and an accession number is added to the usual citation form. The service is assumed to be the publisher if the material was not published before, except that it is unnecessary to state a location for ERIC (Educational Resources Information Center) or other government information services.

UNPUBLISHED THESIS OR DISSERTATION

> Izquierdo, Rene C. "'Anacaona' de Salome Urena de
>
> Henriquez, Poema Epico Sobre La Conquista de America:
>
> Un Analisis Estilistico y Tematico." Diss. City
>
> University of New York, 1991.

Even though a dissertation may be book length, the title is put in quotation marks rather than being underlined. Allow two spaces before and after the dissertation designation. The degree-granting institution is named before the date.

> Engstrom, Erika Julie. "Effects of Sex and Appearance on
>
> Ratings of Source Credibility." DAI-A 52 (Apr.
>
> 1992): 3468-A. University of Florida, 1991.

This entry shows that the work cited is an abstract from *Dissertation Abstracts* (DA) or *Dissertation Abstracts International* (DAI). This example abstract is from *Volume A— Humanities and Social Sciences.* Leave a space after that designation and before the volume number. The page on which the abstract is recorded follows the colon, and the granting institution and date conclude the entry.

Treat a *published* dissertation as a book (provided you know that a book was originally a dissertation) and underline the title; give the publication information after identification of the work as a dissertation.

MIMEOGRAPHED, DITTOED, OR PHOTOCOPIED REPORT

> Byrd, Susan G. "Winter Term Library Program."
>
> Photocopied. Miami: Miami-Dade CC, 1988: n.p.

The letters "n.p." following the colon indicate that there is no page numbering to this document. If there were no publisher, the same two letters would appear after the colon citing the location. If the date of the printed material did not appear on it but was known, it would be put in square brackets.

PAMPHLET BY KNOWN AUTHOR

> Taylor, Lisa. Northern Michigan Restaurant Guide. Ann
>
> Arbor: Momentum, 1992.

PAMPHLET BY UNKNOWN AUTHOR

> Air Travel for Your Dog or Cat. Leaflet. Washington: Air
>
> Transport Assoc., 1991.

PERSONAL OR UNPUBLISHED LETTER

> Wallace, Sharon L.   Letter to the author.   22 Nov. 1993.

A personal letter is presumed to be in the possession of the person to whom it is addressed. If not, the name of the museum or archives where the unpublished letter is located must be given.

> Nightingale, Florence.   Letter to Sir Arthur Landrow.
>
> 3 Feb. 1898.   Sheffield Historical Society, Sheffield,
>
> England.

PUBLISHED LETTER IN NEWSPAPER (OR MAGAZINE OR JOURNAL)

> Garcia, Alfonso.   "To Honor Penny Powers."   Letter.   Miami
>
> Herald 4 Aug. 1993, final ed.: 12A.

Letters from readers to editors are often given a "title" or heading when they are published; if so, the heading may be treated as an article title in your Works Cited entry.

> Hill, Lanaloo.   "Dancing Sheet."   Letter.   Arizona
>
> Highways July 1992: 3.
>
> Voss, Ralph F.   "Responses to Richard Gebhardt, 'Theme
>
> Issue Feedback and Fallout.'"   Letter.   College
>
> Composition and Communication 44 (1993): 256-57.

These two examples illustrate a letter published in a periodical with paging by issue and in one with continuous pagination. Except for identifying the material as a letter, each follows the usual format for articles in periodicals.

GOVERNMENT PUBLICATION

> Cong. Rec.   4 Oct. 1993: H7363.

Only the date and page number are required for citations from the *Congressional Record*. An H before the page number signifies it is the record of proceedings of the House of Representatives; an S shows it is a record of the Senate.

> Department of the Interior, Fish and Wildlife Service.
>
> Biological Evaluation of Environmental Impacts:
>
> Proceedings of a Symposium at the 1976 Meeting of the
>
> Ecological Society of America.   Washington: GPO, 1980.

Show the title of the government agency issuing the document as author if there is no person's name so designated. The number and session of Congress are listed, and publications are abbreviated according to whether they are resolutions (Res.), reports (Rep.), or documents (Doc.) emanating from the Senate (S) or the House of Representatives (H), together with the number of the document.

GPO means "U.S. Government Printing Office," the federal publisher of official documents.

Use the two preceding examples as a guide to citing publications by state governments, the United Nations, or other countries.

PUBLISHED INTERVIEW

```
Bullen, Christine.   "Postcard from Terry McEwen."
    Interview.   Opera News Aug. 1993: 26-29.
```

If an interview has no title in the publication, or if no writer-interviewer is given, use the name of the interviewee as if it were the title. If the interview was published in a book, treat it as if it were a chapter in the book; if the entire book is an interview, put the title and publication after the interviewer's name. If the interview was published in a newspaper or magazine, as in the example above, indication that the piece is an interview is the only variation from the usual periodical publication information.

Nonprint Sources

CARTOON OR ILLUSTRATION

```
Schulz, Charles.   "Peanuts."   Cartoon.   Miami Herald, final
    ed. 8 Aug. 1993.
```

This cartoon panel was on the front page of the comics section, but carries neither page nor newspaper section designation; thus, neither appears in the citation.

Put the title of a cartoon or illustration in quotation marks. Consider the caption of a newspaper picture, or that part of it which may appear in bold type, as its title.

```
"Deco Design."   Photograph.   Miami Herald 16 Jan.
    1993: 7I.
```

PERSONAL OR TELEPHONE INTERVIEW

```
Michaels, David.   Personal interview.   17 Feb. 1993.
Wallace, Edward.   Telephone interview.   17 Nov. 1992.
```

RADIO, TELEVISION, OR RECORDED INTERVIEW

```
Hanks, Tom.   Interview.   Larry King Live.   CNN.   13 Jan.
    1994.
Shula, Don.   Interview.   Chuck Meyer Show.   WIOD, Miami.
    13 Sept. 1993.
```

If the interview is on a local station, put a comma after the call letters of the radio or television station and then the city from which the program originated.

QUESTIONNAIRE, SURVEY, OR POLL

```
CCCC Committee on Assessment.  "Survey of Postsecondary
    Writing Assessment Practices."  Questionnaire. 1992.
Jason Roberts.  Survey Response.  3 Feb. 1993.
```

A large-scale survey and/or its responses is cited by surveyor and title, if there is one. Use the name of a particular respondent's information used in the research paper came from if you know it. Otherwise, your reader will assume that the questionnaire or survey was answered anonymously. If you had a number of signed responses to an inquiring document, arrange them alphabetically by surname, and just use the first one with *et al.*, as in **"Adams, Pat, et al."**

WORKS OF ART

```
Renoir, Pierre-Auguste.  San Marco.  Minneapolis Institute
    of Arts.  Minneapolis.
Hanukah Lamp from Poland.  Jewish Museum.  New York.
Brancusi, Constantin.  Sleeping Muse.  Metropolitan Museum
    of Art.  New York.
```

If your reference to a work of art is not the original piece but a photograph of it, then after the location information cite the illustration number, slide number, or page number of the place (or book) where you saw the picture.

```
Benin Kingdom, Edo peoples, Nigeria.  "Equestrian Figure/
    Private collection.  Illus. 45 in African Arts in
    the Cycle of Life.  By Roy Sieber and Roslyn Adele
    Walker.  Washington: National Museum of African Art,
    1987.
```

This particular citation is not attributed to an individual artist, nor does it have a formal name. Thus, the markers of this sculpture and the title it is given in the book are used as the initial part of this citation.

```
Rodin, Auguste.  Meditation.  Musee Rodin, Paris.  Illus.
    5.6 in Rodin Rediscovered.  Ed. Albert E. Elsen.
Washington: National Gallery of Art, 1981.
```

The citation is of a statue and thus includes the name of its sculptor, its title, and location. Because the statue was a picture in a book, information about the book in which the author of the term paper finds it must be included, as it is here.

SPEECH OR LECTURE

```
"Yaxchilan and Its Blood-Letting Lintels."  Institute of
    Maya Studies.  Miami Museum of Science.  22 Jan. 1994.
```

RECORDED SPEECH OR LECTURE

Tolliver, Johnny E. "Authentic Assessment." National
Council of Teachers of English TE93-27, 1993.

RECORDING OF THE SPOKEN WORD

Wambaugh, Joseph. Finnegan's Week. n.p.: Brilliance
Corp., 2 audio cassettes, n.d.

A Richard Burton Anthology of Classic Poetry. Botsford:
Film Archives, 80221, audio cassette, n.d.

COMPUTER SOFTWARE

Word. Vers. 5.0 Computer Software. Microsoft, 1991.
Macintosh, 5 disks.

If other information is important, such as the operating system for which it is designed, list it in order beginning two spaces after the period following the date. Separate any items by commas, as in the example below.

World Literary Heritage. CD-ROM for IBM. Irvine:
Softbit, 1993. MD-DOS 3.1, Windows 3.1, 2 MB-RAM.

MATERIAL FROM A COMPUTER SERVICE

Knickerbocker, Brad. "Running for Congress Under Greens
Banner." Christian Science Monitor 10 Oct. 1990: 8.
DIALOG file 484, item 01278184.

This record assumes you used a complete printout of the material from the computer service; that is why after the usual concluding period of the entry, you would note the name of the computer service, the file number, and the item number. If you get only the identification or annotation from the computer service, you would not use such information because you didn't get a complete piece of writing. However, if you subsequently get the entire piece, you would include it in the Works Cited following the format usual for that particular printed source.

INTERACTIVE COMPUTER SOFTWARE

The Dream Machine. Written and prod. Geoffrey de Valois,
and Donny Cohen. Dir. Geoffrey de Valois, and Steve
Michelson. Los Angeles: Voyager Co. LaserStacks,
1987. 3 1/2" disc for Macintosh and 2 12" laser
discs, 58 min. each.

RADIO OR TELEVISION PROGRAM

Evening Music with David Garland. WNYC-FM. New York.

   15 Apr. 1993.

Chantilly Lace. Dir. Linda Yellen. With JoBeth

   Williams, Talia Shire, and others. Showtime,

   18 July 1994.

Because the latter, a television program, appeared on a cable channel, the station call letters and city in which it was seen are unnecessary in the citation. (Put them in place of the network, as applicable.) Were the scriptwriter important in the research paper in which this citation appears, it would appear before the name of the director.

FEATURE-LENGTH FILM

Wilder, Billy, dir. The Spirit of St. Louis. With James

   Stewart, and others. Warner Bros., 1957.

Videocassette.

Feature-length films are usually listed by their directors. If the author of the screenplay, an actor, the cinematographer, or another person connected with the film is of major importance in your research, put that name first and give the name of the director after the title of the film. Otherwise, the order is usually: title, director, actors. Add the names of the screenwriter, and producer if those people figure prominently in your research writing; then note the distributor or production company and year of release. Note if the film you consulted for your research was on videocassette or laser disc (and if it is on more than one video or disc); otherwise, it is assumed to be either 16 mm or theatrical production film size such as 35 mm or 70 mm. Give videocassette or laser disc distributor's name if known.

Stewart, James, actor. The Spirit of St. Louis.

   Dir. Billy Wilder. Warner Bros., 1957.

   Videocassette.

Wilder, Billy, and Wendall Mayes, screenwriters.

   The Spirit of St. Louis. Dir. Billy Wilder.

   With James Stewart. Warner Bros., 1957.

   Videocassette.

Waxman, Franz, comp. and cond. The Spirit of St. Louis.

   Dir. Billy Wilder. Prod. Leland Hayward. Warner

   Bros., 1957. Videocassette.

SHORT FILM OR VIDEOTAPE

Hubley, Faith, filmmaker. Tall Time Tales. Santa Monica:

   Pyramid, 1992. 8 min., 16 mm color.

FILMSTRIP OR SLIDE PROGRAM

"IFR Clearance Shorthand." Advanced Pilot Series.
1 filmstrip, 1 audiocassette. Englewood: Jeppesen,
1981. 90 fr. color.

Filmstrips, less used now than before the advent of videocassettes, are likely to be very variable in the production information you can get from them. If you use an entire series of filmstrips for information and can get more information about each of them, use a slightly different form.

National Defense. 2 filmstrips, 2 audiocassettes. Written
by Kate Griggs. Photo ed. Wendy Davis. Prentice-
Hall Media, 1982. Each 84 fr., color, mono, 27 min.

Filmstrips and slide programs are usually written with the medium stated after the title and before other information.

LIVE THEATRICAL PERFORMANCE

Wasserstein, Wendy. The Sisters Rosensweig. Dir. Daniel
Sullivan. With Michael Learned, Linda Lavin, Tony
Roberts. Ethel Barrymore Theater, New York. 6 Apr.
1993.

LIVE MUSICAL PERFORMANCE

Marsalis, Wynton. Gusman Center for the Performing Arts.
Miami. 17 Apr. 1994.

Otello. By Giuseppi Verdi. Production by Elijah
Moshinsky. Cond. Valery Gergiev. With Carol Vaness,
Placido Domingo, Sergei Leiferkus. Metropolitan
Opera, New York. 25 Mar. 1994.

Information about an opera generally lists principal singers according to vocal range: soprano, mezzo, tenor, baritone, bass. However, if the research work you prepare is about a performer, you may put that person's name first, as you might in writing about a performer in a film.

Domingo, Placido, tenor. Otello. By Giuseppi Verdi. Cond.
Valery Gergiev. With Carol Vaness, Sergei Leiferkus.
Metropolitan Opera, New York. 25 Mar. 1994.

BROADCAST OR TELECAST OF MUSICAL PERFORMANCE

Tosca. By Giacomo Puccini. With Maria Gleghina, Luciano
Pavarotti, James Morris, and others. Prod. by Franco
Zeffirelli. Cond. Christian Badea. Metropolitan
Opera. WTMI, Miami. 16 Apr. 1994.

If this were a citation for a paper about the well-known tenor, Pavarotti, his name would appear at the head of the list of singers. It would not, however, replace the title of the work in which he appeared. The call letters on which the performance was heard identifies it as a radio broadcast; were it seen by the research paper author on television, the call numbers would identify the different source.

CD MUSICAL RECORD OR ALBUM

> Bernstein, Leonard. <u>West Side Story</u>. With Kiri Te
>
> Kanawa, Jose Carreras, Tatiana Troyanos, Kurt
>
> Ollmann, Marilyn Horne. Cond. Leonard Bernstein.
>
> 2 stereo CDs Deutsche Grammophon, 415253-2, 1985.

This recording was made with an orchestra assembled for the purpose. If a particular orchestra makes a recording you are citing, write its name after that of the conductor but before the name of the record company.

Many modern audio recordings and many reissues of earlier works are on compact discs, or audio cassettes. Should you need to cite a recording which is on LP, the number may indicate it. In the interest of accuracy, you should, therefore, state the form of recording you used for research before stating the identifying number and name of the recording company.

> To the Extreme. Vanilla Ice. Audiotape K4-9532, SKB
>
> Records, 1990.
>
> Brahms, Johannes. Symphony #1 in C Minor, Op. 68. Cond.
>
> Klaus Tennstedt. London Philharmonic Orchestra.
>
> Stereo CD 7 47029 2, EMI, 1984.

The name of a soloist, if there is one, will appear before that of the conductor. Although record titles are generally underlined, that is not done if the composition is identified by form and key.

CHAPTER 10

Final Presentation

MANUSCRIPT PREPARATION AND PROOFREADING

Your paper is written, the revisions made, and now you are ready to do the last few tasks to make a final copy of your paper and put it in presentation form. Follow the few guidelines in this chapter and your paper will make the best possible impression on your audience (and on the instructor who will grade your work).

Not all the sections of this chapter will apply to you. For instance, business, technical, and scientific research papers sometimes have a synopsis or abstract of the study included with the presentation. You may not need them. However, if you read through the entire chapter, you will see what possibilities exist for various kinds of research papers.

Check the sample research paper at the end of this chapter, on pages 230–46, if you are working with MLA style. In it, you will see examples of the details that have been explained throughout the book, so you can use it as a model for your own paper. (If you are working with the APA style, Chapter 11 explains documentation specifics and has a sample research paper in that style on pages 247–56.) You will find two kinds of commentary in the margins of both sample papers:

- **Form** information is in color.
- **Content** comments in black are about the substance and organization of the papers.

Proofread your entire paper carefully when you finish writing the final draft. An author is responsible for the accuracy of all work, so even though spelling and punctuation variations may be typing errors, they will not be so judged when people read your paper. Therefore, it's imperative to *correct any errors*, especially in going over a final draft.

If you are using a typewriter, read each page carefully before removing it from the machine. Then, you can white-out minor errors and retype letters or words as needed and still keep lines even. If something short has been omitted, type it in directly above the line where it should have been and use a caret (^) to show where the insert goes. Retype pages on which there are long insertions or changes. Don't crowd lines so much that they're unreadable. And never write in the margins.

If you have been writing on a word processor, final preparation of your research paper should be easy. Do the last round of editing and proofreading from a hard copy, because typos (typing mistakes) and other errors are usually more apparent on it than they are on screen. Afterwards, transfer spelling, punctuation, and grammar corrections (or any last-minute revisions) to the written work on-screen. If you have a spell checker or a grammar checker on the computer, be sure you have used them so appropriate corrections will already be on your disc before the last printout.

Take time to proofread your entire research paper before turning it in, because you may catch additional errors when you look at the whole work. If you find any previously overlooked mistakes, make the corrections—very carefully and neatly—in black ink.

TYPING/WORD PROCESSING

Type or word process your paper in a standard serif or sans-serif type, *never* in a script or other fancy typeface. Use *only black type*, never any color, for the text of your research paper. If you are using a typewriter, make sure the type is clean and the ribbon prints a dark, clear image. Use plain white 8-1/2 × 11-inch paper of good quality. Do not use "erasable" paper, because type on it smudges and becomes hard to read; it's also hard for your instructor to write comments on. Onionskin (or other thin paper) is hard to handle and makes reading difficult, so never use it, either.

If you write your paper on a computer, a laser printer will give the best-quality printing; ink-jet printers also give good results. If you use a dot-matrix printer, use a setting as close as possible to "letter quality," and be sure the ribbon is fresh or, if possible, new. Standard white pin-feed computer paper is acceptable, provided you tear off the perforated edges cleanly after your work is printed.

Accent marks or other symbols you can't type or print should be added afterwards in black ink using a fine- or medium-point pen.

Follow these spacing customs for final typing or printing:

- Type or print on only one side of each page.
- Leave one-inch margins at the top and the bottom as well as on the sides of all text.
- Double-space throughout all parts of the research paper, including long quotations and Works Cited entries.
- Indent the beginning of each new paragraph five spaces from the left margin.
- Long quotations (five or more typed lines of prose, four or more lines of poetry) are indented ten spaces from the left margin and shown without quotation marks.
- Prefer to set a computer to print ragged right (rather than with justified right margin), because that form is easier to read.

PAGE NUMBERING

Number all pages consecutively *in arabic numerals* throughout the re-search paper, beginning with the first page of text and including appendixes and Works Cited.

Number *front matter pages,* such as the outline, preface, or other material, consecutively in *small roman numerals.*

Page numbers should be set 1/2 inch down from the top of each page and so they line up at the right-hand margin of the text (that is, one inch in from the right-hand edge of the paper). Do *not* use periods or abbreviations for "page" with the number. However, *do* put your last name immediately before the page number. (See the sample research paper in this chapter on pages 230–46 as examples.) Additionally, use your first initial if there is more than one person with the same last name in your class.

FIRST PAGE OF THE RESEARCH PAPER TEXT (MLA)

All the necessary identification for you and your research paper are on the first page of the text. That is, in MLA style there is *no separate cover page.* One-half inch down from the top of the paper and ending at the right-hand margin one inch in from the end of the paper, put your last name (and first initial, if needed) and the arabic numeral "1," as noted in the above section (and shown on page 232).

In the upper left-hand corner of your paper, one inch down from the top and one inch in from the left side of the paper, type the following **personal identification information** in double spacing:

- Your full name
- The name of your instructor
- The course abbreviation and number for which you wrote the paper (and the sequence number of your section, if so requested by the instructor)
- The date the paper is due

Allow a double space, and **center the title** of your paper. Use capital letters to begin each word except articles, conjunctions, and short prepositions. *Do not* put the title in all capitals, enclose it within quotation marks, underline it, or put a period at the end. However, if the titles of books, films, short stories, poems, or other pieces usually underlined or put in quotation marks are part of the title of your paper, use them as appropriate.

EXAMPLES

`Nonviolent Tools for Environmental Activists`

and

`Story into Film: "Pickets" and` <u>`A Time Out of War`</u>

If your title requires more than one line of type, double-space between the lines.

Before beginning the text of your paper, use a double space to separate it from the title. Therefore you can keep your typewriter or computer set to double spacing throughout the paper.

Begin the text with the usual five-space indentation from the left margin for the first paragraph. If you begin with a long quotation without introduction, however, follow the ten-space indentation from the left margin that you would use anywhere else in the research paper.

OUTLINE

The outline from which you wrote your research paper is often included with the presentation text so an instructor can see the content and organization of your paper before reading it. Because it is preliminary to the research paper, it is usually put before the paper itself. Since the outline is before the first page of the text, which bears your personal information and the paper's identifying information, repeat that information on the first page of your outline. That is, observing standard margins and double spacing, put your name, instructor, course, and date at the top left corner. Use small roman numerals to number pages in an outline, even if there is only one such page; put them, with your name, ½ inch down from the top of the right-hand corner of the page and ending one inch in from the edge of the paper.

Double-space all typing (or printing) in the outline, and adhere to the same margins as in the text of the paper.

Center the title of your paper, and follow it with a double space. Usually, begin the outline with the thesis statement of the paper, so labeled and double spaced; then begin the outline. See pages 230–31 for an example of the outline of the sample research paper in this chapter. You do not need to label this page as an outline, because anybody looking at it can see that it is one.

THE TEXT (MLA STYLE)

Follow the information about writing your paper in Chapter 7 and the conventions of documenting it you read about in Chapter 8. Take one last look before submitting your work to make sure that you have acknowledged all material that isn't original, that pages are numbered consecutively, and that you have been consistent in using the preferred documentation system.

Underlining in typing means that if the words were set in printer's type they would be italicized—the custom for the titles of many works, for foreign words and phrases, and for words you want the reader to note particularly. If your word processing program and the printer you use have italics capability, use them instead of the underlining.

If you are printing your research paper from a computer disc, don't get fancy with boldface or multiple typeface changes, even if your computer and printer support such variations. Just keep the text simple and readable.

ILLUSTRATIVE MATERIALS: CHARTS, TABLES, GRAPHS, AND OTHER VISUALS

Put illustrative materials as close as you can to the portion of the text they illustrate or refer to; doing so makes your research paper easy to read and understand. If you haven't included them while you were drafting the text but find, upon rereading, that some would be helpful, add them before the final printing or typing of the text. Since visual representation of some ideas, expecially complexities, is often helpful to readers, plan on using whatever will fit your subject. A map to show population change, a graph to illustrate the relation between interest rates and employment, a table to show attendance at professional football games, some bars of music, an original drawing or photograph—all these are the kind of illustrative materials you can use with your research paper.

Consider creating your own visuals if you haven't found any that are suitable. You can draw, photograph, or create a montage of cutouts. Many computer programs can accommodate visuals, format them for you, or enable you to draw them yourself. Some computer programs are particularly suitable for a variety of kinds of charts, graphs, and other visuals.

Follow instructions for labeling tables and figures and citing sources for those you borrow from other sources, as explained on pages 191–93.

As a final check, be sure all the components of any illustrative materials you incorporate are clearly labeled.

COMMENT NOTES

Comment notes are brief elaborations, comments on the text, or a series of sources that would interrupt the text if written as parenthetical documentation. As explained in Chapter 7, page 175, you may make such comments at the end of the text of your paper. They will be coordinated with the appropriate place within the text by consecutive superscript arabic numbers.

Treat comment notes as endnotes. Begin them on a new page immediately after the research paper text concludes, but continue your name and consecutive page numbering as throughout the text. **Center the title "Notes"** (without the quotation marks) one inch from the top, and type the notes double spaced.

Begin each note with the superscript (or superior) number indented five spaces from the left margin. Skip one space and then type the required information. Second and subsequent lines begin at the left margin to maintain the *paragraph indentation* used in Notes. See an example of comment notes as part of the sample research paper on page 244.

If you use comment notes or other endnotes, make a final check to be sure the note numbers correspond to appropriate places in the text of your paper.

ENDNOTES

Some instructors still prefer that students following MLA form provide endnotes for text citations rather than parenthetical documentation. This is explained and illustrated in Chapter 8 on pages 194–201. If you are using this system, the documentation notes may be interspersed with comment notes. Follow the page setup described in the preceding section, beginning the information on a page headed Notes.

WORKS CITED

The Works Cited listing concludes the research paper and follows any Notes you may show. The forms to use for this listing were described in Chapter 4 so you could record the information accurately on preliminary citation cards. The **conventions** of the Works Cited list are detailed in Chapter 9 on pages 204–20. Further **conventions for entries** were detailed on page 203. Use this information as a guide.

If you require more than one Works Cited page, continue with the page numbers but do not use a heading. For an example of the proper format, see pages 245–46 of the sample research paper.

Notice that in your research paper you will be using a composite list of all sources cited without divisions by medium. Longer papers and books sometimes divide sources into Primary Sources and Secondary Sources, or into groups such as Books, Periodicals, Computer Software, Films, and so on. However, all student research papers should use a single, alphabetized list of works.

ANNOTATIONS

An annotation is a short statement that tells what is important or characteristic about a source. It is particularly helpful to anyone who wants to decide whether or not to consult a source you have used in preparing your research paper. Since each tells something of the contents of a source or makes some other comment, a reader can decide what is of special interest.

Keep annotations brief; one or two remarks suffice. Begin each annotation two spaces after the period ending the citation. Customarily, an annotation is not a complete sentence, though it begins with a capital letter and ends with a period.

Head the page on which they begin "Annotated List of Works Cited" (or "Annotated List of Works Consulted"), rather than simply Works Cited. Otherwise, follow all the conventions you have already read about in Chapter 9 and immediately before this section.

If you know you will have to supply annotations to the works you cite in your paper, you should write comments on the preliminary citation card for each source as you use it. The questions you answer in evaluating your source materials (see pages 108–11) will also help you think of comments you might want to make in annotations. The following list shows the kinds of comments you might make in annotations and gives examples of each. You may also combine the various sorts of comments.

1. **State the general content of a source.**

    `Supports the author's contention that` `Painted Veils` `was written in only six weeks.`

2. **Make a judgment about the source.**

   `Particularly clear explanation of the legal basis of the`
   `suit.`

3. **Point out valuable properties or qualities of the source.**

   `Contains photographs by the author.`

4. **Note the viewpoint or bias of the author.**

   `Lacks suggestions about or allowances for alternate`
   `solutions.`

5. **Tell something helpful about the author of the source.**

   `Author is former airline pilot with extensive experience`
   `in teaching safety classes.`

Look at the annotated bibliographies in some of the sources you use for your research work, and you may discover additional kinds of information an annotation can contain.

The Works Cited listing in the sample research paper in this chapter is not an annotated one, but here are examples of what some of the entries would be like if it were.

Nader, Ralph. Ralph Nader's Civic Curriculum, Draft.
     Washington: Center for Study of Responsive Law, 1991.
     Designed for teachers and other leaders to show them
     how to promote nonviolent activism.

Rauber, Paul. "No Second Warning." Sierra Jan./Feb.
     1992: 24+. Violent acts against environmentalists
     planning nonviolent activities.

Riding, Alan. "France Suspends Its Testing of Nuclear
     Weapons." New York Times 9 Apr. 1992, Intl. ed.: A4.
     Was result of government courting two increasingly
     powerful environmental groups.

APPENDIX

An appendix contains additional illustrations or other materials that amplify the text without interrupting it. That is, you might use it to show a series of charts or tables useful to readers' understanding without breaking their concentration as they read the text of your paper. In this book, there is an appendix that gives a selected list of reference works so you can see the extent and variety of library materials you might use, and another appendix that shows you words and abbreviations commonly used in academic research. Both are supplemental to the text, so they are the sort of information that can safely be put in appendixes. (An alternate form of the plural word is "appendices.")

If your paper requires an appendix, or several of them, give each a sequential designation using capital letters. Put them immediately after the text and before the Notes or Works Cited in a research paper because, strictly speaking, appendices are supplements to the text. Head the first one "Appendix A" and use an identifying label; center it an inch down from the top of the paper; use the same form but with a different letter for subsequent appendices. Continue with successive page numbers as you do throughout the text and other material in your research paper.

OTHER OPTIONS: PREFACES, STATEMENTS OF PURPOSE, SYNOPSES, AND ABSTRACTS

Few undergraduate papers require any of these options. Nor will you usually be asked to include more than one of them in the final presentation of your research work. Each precedes the paper itself (or the outline), and is typed in double spacing, and the pages are numbered consecutively in small roman numerals, just as all material ahead of the text is.

A preface is a brief introduction telling the audience what it can expect to find in the paper. Most prefaces are no more than half a page long. If you are asked to include a table of contents with your paper, the preface follows it.

A statement of purpose tells what you propose to do or show in the text that follows. Sometimes it also tells the reason you undertook the research being reported—that is, it tells the purpose you hope to achieve by doing this project. Papers on scientific or science-related subjects often begin with a statement of purpose.

A synopsis (the plural is "synopses") **or abstract distills details of the content of a research paper.** Both differ from the preface because they give more information about the content and are also likely to stress the purpose for which the research was undertaken. Neither is longer than one page.

Center the heading telling what is on the page (that is, "Synopsis" or "Abstract" or other—but without the quotation marks shown here) in capital and lowercase letters, one inch down from the top of the paper. Then double-space before beginning the writing, which is also double spaced. Observe the same one-inch margins around the material as you do in typing the text.

FASTENING PAGES

Use a paper clip at the top left-hand corner to fasten together the pages of your completed research work. The clip is easy for a reader to remove and thus frees the pages to turn. Or a reader may want to put the Works Cited list alongside the text for handy reference. Since all pages are numbered and contain your name, the paper can readily be reassembled.

Some instructors want to have papers submitted in one of the many kinds of inexpensive covers or binders that protect your work as well as hold it together. Others may even prefer to have papers stapled together.

Ask your instructor which method of fastening pages is preferred.

SAMPLE RESEARCH PAPER IN MLA FORM

On the following pages is a research paper written by a student who followed the process described in this book. It includes the outline, the paper itself, an example of comment notes, and a Works Cited listing. You may recognize some parts as those you have already read as examples throughout this book.

In the margins of each page you will see two kinds of comments:

- Comments printed in **color** are about **form**.
- Comments printed in **black** are about **content**.

Use the comments as a guide to preparing your own research paper for final presentation.

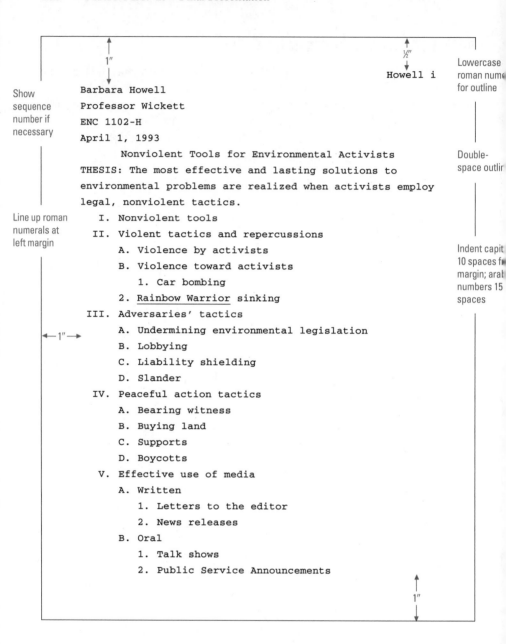

Show sequence number if necessary

Line up roman numerals at left margin

←1″→

1″

½″

Howell i

Lowercase roman numerals for outline

Double-space outline

Indent capitals 10 spaces from margin; arabic numbers 15 spaces

Barbara Howell

Professor Wickett

ENC 1102-H

April 1, 1993

   Nonviolent Tools for Environmental Activists

THESIS: The most effective and lasting solutions to environmental problems are realized when activists employ legal, nonviolent tactics.

  I. Nonviolent tools

 II. Violent tactics and repercussions

  A. Violence by activists

  B. Violence toward activists

   1. Car bombing

   2. Rainbow Warrior sinking

III. Adversaries' tactics

  A. Undermining environmental legislation

  B. Lobbying

  C. Liability shielding

  D. Slander

 IV. Peaceful action tactics

  A. Bearing witness

  B. Buying land

  C. Supports

  D. Boycotts

  V. Effective use of media

  A. Written

   1. Letters to the editor

   2. News releases

  B. Oral

   1. Talk shows

   2. Public Service Announcements

1″

C. Blatent attention-getters
   1. Students
   2. Demonstrations
VI. Educational projects
VII. Legislative tools
   A. Environmental Education Act
   B. Freedom of Information Act
   C. Citizen action suits
   D. National Environmental Policy Act
VIII. Tools of environmental organizations
   A. Lobbying
   B. Voting-record scorecards
   C. Candidate "watches"

_{1"}

_{½"}

Howell 1

Last name
page num

Barbara Howell

Professor Wickett

Double-space
heading

ENC 1102-H

July 1, 1993

Consecuti
arabic nur
for pages
throughou

Nonviolent Tools for Environmental Activists

Indent each
paragraph 5
spaces from
left margin

Few causes today are as complex and eminently
important as those that involve the environment.
Increasing numbers of people are becoming aware of the
finiteness of Earth's resources and civilization's abuse
of those resources. Although there is agreement about
"the problem," those who are moved to take action have
differing ideas of how to achieve "the solution." The
most effective and lasting solutions are realized when
environmental activists employ legal, nonviolent tactics.

Center title

Double-sp
throughou
paper

Thesis
statement
appears early
in paper

Ragged rig
margins
preferred

Text explains
terminology

The term "nonviolent" should not be confused with
"nonconfrontational." Environmental activism demands
direct (i.e., confrontational) action on environmental
issues, but it is more effective if implemented by a
group rather than by an individual. Although their
policies and priorities vary, most environmental groups
choose nonviolent means to achieve their objectives. The
strategies employed by these groups range from direct
action to public awareness, from education to actual
legislation and, more often than not, a combination of
all four.

Unfortunately, many people are frustrated by the

←1"→politics and time-consuming procedures involved in
environmental legislation. They perceive "the problem"

About
←1"→

1"

as critical and in need of an immediate solution.
Often these people are in the throes of newly found
environmental awareness and are ready to use any means
to achieve their goals. Too often the means chosen are
violent or destructive; the solutions imagined or
temporary; the results counterproductive in terms of
lasting change.

Note parallel
sentence
structure

Pouring sugar in a bolldozer's fuel tank, spiking
trees, and throwing blood on women wearing fur coats may
draw attention to the issues of development in sensitive
areas, mismanagement of the national forests, and the
plight of endangered and "farmed" animals, but they do
nothing to address the causes. They only serve to
aggravate the symptoms.

Inevitably, the state will buy another bulldozer--
at taxpayer expense--and continue the project, forgotten
spikes will lie in wait to injure some unsuspecting
logger, and the fur-wearer will be more determined to
wear whatever she chooses. Only through legislation and
education will unchecked development of the wilderness
cease, Forest Service policies change, and consumer
demand for furs becomes a thing of the past.

or's name
rated into

Contrary to Dave Foreman's statement that Earth
First!'s "militant presence will make it easier for
guys like you [a Sierra Club member] to deal with the
bureaucrats in smoke-filled rooms" (McBride 14), violence
only invites more violence. Earth First! discovered this
first-hand with the 1990 car bombing and injuring of two
of their directors. Oakland police had disregarded

Square
brackets show
interpolation

previous reports of death threats and tried to prove

Parenthetical documentation supports a specific

the group members had planted the bomb themseleve (Rauber 24-30). This illustrates another way that violent tactics are counterproductive and divisive of individuals with the same ultimate goal--a healthy planet on which to live.

This is not to say that peaceful tactics are without risk. Even Greenpeace's Quaker tactic of "bearing witness" (Christrup 13) to environmental atrocities has repeatedly put activists in the line of fire between whales and whalers, seals and hunters, Earth and nuclear devices.

Series of documentations

There is adequate evidence (Christrup 18; Greenpeace 1; Nader "Curriculum" 109; Riding) that relentless protests of France's nuclear testing in the South Pacific resulted in the bombing and sinking of Greenpeace's Rainbow Warrior and the death of photographer Fernando Pereira in July 1985. Undaunted by this tragic loss, Greenpeace sued the French government, eventually winning $8 million, and on April 8, 1992, France finally announced a moratorium on nuclear testing for at least one year.

Author's name is part of text

In Christrup's article, Twilly Cannon, a former Greenpeace director, described the perils involved in documenting damage to fish populations by Asian driftnetters as

Block indent for quote of more than 4 lines

the most dangerous small-boat conditions I'd ever been in. We had to stay night and day alongside the driftnetters. There was heavy fog and the Rainbow Warrior's radar couldn't see us behind the waves. But we came out with hard evidence of the destructiveness of those nets. (19)

There are other dangers in fighting this good fight. For example, the major offenders of the environment, such as chemical, utility, oil, mining, and timber companies, have been launching large-scale "green-washing" public relations campaigns. Some are founding powerful lobby groups with benevolent-sounding names. "The Foundation for Environmental and Economic Progress" and "The Endangered Species Act Coordinating Council" are two such groups with the real goal of undermining the Endangered Species Act (D'Esposito).

In Chemicalweek, the "Environment Newsletter" column warns chemical colleagues of the birth of activist groups formed to keep the public updated on Union Carbide and DuPont activities ("New Green").

Another article ("New Group") informs readers of the existence of the "Superfund Action Coalition" that was formed to

eliminate retroactive liability under the Superfund[1] cost-effective strategies. The coalition, made up of industrial companies and associations, is reacting to liability assessed for 'blameless industrial activity that occurred 20, 50, or even 100 years ago' [an unnamed] spokeswoman says.

Environmental activists need to use education and action to meet such threats.

Margin annotations:

—mentation block
ation period

Article title shortened in text

—ation
—s in middle
—ntence

Superscript number coordinates with "Notes"

—t block
—e 10 spaces
left margin

Clarification comment in square brackets

Howell 5

Even Rachel Carson's widely read and praised book
did not move people to militant environmental action. No
wonder, then, that according to Brooks (40),

> When <u>Silent Spring</u> was published, the National
> Agricultural Chemical Association did not
> attempt to deal with the hazards that the book
> exposed. Instead it appropriated a quarter of
> a million dollars in an attempt to prove--
> unsuccessfully--that Rachel Carson was a
> 'hysterial fool.'

With adversaries like that, today's environmental
activists must be resourceful, knowledgable, and well
organized. They must have an array of nonviolent tools
at their disposal. As McCloskey (12) writes:

> . . . it is not enough to simply protest the
> status quo. Protests can lay the groundwork,
> but in a mass society changes are made only
> when the controlling institutions are forced
> to make them through the political process.

That process has worked often. Since its founding in
1955, the Nature Conservancy has purchased over 5.5
million acres (1,300 preserves) in unique or sensitive
areas of the United States, Canada, Latin America, the
Caribbean, and the Pacific ("Nature Conservancy"). This is
an excellent way to preserve land and control its use.

<u>The Grass Roots Primer</u> (249-50) relates a success
story from Middletown, New Jersey, in which the Nature
Conservancy helped a small citizens' committee preserve
undeveloped land. The Conservancy was helpful because

Margin annotations:

Source citation
appears before
quotation

Single marks for
quote within
quotation

Numerical
clarification
helps reader

First of three
digits omitted,
not repeated

1) It held the option and later took title to the land, thus relieving [their] committee of the burdens of real estate ownership.

Words added in brackets for sense

2) It served as a repository for and kept an accounting of the funds [they] collected.

3) By being both prestigious and tax deductable, it increased the number and amount of contributions.

Transitional sentence

Bearing witness and buying land are only two of the many strategies used by environmental activists today. Throughout a telephone interview, Cannon stressed the importance of utilizing a variety of tactics. "Like tools in a toolbox," he said. "We pull out whatever tool is appropriate for the job." A few tactics are like hand-tools: successfully operated by one person. However, most require the power produced by a group.

Short quotations treated as part of text

An influential tool held by every man, women, and child is the decision of which companies to buy--or not buy--consumer goods from. For instance, alert citizens are finding it is as important to support the companies that use recycled materials as it is to boycott the products of companies that pollute or commit various "crimes" against the environment.

Transitional word

Another powerful activist tool is the pen and the ability to wield it. Ralph Nader's Civic Curriculum (148-52) provides many suggestions for using the media effectively. One place to begin is with a letter to the editor of a newspaper, for it can be read by the public. Further, legislators often use such letters to keep a finger on the pulse of their constituency.

Citation begins sentence

Environmental activists can put out news releases to
get publicity in support of their events and activities
that might otherwise slip by unnoticed by the public.

Hand delivery of letters and releases is a good
tactic in this age of faxes and bulk mailings. The
determination conveyed by this simple act may also
persuade an editor or feature writer to write on the
subject.

Most radio and television stations program talk
shows, some of which are call-ins. In addition to
inviting listener/viewer comments--to which environmental
activists can always respond--such shows are receptive to
ideas for topics. Protecting the environment, especially
with local ramifications, is usually an appealing subject
for local broadcasters. Talk shows are also a good tool
for informing the public of local environmental problems
and prompting it to action.

Free publicity is also available through Public
Service Announcements (PSAs). A PSA cannot be used
to state an opinion, but it can be used to announce
meetings or convey other such information. All radio
and television stations are required by law to devote
a certain amount of broadcast time to PSAs, so
environmental activists should find out about deadlines
and specifications on local stations.

Another way to get media attention is through
unusual stunts and demonstrations. Chaining oneself to an
ancient tree tugs on the heartstrings of the masses, but
it has been done often. Stunts like the Sierra Club's
peanut-shell caper in 1969 (Stallings 90) creatively

Date helps
readers fo
on time

Howell 8

spotlight environmental ills in need of a cure. For this
event, activists flushed peanut shells at Miami City Hall,
then watched them float around in nearby Biscayne Bay
outside the sewage treatment plant.

Public demonstrations show unity and strength in
numbers. They appeal to the bandwagon mentality of their
observers and are good attention-getters. Effective
demonstrations can show the multigenerational makeup of
today's pro-environment activists. They are even more
effective if followed closely by a public education
campaign and/or legislative action.

Education is an important strategy employed by
ecology-minded groups and individuals everywhere because
the values required to preserve the biodiversity and
health of the planet must be taught. Environmental
education is helping millions of people discard the age-
old belief that the Earth is ripe for exploitation and
replacing it with a new understanding of the interrelated
complexity of the planet. As John Muir[2] said one hundred
years ago, "When we try to pick out anything by itself we
find it hitched to everything else in the universe" (qtd.
in Mitchell 23).

Educators today are beginning to address the need
for programs that are "interdisciplinary/integrated/
involved" (Fanning 6-7). The interdisciplinary sciences,
such as biology, chemistry, ecology, etc., are beginning
to be taught as part of a larger whole (that is,
integrated) with seemingly unrelated subjects, such as
political science, business, law, marketing. This gives
students a purposeful outlook toward their chosen

Superscript
number
coordinates
with "Notes"

:ation
eared within
r material
or found

careers. "Involved" means that once integrated, these
professionals of the future must stay active in the
community and be environmentally ethical.

This holistic approach is currently implemented at
all educational levels. Kindergarteners plant trees
and encourage their parents to recycle. Middle school
students may petition their school board to purchase
books made from recycled paper, while high school
students discover ways to increase the energy efficiency
of their schools.

That the slogan "Reduce, Reuse, Recycle" echoes in
the halls of America's schools is partially to the credit
of the Environmental Education Act of 1970. Among this
Act's goals are to foster environmental awareness in
every citizen through the funding and developing of new
curricula for students, and training programs for
teachers, government employees, and society in general.

In reporting on anthropologist Margaret Mead's
testimony in favor of the EEA (Environmental Education
Act) before House and Senate subcommittees, Brezina (48–
49) stated, "we would have to learn . . . 'what a long-
term, continuous, and ultimately boring activity caring
for the environment will be. . . . very much like good
housekeeping, you know, and the dishes are never done.'"
Mead went on to say, "'A short-term perspective won't
protect the environment. We will have every polluter back
polluting cheerfully in five years unless we build
structures that last.'"

Ellipsis shows omission from original

Period ends previous sentence, ellipsis begins new one

Quotation within quotation

Howell 10

But building "structures that last" is often easier
said than done. As Nader points out in his "Introduction"
to Ecotactics,

> . . . corporate and government polluters crave
> secrecy and deny citizens access to the records
> of that which is harming their health and
> safety.

> State and federal agencies keep undisclosed
> data on how much different companies pollute.
> Thus has industrial lethality been made a trade
> secret by a government that presumes to be
> democratic. (15)

Fortunately, there exists a great tool--which can be
used by anyone--called the Freedom of Information Act
(FDIA). This Act gives the public access to federal
government information and documents from which can be
acquired sufficient evidence that an activist can initiate
a Citizen Action Suit to force government agencies to
enforce existing laws. These efforts have led to new
legislation, as well.

But once again, education is the key. According to
Sive (527), the prepared activist is one who has read
"all the constitutional provisions, federal and state
statutes, ordinances, agency regulations, etc. that
pertain to [their] case . . . circumstances and findings
of all the relevant court decisions on all levels . . .
to date, meaning today'" [emphasis added].

The National Environmental Policy Act of 1970
(NEPA)[3], which established the Environmental Protection

Howell 11

Agency, also requires all federal agencies to prepare an environmental impact statement (EIS) for every project <u>before</u> beginning work on it. This includes many private and state projects that must be licensed by a federal agency.

Kimbrell points to one case where the Army closed an electronic warfare facility in Woodbridge, VA, rather than subject it to the scrutiny of an EIS and other NEPA regulations.

> NEPA has stopped or slowed . . . a large
> variety of other federal projects that would
> have harmed the environment.
>
>   It is one of the most powerful legal weapons
> in the environmentalist's arsenal. (154)

New paragraph within quotation indented 3 spaces

All major environmental organizations stay abreast of pending legislation. Activists continually lobby and keep other environmentalists up to date on imminent votes in the legislatures, urging them to write, call, and visit their representatives about these issues.

Activist groups also keep "scorecards" on legislators, recording how they vote on environmental issues. Surveys[4] are given to untried candidates ("Sierra"); the results are widely publicized. An increasing number of incumbents are finding themselves running against "Green" candidates ("Let's Party"). This activist tool will prove to be a cornerstone in getting future legislation passed.

No page number needed; article on one page

Paper concludes with summarizing paragraph

Nonviolent action, education, legislation: these are tools readily available to everyone who cares about the

environment. They can be used by people of all ages,
in all places, and do not cost anything except time and
personal commitment. Yet these are the very tools that
can build a sustainable society for both the immediate
and long-range future.

Howell 13

Notes

[1] "Superfund" is the common name for The
Comprehensive Environmental Response and Liability
Act (CERCLA) of 1980. It was revised in 1986.

[2] John Muir founded the Sierra Club in 1882.

[3] NEPA Section 102 (a) requires an environmental
impact statement and public participation in planning
stages of a project (in addition to other requirements).

[4] Among topics on a Miami-group Sierra Club
candidate questionnaire were these:

Solid Waste	Energy
Wetlands	Population
Growth Management	Toxics
Coastal Protection	Biodiversity
Global Warming	Land Acquisition

Howell 14

Works Cited

Brezina, Dennis. <u>Congress in Action: The Environmental
    Education Act</u>. New York: Macmillan, 1974.

Brooks, Paul. "Notes on the Conservation Revolution."
    <u>Ecotactics: The Sierra Club's Handbook for
    Environmental Activists</u>. Ed. John G. Mitchell and
    Constance L. Stallings. New York: Simon, 1970.
    36-42.

Cannon, Twilly. Telephone interview. 23 Jan. 1993.

Christrup, Judy. "Our Twentieth Anniversary."
    <u>Greenpeace Magazine</u> Jan./Feb./Mar. 1991: 13-19.

D'Esposito, Steve. <u>Greenpeace Letter</u>. Apr. 1992.

Fanning, Odam. <u>Opportunities in Environmental Careers</u>.
    Chicago: NTC Pub., 1991.

"Greenpeace Hails French Nuclear Testing Moratorium."
    <u>Greenpeace Newsletter</u> Jul./Aug./Sept. 1992: 1.

Kimbrell, Andrew C., and Edward Lea Rogers. "The
    Environment, The Law, and You." <u>The Green Lifestyle
    Handbook</u>. Ed. Jeremy Rifkin. New York: Holt, 1990.
    151-62.

"Let's Party." <u>Buzzworm: The Environmental Journal</u>
    Mar./Apr. 1992: 12.

McBride, Stewart. "The Eco-Pranksters." <u>This World</u> 16
    Jan. 1983: 12+.

McCloskey, Michael. "Foreword." <u>Ecotactics: The Sierra
    Club's Handbook for Environmental Activists</u>. Ed.
    John G. Mitchell and Constance L. Stallings. New
    York: Simon, 1970. 11-12.

Mitchell, John G. "On the Spoor of the Slide Rule."
    Ecotactics: The Sierra Club's Handbook for
    Environmental Activists. Ed. John G. Mitchell and
    Constance L. Stallings. New York: Simon, 1970.
    23-35.

Nader, Ralph. "Introduction." Ecotactics: The Sierra
    Club's Handbook for Environmental Activists. New
    York: Simon, 1970. 13-19.

---. Ralph Nader's Civic Curriculum. Draft. Washington:
    Center for Study of Responsive Law, 1991.

"New Green Groups Target CPI." Chemicalweek 5 Feb. 1992:
    45.

"New Group Eyes Superfund." Chemicalweek 5 Feb. 1992: 45.

Our Endangered Plants and Animals Need You and the Nature
    Conservancy. Leaflet. Arlington: Nature
    Conservancy, n.d.

Rauber, Paul. "No Second Warning." Sierra Jan./Feb.
    1991: 24+.

Riding, Alan. "France Suspends Its Testing of Nuclear
    Weapons." New York Times 9 Apr. 1992: A4.

Robertson, James, and John Lewallen, eds. The Grass
    Roots Primer. Covelo: Yolla Bolly, 1975.

Sierra Club Political Committee Meeting. Coral Gables,
    FL, 5 Mar. 1992.

Sive, Mary Robinson. Environmental Legislation: A
    Sourcebook. New York: Praeger, 1976.

Stallings, Constance L. "It's June in December."
    Ecotactics: The Sierra Club's Handbook for
    Environmental Activists. Ed. John G. Mitchell and
    Constance L. Stallings. New York: Simon, 1970:
    88-94.

Margin notes: 3 hyphens and period signify same author as previous entry · No date of publication shown · Nonprint source · No author shown on original

APA and Other Styles

"APA" stands for the documentation style of the American Psychological Society, a widely used research paper format. The *Publication Manual of the American Psychological Association*, 3rd ed. (Washington: APA, 1983) is the standard for most of the social sciences as well as for other fields, including research in the humanities. It is an author-and-date system; that is, citations in the text acknowledge the author(s) and the date a particular work was published. Although the APA system differs somewhat from the MLA system, you will find it easy to use and comfortable to make the transition if called upon to do so. This chapter highlights and illustrates some characteristics of the **APA format system first**, then notes elements of other systems, should you need to use one of them.

APA FORMAT AND PAGE NUMBERING

Either type or computer print your research paper, following these conventions:

1. **Margins should be 1½ inches at the top, bottom, left, and right of each page in an APA-style research paper.**

2. **Use double spacing throughout** the text of the paper itself and on other pages that go with it.

3. **Prefer to use a ragged right margin for readability** rather than a justified right.

4. **Indent the beginning of each paragraph by five spaces** from the left margin, and **indent each line of a long quotation** (that is, one of more than 40 words) **by ten spaces** from the left margin.

5. **Do not hypenate words,** even if your computer program will do so automatically. Rather than break words, let lines run short of the margin.

6. **The usual order of pages for the research paper** is this:
   - title page
   - (outline—if requested by instructor)
   - (abstract—if requested by instructor)

text

- references
- appendices—if required for the paper
- notes—if not included in parenthetical documentation

However, you may not need to include some of these elements in the particular assignment you are doing.

7. **Pages, including the title page, are numbered consecutively with arabic numerals at the top right corner of each page.** Any pages before the text should be part of that numbering system. (Although the APA recommends small roman numerals for pages before the text, use arabic numerals to avoid confusion.)

8. **A shortened form of the title is placed above page numbers** in papers submitted for publication to journals that use the APA style, so you may follow that custom in a research paper submitted for a class. **End this abbreviated title flush with the right-hand margin** at 1½ inches from the edge, **and 1½ inches down** from the top of the paper. **The page number should be a double space below the title** and should end flush with the right-hand margin.

9. **Endnotes are usually permitted** by instructors whose students prepare undergraduate research papers. However, footnotes (that is, notes shown at the bottom of the pages as needed) are recommended for theses and dissertations.

APA FORM TITLE PAGE

Prepare a separate title page containing the title of your paper, your name, and the course for which it is being submitted. Center all this information, and write it in capitals and lowercase letters. Begin paging the research paper with this title page: put the number "1" and a short form of the title at the top right and with the spacing for page numbering described in the previous section.

Put the title on a line at the approximate center of the page. Ideally, the title will not be very long; but if it is, double-space between the lines. Allow a double space below the title, and center your complete name, after another double space, put the title and/or number of the course for which you are submitting the paper. Some instructors may also request that you write their name and/or the due date of the research paper below the other information. (These recommendations differ in a few respects from what the APA *Publication Manual* suggests, but the information given in that book presupposes manuscripts submitted for publication in refered journals.) See the title page on page 257 of the sample research page in this chapter as an example.

REFERENCE CITATIONS IN TEXT

The APA system calls for **parenthetical documentation** within the text of the research paper. However, to each citation of **author's name (or title of a** work) and page number or other locator is added *the date of its publica-tion*. The full publication information for both print and nonprint sources is given in a listing titled References, which begins at the end of the research paper.

Acknowledging Ideas and Short Quotations

The APA format uses numbers of words to distinguish between short and long quotations. In this format, a **short quotation contains fewer than 40 words** and therefore does not have to appear as a separate block. Parenthetical documentation is usually used, and follows the conventions noted in the preceding paragraph.

Just as in acknowledging borrowed ideas, the source of a short quotation may be acknowledged anywhere within a sentence. If the quotation or passage to be cited occurs *at the end of a sentence*, put the documentation *before* the period. If the quotation or other borrowed idea is *in the middle of a sentence*, put the parenthetical documentation immediately after what needs to be cited, then continue the sentence. If you want to let readers know the source of an idea or quotation so that they don't think it's your own, put the parenthetical documentation as an *introductory notation*. The examples that follow illustrate such placements.

CONVENTIONS OF APA IN-TEXT DOCUMENTATION

In-text documentation may be either parenthetical, partially parenthetical, or completely within the context of the wording of the paper. However, the following conventions apply, whichever method is chosen—and there ought to be variety in the ways you cite sources in order to maintain liveliness in your writing.

1. **Citation information for a complete work consists of the author's name (or the title of a work) and the date of publication.**

    EXAMPLES

    A summary of how the Social Security system works (U.S. Dept. H&HS, 1988) is written in easy-to-understand language.

    or

    Social Security: How it works for you (1988) is an easy-to-understand summary of how the system works for individuals.

2. **Anonymous works are acknowledged by title** (or a shortened form of it) **and date of publication**. If a shortened form is used, readers can, of course, find the complete title in the References listing.

    EXAMPLE

    Social Security (1988) is an easy-to-understand summary of how the system works for individuals.

COMMENT

This work has a subtitle, which makes the whole title rather long. It may be shortened, as here. Anyone looking for it will find the complete title on the References page.

EXAMPLE

Solutions to environmental problems are categorized and described in vivid terms in **Endangered** (n.d.).

COMMENT

The complete title of this leaflet is *Our Endangered Plants and Animals Need You and the Nature Conservancy*, so a shortening of the title is certainly called for. The abbreviation "n.d." within parentheses where the date would ordinarily appear shows that there is no date on this leaflet.

3. **Precede acknowledgment of a specific page by the abbreviation "p." before the page number.** Use the abbreviation "ch." if you are acknowledging an entire chapter in a book.

EXAMPLES

Another way to receive larger benefits is for people over 65 to delay filing for benefits in the future (Rovner, 1990, p. 2836).

and

APA format is explained separately (Roth, 1994, ch. 11).

4. **If a work has two authors, give both names every time the work is referred to in the text.** If there are three to five authors, name all of them in the first reference; in later citations use only the last name of the first author followed by "et al." Should you cite a source that has six or more authors, for all references write only the surname of the author listed first followed by "et al." Use the word "and" if the names are given in the text, but prefer an ampersand (&) in parenthetical citations and in the reference list.

5. **If you recorded material by two authors with the same surname, distinguish between them by always noting the initials of each one, even if the years of their publications are different.**

EXAMPLE

J.R. Aldama (1992) and C.L. Aldama (1993) studied the comparative development of . . .

6. **When citing two or more publications by the same author or authors within the same parentheses, put the dates of publication in chronological order.** Give the name(s) only once.

EXAMPLE

Staging variations (Domingo, 1978, 1988, 1992) are well documented.

7. **Two or more works by the same author(s) published in the same year are shown by assigning each a lowercase letter, alphabetically by title,**

to distinguish them in parenthetical documentation. Use the same letters when you cite those works in a Reference listing; see page 253.

EXAMPLE

```
C. Matz describes computer-generated musical notation in
several publications (1993a, 1993b, 1993c) addressed to
those not in the music business.
```

NOTES AND ENDNOTES

Content (commentary) notes supplement the text, tables, or other visuals in the research paper without interrupting it. You can also use such notes if parenthetical documentation would be unduly long. Although such notes may be at the bottom of the page on which the material they supplement appears (hence, "footnotes"), the spacing to do so is awkward. Therefore, you may list content notes separately and after the References listing for the paper.

In the text of the paper, use a consecutive superscript arabic numeral to mark each place at which you want to make a comment note. The numeral may be either within a sentence or at the end of it, *before* the period. Allow a space after the numeral and before continuing with what you write. Each note must be matched with its explanation on the note page.

Begin the notes on a separate page—still numbered consecutively—which you head "Notes" (without the quotation marks, of course) in the center of the page and 1½ inches down from the top of the paper. Double-space after that and, beginning five spaces in from the left margin, put the matched superscript number for each note. Begin the note immediately after that number, without allowing an additional space. Since notes are written in paragraph indentation, second and succeeding lines will be at the usual left side margin of the paper. All text for notes is typed double spaced.

APPENDICES AND OTHER MATERIALS

Follow the format and typing instructions already given for the MLA style adjuncts on pages 227–228 if you need to set up these possible additions to an APA style research paper. Of course, retain the page heading and numbering system of APA.

REFERENCES IN THE APA FORMAT

The APA equivalent of the Works Cited listing is called "References"; the word is typed 1½ inches down from the top of the paper and at the center of the first line of a new page. Type all information in the References with double spacing. Allow *one space* after periods and commas, none after closing parentheses.

The References are presented in *hanging indentation* form. That is, start the first line of each entry at the left margin, but indent succeeding lines of each entry *three spaces* from that margin.

Put all references in alphabetical order by author's last name. If no author is given, alphabetize the entry by title. Titles beginning with *A, An,* or *The* are typed that way, but alphabetizing is by the next word.

Each entry in the References list contains four units, in this order, and each unit ends with a period:

- author
- date of publication
- title of work
- publication information: location and name of publisher for books; volume and page numbers for periodicals

Variations for nonprint references should incorporate as much of these units of information as possible. Also, add what is special to each medium, such as film director or musical performer.

Only proper nouns and the first word of a title (and of a subtitle) are capitalized. No quotation marks are used in a list of References. Book and periodical titles are underlined. Months are written out in full, *not* abbreviated.

The following list summarizes some of the other customs you are expected to adhere to in the APA style for References.

1. **The Author(s)**

    1.1. **Give the surname followed by a comma and the initials of each author**, no matter how many there are. Use commas between the names and an ampersand (&).

    EXAMPLE   Kaufman, I.S., & Nimar, S.

    1.2. **One or more editors of a book are indicated by the abbreviation Ed. or Eds. in parentheses** after the name of the last editor shown.

    EXAMPLE   Leiblie, L., Leiblie, D., & Glass, C. (Eds.)

2. **The Date of Publication**

    2.1. **Enclose in parentheses the year of publication of a book.** Put a period immediately after the close of the parentheses.

    2.2. **Put a comma after the year of publication of a magazine or newspaper, then give the month—written out in full—and the date. Enclose the whole in parentheses.** End this part of the entry with a period.

    EXAMPLES   Roth, R. N. (1994).

                    (1993, July/August).

                    (1993, August 11).

3. **The Title**

    3.1. **Two or more works by the same author(s) are listed in the order of publication. Repeat the name of the author(s) for each entry. If the works were published in the same year**, assign each a lowercase letter based on alphabetizing the titles, and put it next to the date of each piece of work.

EXAMPLES

```
Michaels, D. (1994a). Living in the 21st century . . .

Michaels, D. (1994b). Mastering model making . . .
```

3.2. Notation of a special edition of a book, such as revised (rev.), alternate (alt.), subsequent (7th ed.), and so on, **is enclosed in parentheses after the title.** End that unit of information with a period.

4. Publication Information

4.1. Unless the city in which a book publisher is located is well known, show the state where the publisher is located. Use standard two-letter Postal Service abbreviations. If a book was published outside of the United States, abbreviate the name of the country, unless the city is well known (such as London, Athens, Rome). Separate the location from the name of the publisher with a colon. End the unit with a period.

EXAMPLE   `Belmont, CA: Wadsworth.`

4.2. An article or chapter within a book is treated as an article through the first three units of author, date, and title. Then, add the word "In" and give the author's or editor's name (if it is different from the author or editor of the complete book), the book title in which it is found, then parentheses enclosing the abbreviation "pp." with the page numbers on which it appears. Finally, give the publisher's location and name, followed by a period.

EXAMPLES

```
Kalat, J. W. (1990). Intelligence and its measurement.
    In Introduction to Psychology (2nd ed.). (pp.
    349-356). Belmont, CA: Wadsworth.
Gornick, V. (1990). Mama went to work. In J. Zandy
    (Ed.), Calling home: Working-class women's
    writings, an anthology (pp. 149-153). New
    Brunswick, NJ: Rutgers University Press.
```

Only invert the name (or names) in the author position.

4.3. Omit such words as "Company" and "Incorporated," but do spell out the names of university presses and of publishing companies.

4.4. A journal article in a periodical with continuous pagination shows the name of the publication and volume number (each underlined but separated by a comma), then a comma and the page numbers of the article, followed by a period.

EXAMPLE   `College Composition and`
`Communications, 44, 201-02.`

4.5. A journal article in a periodical with *pagination by issue* adds the number of the issue in parenthesis after the volume, and the comma comes after that item.

EXAMPLE   Computers and Composition, 10(1), 55-57.

4.6. Magazine and newspaper articles show all the page numbers on which the entry appears, preceded by an abbreviation of either "p." (if the article is on only one page) or "pp." (if it is on several, even discontinuous, pages). If pages are not continuous, show all pages but separate them by commas in the following way.

EXAMPLE   pp. 12, 25, 30-32.

Print Resources

The following are some selected examples of the APA system of noting reference works. If you do not find a model in this brief section of a source you need to list, consult the *Publication Manual of the American Psychological Association* (3rd ed.). (1983). Washington, DC: APA.

BOOK BY SINGLE AUTHOR

Koontz, D. R. (1992). Hideaway. New York: Putnam.

BOOK BY TWO OR MORE AUTHORS

Coe, S., Teasdale, D., & Wickham, D. (1992). More than a game: Sport in our time. New York: BBC-Parkwest.

BOOK EDITED OR COMPILED

Levy, P. B. (Ed.). (1992). Documentary history of the modern civil rights movement. Newport, CT: Greenwood Publishing.

EDITION OF A BOOK

Roth, A. J. (1994). The research paper: Process, form, and content (7th ed.). Belmont, CA: Wadsworth.

CHAPTER IN A BOOK OR ARTICLE IN A COLLECTION

Mannes, Myra. (1992). How do you know it's good? In H. Brent & W. Lutz (Eds.). The Horizon Reader (pp. 799-805). New York: St. Martin's.

This entry illustrates that when the names of editors are not in the author position, they are preceded by the word "In" and *are not inverted*. Because the reference is to only a portion of a book, the pages on which it appears are shown after the title of the book and with the abbreviation that indicates they are pages within a work.

ARTICLE IN A MAGAZINE OR JOURNAL WITH CONTINUOUS PAGINATION

> Rust, V. D. (January 1992). Educational responses to
>
> reforms in East Germany, Czechoslovokia, and Poland.
>
> Phi Delta Kappan, 73, pp. 386-89.

MAGAZINE ARTICLE WITH PAGINATION BY ISSUE

> Tobias, A. (1993, July 26). A tax increase you can avoid.
>
> Time, p. 53.

NEWSPAPER ARTICLE BY KNOWN AUTHOR

> Hoversten, P. (1993, August 11). 'One shot in a lifetime'
>
> opportunity. USA Today, pp. 1A, 2A.

This entry illustrates an article extending for more than one page.

Nonprint Resources

FEATURE LENGTH OR SHORT FILM OR VIDEOTAPE

> Spielberg, S. (Producer & director). (1993). Jurassic park
>
> [film]. Hollywood: Universal Pictures.

If the producer and director are different people, show the function of each in parentheses after the name. If the director, actor, writer, or title of the film is most important for purposes of your research paper, put that designation first in the entry.

In the square brackets after the film title, specify the medium—that is, state if the work is a film, videotape, filmstrip, or slide series.

INTERACTIVE VIDEO

> Rain forest. (1991). National Geographic Society [1 laser
>
> disc, 2 computer discs]. Washington, DC: National
>
> Geographic.

This entry specifies the laser disc and computer program designed to be used together.

If an author or director of the program is featured, rather than the title, begin the entry with that person's name followed by his or her function in parentheses.

CASSETTE RECORDING, CD, AUDIOTAPE, OR RECORD

```
Ogbu, J. (Speaker). (1992). Understanding cultural
    diversity and learning. (Cassette Recording No. 71168-
    1288). Urbana, IL: NCTE.
```

SAMPLE RESEARCH PAPER IN APA FORM

On the following pages is a research paper written by a student who used the APA style because it is on a social science-related subject. **Marginal notes** point out matters of **form in color** and of **content in black.**

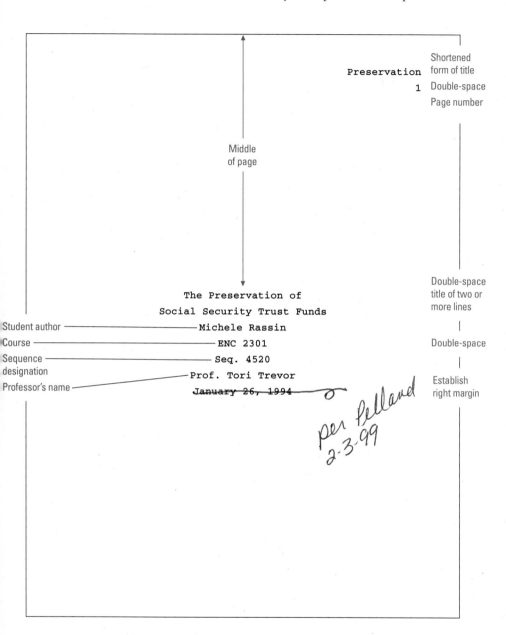

Shortened form of title

Preservation

1   Double-space

Page number

Middle of page

The Preservation of
Social Security Trust Funds

Double-space title of two or more lines

Student author ——————— Michele Rassin

Course ——————————— ENC 2301   Double-space

Sequence designation ——————— Seq. 4520

Professor's name ——————— Prof. Tori Trevor   Establish right margin

~~January 26, 1994~~

per Pelland
2-3-99

1½" Margin

Preservation

2

The Preservation of Social Security Trust Funds

←1½"→
Margin

THESIS: Social Security trust funds need to be preserved

←1½"→
Margin
          so future generations can receive what has been

          promised to them.

     I. History of Social Security funds

         A. Founding

         B. Collapse

Double-space
throughout
outline
         C. Recovery

         D. Considerations

     II. Effects on recipients

         A. Younger generation

            1. Taxed more

            2. Pay more income taxes

         B. Low-income earners

         C. Older generation

            1. Receive more than paid

            2. Life expectancies

            3. Larger benefits

    III. Surplus of trust fund

         A. For elderly

         B. For young generation

         C. Claims on surplus

            1. Reserves promised

            2. Congressional spending

     IV. Future prevention of surplus

         A. Relieving burden on payroll taxes

            1. Tax as income tax

1½" Margin

Running head
on each page
(limit length)

    2. Tax corporations

    3. Tax millionaires

B. Privatization

C. Euthanasia

D. Immigration

1½″ Margin

Preservation

4

Double-spa

Title on 1st Page of Text

Indent each paragraph 5 spaces

In the 1990s, people are living longer and depending more on the government. Each day, the U.S. Congress is voting for or against spending money for the good of the people. Unfortunately, Congress is spending more than it can afford to, which affects the well-being of the American people depending on Social Security. Because we have a government that rules for the people, it needs to use funds accrued for the people who need it the most.

Cite source by author, year, page(s) in parentheses

In 1990 more than 36 million people received benefits averaging more than $660 a month (Miller, 1991, p. 145), but these benefits given were not based on need. Nor will they be available unless Social Security funds are preserved so future generations can receive what has been promised to them.

Type entire paper doub space

Thesis statement of paper

The concept of Social Security benefits for the elderly resulted from economic instability during the Great Depression. In the 1930s, Francis E. Townsend set up a program that included a $200 monthly pension for people aged 60 and older. In support of Townsend's program, 5,000,000 elderly people nationwide joined in the Townsend Club demanding the program be put forth. In responding to the demands of the people, President Franklin D. Roosevelt set up a committee on economic security to examine the possibilities for pension funds.

General knowledge needs no source cita

Finally, Congress revised the committee's possible solutions for the program and on August 14, 1935, established the Social Security Act. This legislation declared that the foundation of the pension would be financed by a payroll tax on employers and employees. The Social Security Act was the basis for old-age pension funds, and has been revised several times since then. Amendments to the Act expanded it to include dependents, disabled, and other groups. Amendments also have elaborated the types of coverage and adjusted both taxes and benefits to keep pace with inflation.

The 1935 Act concentrated on problems occurring at that time. However, by the early 1980s there had to be drastic changes in order to compensate for different times. In 1982, the Social Security System almost became insolvent. As Donian pointed out (1988, p. 26), there was a deficit in the Social Security Trust Fund of $7.9 billion. In order to compensate for this deficit through the Social Security financing reforms of 1983, Congress raised Social Security taxes and lowered benefits. This recovery action by Congress eliminated the short-term risks of insolvency and began the upward trend towards a surplus.

In order to receive compensation from Social Security, one must first pay a fair amount of taxes. In 1990, a 7.65% tax rate was imposed on income earnings up to $51,300 (Miller, 1991, p. 145). However, the employer had to match equally the employee's contribution at that tax rate. As Miller goes on to say, the result is actually that the employer's contribution is really paid-- at least in part--by the employee's receiving a reduced wage rate.

Author name is in text; unnecessary in citation

Citation in
middle of
sentence

In order to receive benefits, one must first have earned "credits" for certain amounts of work. For example, (U.S. Dept. H&HS, 1988, p. 9) in 1988 a person earned one credit for each $470 of earnings and a maximum of four credits for $1,880 or more earned. Once an individual earns a certain number of credits, that person is considered fully insured. No worker reaching age 62 in 1991 could be fully insured with less than ten years of credit. However, once acquiring those years of credit, a person was then sure of being fully insured for receiving benefits.

Some people can also receive full benefits for other reasons (U.S. Dept. H&HS, 1988, p. 6). If a child under 16 is in a parent's care, the parent can receive spouse's benefits even if not yet 65 years old. Disabled people can also receive Social Security benefits under certain conditions. Such a financial assurance could be very beneficial since "3 of every 10 young men who start working today will die or become severely disabled before reaching normal retirement age" (U.S. Dept. H&HS, 1988, p. 5).

Period after
citation that
ends sentence

Even though recipients of Social Security receive contributions, the younger people are paying more in Social Security taxes than they realize. Because the young are not writing a check to the Social Security Administration, they do not consider how much they are paying in taxes. The money, instead, is taken automatically out of their paychecks.

Begins II
of outline

In addition, because of legislation, the younger
generations are paying more in Social Security taxes.
As a result of President Reagan's bait-
and-switch tax cuts, 69 percent of American
families emerged from the eighties paying more
in Social Security taxes than they do in income
taxes--which is the main reason that the poorer
60 percent of families pay more in federal
taxes than they did in 1980. (Bennet, 1991,
p.30)

Furthermore, despite the Reagan tax cuts "low-income
workers [are] paying as much as 28 percent more in taxes
than they did in 1980" (Bennet, 1991, p. 29).

Moreover, low-income earners pay a lot of payroll
taxes to then receive meager Social Security benefits.
Choi points out that the benefits are reduced further as
a result of low-income earners' comparatively shorter
life expectancy, even after age 65. Further, low-income
earners are more likely to retire early due to ill health
and are less capable of working after retirement, so they
thus get reduced Social Security benefits (1989, p. 149).

Not only do low-income earners pay more in taxes,
but also single persons, unrelated people sharing the
same house, and childless couples also do not get tax
cuts. Although tax burdens rose for childless couples
since 1985, tax burdens dropped for poor Americans with
children (Bennet, 1991, pl 31). Taxes also dropped 4.6
percent (Bennet 1991, p. 30) for the richest fifth of the
population.

(Margin annotations:)

notations of 40
more words
block indent

quare brackets
close word
ded so
otation makes
se

Source noted
after final period
of indented
quotation

Tables integrated into text

Many young people feel they will not get back as much in benefits as they paid in, but most people will receive more in benefits than they paid in taxes (U.S. Dept. H&HS, 1988, p. 11). The lifetime Social Security benefits for persons who retired December 1987 can be seen in Table 1. The figures are shown by race, sex, and socioeconomic status.

Tables usually present quantitative data

Tables need clear, brief titles

Table numbered consecutively throughout paper

Table 1

Lifetime Social Security Benefits for Retirees in December 1987

Underline titles of tables

Separate labels from statistics with underlining or italics

White Male		White Female		Black Male		Black Female	
$862	$434	$862	$434	$862	$434	$862	$434[1]
$98,990	$49,839	$98,990	$49,839	$98,990	$49,839	$98,990	$49,930[2]
91,242	45,939	104,519	52,623	87,076	43,841	100,516	50,608[3]
93,733	44,622	106,118	51,783	89,764	42,420	102,279	49,682[4]

Content footnote numbers after material noted and ½ space above line of type

Note: From "Differential life expectancy, socioeconomic status, and Social Security Benefits" by N. G. Choi, 1989, Social Work, 34, p. 149.

Source of table is below it and in this form

Under the current law, people who were 62 to 64 years old in 1990 and drawing from the Social Security trust fund were treated differently from those aged 65 to 69. The following is called the "earnings test" and is used to determine how much benefits one is entitled to receive:

> In 1990, people from 62 to 64 may earn up to $6,840 before benefits are reduced. For every $2 earned in excess of $6,840, benefits are reduced by $1. For people from 65 to 69, the

1990 earnings limit is $9,360. For this older
group, benefits are reduced by $1 for every
$3 earned in excess of the limit. (Rovner,
1990, p. 2836)

A hypothetical example of how the earnings test
affects individuals can be seen in Table 2. Both John and
Ida are in line for $4,000 in annual Social Security
benefits before the retirement test is applied.

Table 2

Benefits 63- to 67-Year-Olds Will Receive

John, age 63		Ida, age 67	
Earnings in 1990	$7,840	Earnings in 1990	$9,960
Exempt amount for		Exempt amount for	
under 65	6,480	over 65	9,360
Excess over exmpt		Excess over exempt	
amount	1,000	amount	1,000
Benefit cut = 50% of		Benefit cut = 33% of	
excess	500	excess	200
Benefits John receives		Benefits Ida receives	
in 1990	3,500	in 1990	3,800

Note: From "How earnings test works" by J. Rovner, 1990,
Congressional Quarterly Weekly Report, 48, p. 2836.

Individuals who continue to work at jobs that pay as
much or more than they earned throughout their working
lives get higher benefits when they do retire. Another way

Underline title

to receive larger benefits is for people over 65 to delay
filing for benefits in the future (Rovner, 1990, p. 2836).
Then, one does not have to worry about receiving money
since there has been, and will be, a surplus in the
Social Security trust fund.

MaNamee indicates that in fiscal 1989, Social
Security trust fund tax receipts exceeded benefit payments
by $30 billion. Furthermore, the cumulative surplus will
hit $506 billion by the year 2015 and <u>$12.4 trillion</u>
[emphasis added] by 2030 (1988, p. 61). Even though there
is a surplus and will continue to be one, the trust funds
need to be preserved so future generations can receive
what is promised to them.

Author comment
in square
brackets

> By law, surplus payroll revenues are
> invested in Treasury Securities--in other
> words, it is lent to finance other government
> operations, and an IOU is deposited in the
> Social Security trust fund. No financial
> investment is more ironclad than the U.S.
> Treasury bonds. The Social Security IOUs will
> be paid back. . . . (Cloud, 1991, p. 1041)

Quotation stop
in mid-senten

Even though the IOUs will be paid back, a surplus will
remain only as long as Congress leaves it alone.

Congress does not want to cut spending, nor does it
want to raise taxes, but that only leaves it to take the
money out of something else to fix the deficit.

> If Congress keeps its hands off, estimates
> Budget Director James C. Miller III [his job at
> the time he wrote this], the cumulative surplus

Author comm
in square
brackets

would equal the total amount of federal debt
outstanding by around 2005. . . . [Moreover,]
Robert M. Ball, former Social Security
commissioner and key author of the 1983
reforms, warns that the reserve is needed to
pay benefits already promised after 2030.
(McNamee, 1988, p. 61)

Transition supplied in square brackets

The surplus now being collected by the Social
Security trust fund to pay benefits when younger
generations retire early in the next century or so is
actually being frittered away on day-to-day government
expenses and, according to Democratic Senator Daniel
Patrick Moynihan of N.Y., "it is our purpose to restore
integrity to that system" (Hager, 1991, p. 1041).

If Congress does not spend the surplus in the Social
Security trust fund, there will be a short-term
preservation of the funds. However, to spare the future
surplus of the trust fund, some actions need to be taken
so future generations can receive what is promised to
them.

Transition to IV of outline

One preventive measure that can be taken is to make
payroll taxes less of a burden. This can be achieved by
treating benefits as ordinary income and taxing them at
normal rates. With this idea, there must be a provision
to avoid the double-taxation of workers' original
contributions. Treating benefits as ordinary income tax
would raise $75 billion dollars by 1995 (Bennet, 1991,
p. 31).

Bennet also points out that a second way to make payroll taxes less of a burden is to raise taxes to 38% on corporations and individuals making more than $250,000. This concept, proposed by the Citizens for Tax Justice, would raise $30 billion or more a year (1991, p. 31).

A final idea to relieve the burden of payroll taxes is a surtax on millionaires, an idea supported by Vice President Al Gore when he was a senator (Bennet, 1991, p. 31). Although a tax on millionaires has not been made, the Senate Budget Committee approved an amendment in 1991 that "urged that the proceeds from any new tax on millionaires be used to reduce the tax burdens on families by increasing the dependent exemption and tax credits for children" (Hager, 1991, p. 1042).

Not only would making payroll taxes less of a burden prevent future surpluses, but also certain organizations feel privatization would prevent future surpluses. Organizations of "Libertarians and free marketers for whom a government-sponsored retirement plan has always been an outrage, want to privatize the whole thing" (Donian, 1988, p. 26).

A further startling proposal that Donian reports (1988, p. 26) is euthanasia, which would also prevent future surpluses of the Social Security funds. As explained by supporters, "Opponents of birth control and abortion . . . have long named that euthanasia would be the next step, and if it is, one unintended consequence

Wording omitted from quotation as not needed to make point

would be to postpone or even cure the long-term Social
Security deficit."

Finally, encouraging immigration would also help the
long-term balance of the Social Security trust fund. This
unusual, and probably "tongue in cheek," suggestion would
provide an effective solution because although there
would be more Americans to dip into Social Security
later, a previous generation would not, inasmuch as, for
the most part, newly arrived workers leave their parents
back in the old country, thus eliminating that generation
as recipients of Social Security monies.

The Social Security system has problems of
inequality, and surplus that never existed before the
1981 insolvency is now present because Congress spends
more today than ever before without regard for the
deficit. If Americans are to retain the well-being of
dependents, of the elderly and the disabled, and of other
groups, Americans ought to be concerned with retaining
the Social Security surplus in existence and giving the
reserves to the people who need it the most and who were
promised it.

Quotation marks
signify familiar
words used in
special way

Thesis reiterated
in conclusion

Start reference
list on new page
and center title

Hanging
indentation with
first line of entry
at left margin

Each
succeeding line
of entry indented
3 spaces

Double-s▮
througho▮

References

Bennet, J. (1991, June). The W-2 step; The democrats
are right that the Social Security tax is unfair, but
they're wrong about how to fix it. Washington Monthly,
pp. 29-32.

Choi, N. G. (1989, March). Differential life
expectancy, socioeconomic status, and Social Security
benefits. Social Work, pp. 147-150.

Cloud, D. S. (1991). Who's accountable for Social
Security? Congressional Quarterly Weekly Report, 49,
1041.

Donian, T. G. (1988, May 30). Boom and bust: That's
what seems to be in store for Social Security.
Barron's, pp. 11, 24.

Hager, G. (1991). Senate ok's fiscal blueprint, rejects
payroll tax cut. Congressional Quarterly Weekly
Report, 49, 1040-1043.

McNamee, M. (1988, March 21). Can Washington keep its
hands off Social Security's bulging coffers? Business
Week, p. 61.

Miller, R. L. (1991). Economics today (7th ed.) New
York: HarperCollins.

Rovner, J. (1990). How earnings test works.
Congressional Quarterly Weekly Report, 48, 2836.

U.S. Department of Health and Human Services. (1988).
Social Security: How it works for you. Baltimore: SSA.

Notes

^{1}\$862 and \$434 represent PIA's [Primary Insurance Amounts] of a lifetime maximum-taxable-wage worker and a lifetime minimum-wage worker, respectively, who otherwise had the same work history.

^{2}Lifetime benefits were calculated based on the average life expectancy across sex and race (61.8 years).

^{3}Lifetime benefits were calculated based on differential life expectancies by sex and race only.

^{4}Lifetime benefits were calculated based on differential life expectancies by sex, race, and socioeconomic status.

enter heading
new page

dent first
e of each
te 5 spaces

perscript
mbers
respond with
se in text

Double-space
notes

OTHER RESEARCH DOCUMENTATION AND REFERENCE SYSTEMS

Although *The MLA Style Manual* is widely accepted as the source of both student and professional research writing style for the humanities and the *Publication Manual of the American Psychological Association* for writing in the social sciences, many of the natural sciences publish their own style manuals. There are the *CBE Style Manual: A Guide for Authors, Editors, and Publishers in the Biological Sciences*, 5th ed., the *Handbook for Authors of Papers in American Chemical Society Publications*, and style manuals for mathematics, geology, physics, and other academic disciplines. *The Chicago Manual of Style* is widely used in publishing, and the Government Printing Office issues a *Style Manual*. Most libraries have copies of these materials for you to consult, should you need to.

Footnotes

You have already read on page 249 about notes and how they are coordinated with superscript numbers in the text. Sometimes such notes are put at the bottom of the page of text on which the information needs to be noted (hence, footnotes). The forms for writing these are the same as for other notes, whether you use MLA, APA, or another style. Although a long-standing research technique, they are difficult to space properly.

If you use footnotes, separate the beginning of footnotes on a page from the text with four spaces (that is, two double spaces), and type them single space in paragraph indentation format.

Some computer programs are available that allow for footnotes. Or you can preview the set-up of a computer-written page and make adjustments for the footnotes before you print.

Between-Line Documentation

One method of citing information that is sometimes used in theses and dissertations—but probably not in undergraduate papers—puts full citation information and notes at the point where the reader needs the information, even though it is in the middle of a page. The arabic superscript number, successive throughout the paper, appears at the appropriate place in the text, then a line from margin to margin is put across the page as soon as possible beneath it, the coordinated superscript information is written double spaced in paragraph indentation, and another margin-to-margin line encloses the information. The text then continues after the usual double space.

Author-and-Date System

This is essentially the same as APA documentation, though it may be explained as coming from a different source. That is, in crediting a source, the author (or title) and date of publication are of primary importance. If the reference is to a particular page, that is also listed, usually after a comma that follows the date. Use the APA examples in this chapter for both the in-text documentation and the list of Resources.

Full In-Text Documentation

Another possibility for documenting sources is to give complete information in the text of your paper. Because it is fairly cumbersome and interrupts the flow of reading, the method is seldom used. However, full in-text documentation might be convenient if you have only a few sources to acknowledge.

In this system, enclose within parentheses the documentation information you do not mention in the text, and put the publication information in square brackets within the parentheses.

EXAMPLE

The Grass Roots Primer (James Robertson, and John Lewallen, eds. [Covello: Yolla Bolly, 1991], 24) relates a success story from Middletown, New Jersey, in which the Nature Conservancy helped a small citizens' committee preserve undeveloped land.

If you use this full in-text documentation, it may not be necessary to prepare a separate Works Cited list because the information will be redundant. Check with your instructor for guidance.

Numbering Sources

This system is widely used in the natural sciences, such as medicine and health-related fields, chemistry, physics, computer science, and mathematics, as well as in technological writing. **Documentation in the text is a sequential, underlined arabic numeral followed by a comma, a space, and then the exact page reference.** The whole is enclosed within parentheses.

Each **numeral is then coordinated with a numbered entry in a list of Works Cited at the end of the paper.** Resources, then, are *listed in the order in which they are cited in the text* rather than alphabetically.

EXAMPLES IN THE TEXT

As John Muir said, "When we try to pick out anything by itself we find it hitched to everything else in the universe" (qtd. in 1 23).

and

Educators today are beginning to address the need for programs that are "interdisciplinary/integrated/involved" (2 6-7).

The Works Cited for these two sources would be written this way:

1. Mitchell, John G.   "On the Spoor of the Slide Rule."
   Ecotactics: The Sierra Club's Handbook for Environmental
   Activists.   John G. Mitchell and Constance L. Stallings,
   eds.   New York: Simon, 1990.

2. Fanning, Odom.   Opportunities in Environmental Careers.
   Chicago: NTC, 1991.

Note that although there is a period after the number in the Works Cited listing, none is used after the underlined number in the parentheses within the text.

Selected List of Reference Works Available in Libraries

To list all the reference materials available in even a moderate-sized library is impossible! Reference materials are constantly being updated and new titles are bring added. Periodicals begin or cease publication. New information and retrieval systems are being installed as more libraries switch to computers—and beyond. So as soon as any list is compiled for a book like this, it is out of date. Besides, how could such a list be compiled at all!

What follows, then, is a *selected* listing of sources found in most libraries that is likely to help students in preparing research papers. Effort was made to include recent volumes and editions, though many libraries will contain additional resources. Materials published regularly are followed by the year that publication began. The titles of most volumes are self-explanatory, so full citations and annotations are omitted. If you do your research in a particularly large library or in one devoted to a special subject, be prepared to find many, many additions to this list.

Most materials named here are either published as books or are indexes of published periodical articles. Computer information retrieval services can direct you to hundreds of thousands of items in minutes. And it is also possible to locate unpublished documents, for example, by consulting the ERIC [Educational Resources Information Center] indexes compiled by government-funded centers that gather, catalog, and reproduce such materials for educators. Furthermore, media centers and audiovisual departments usually have extensive lists of catalogs and sources of information that are not included in this listing; the same is true of computer centers.

Every business, profession, and hobby has at least one (and usually several) journal, magazine, or newspaper published for people concerned with it—publications ranging from *American Waterworks Association Journal* to *Volume Feeding Management*. Obviously, to list all such periodicals is impossible! The library where you do most of your research will have a listing of those it subscribes to and facilities for locating periodicals you need to consult.

The following, necessarily selected list, is offered only as a guide to the many materials available and is by no means complete or exhaustive in any category. If publication of a title is regular, the beginning date is noted next to it; otherwise,

the latest publication date, as of this book printing, is shown. The list is divided
into five main groups with numerous subgroups.

I. GENERAL REFERENCE WORKS
   A. General
   B. Atlases
   C. Biographies
   D. Dictionaries
   E. Encyclopedias
   F. Periodical Indexes

II. SCIENCE AND TECHNOLOGY
   A. General
   B. Agriculture
   C. Biology
   D. Chemistry
   E. Computer Sciences
   F. Electronics
   G. Energy
   H. Engineering
   I. Environmental Studies
   J. Geology
   K. Health and Physical Education
   L. Mathematics
   M. Medicine
   N. Physics

III. SOCIAL SCIENCES
   A. General
   B. Business
   C. Criminology
   D. Economics
   E. Education
   F. Ethnic Studies
   G. Geography
   H. Health
   I. History
   J. Political Science
   K. Physical Education
   L. Psychology
   M. Social Work
   N. Sociology

IV. HUMANITIES
   A. Art and Architecture
   B. Foreign Languages
   C. Language

D. Literature
E. Journalism
F. Mass Communications
G. Music and Dance
H Philosophy
I. Religion
J. Speech
K. Theater
L. Women's Studies

V. VOCATIONAL STUDIES
A. Aviation
B. Fashion
C. Interior Design
D. Medical and Allied Health
E. Office Technology
F. Travel and Tourism Management
G. Recreation

I. GENERAL REFERENCE WORKS

A. General

Britannica Book of the Year. Since 1938
Chase's Annual Events. Since 1958
Dissertation Abstracts International. Since 1967 (Formerly
   Dissertation Abstracts. Since 1938)
Europa Year Book: A World Survey. 2 vols., since 1959
Facts on File: World News Digest. Since 1940
Familiar Quotations. 1992
Guide to Popular U.S. Government Publications. 1990
Information Please Almanac. Since 1947
Monthly Catalog of United States Government Publications.
   Since 1895
New York Public Library Desk Reference. 1989
The Reader's Adviser. 6 vols., 1988
Statesman's Year-Book. Since 1864
Statistical Abstract of the United States. Since 1878
United States Government Manual. Since 1935
Vertical File Index. Since 1935
World Almanac and Book of Facts. Since 1868
Year Book of the United Nations. Since 1948

B. Atlases

Atlas of American History. 1987
Atlas of Florida. 1992 (Most states have such atlases)
Chambers' World Gazeteer. 1988

Columbia Lippincott Gazateer of the World. 1962
Commercial Atlas and Marketing Guide. Since 1876
The National Atlas of the United States of America. 1970
National Geographic Atlas of the World. 1990
Oxford Atlas of the World. 1992
Rand McNally Cosmopolitan World Atlas. 1987
The Times Atlas of the World, 9th Comprehensive ed. 1992

C. Biographies

American Men and Women of Science. 8 vols., 1990
Biography Almanac. 2 vols., 1983
Biography and Genealogy Master Index. Since 1980
Biography Index: A Cumulative Index to Biographical Material in Books and Magazines. Since 1946
Chambers' Biographical Dictionary. 1986
Current Biography. Since 1940
Dictionary of American Biography. With supplements, 1946
Dictionary of National Biography. 22 vols., 1885–1971
Dictionary of Scientific Biography. 16 vols., 1980
Directory of American Scholars. Since 1942
International Who's Who. Since 1936
McGraw-Hill Encyclopedia of World Biography. 12 vols., 1973. Supplements, 4 vols., 1987
The National Cyclopaedia of American Biography. Since 1888
New Century Cyclopedia of Names. 3 vols., 1954
The New York Times Biographical Service. Since 1970
Twentieth Century Authors. 1942. With supplements, 1955
Who's Who. Since 1848
Who's Who in America. Since 1899
Who Was Who in America. 1942–1985

D. Dictionaries

Acronyms, Initialisms and Abbreviations Dictionary. 1992
American Heritage Dictionary. 1992
Black's Law Dictionary. 1990
Black's Medical Dictionary. 1992
Cancer Dictionary. 1992
The Concise Oxford Dictionary of Proverbs. 1992
Dictionary of Advertising. 1988
Dictionary of Computer Terms. 1992
Dictionary of Economics. 1992
Encyclopedic Dictionary of Sociology. 1991
HarperCollins Dictionary of Electronics. 1991
Henderson's Dictionary of Biological Terms. 1989
International Dictionary of Medicine and Biology. 3 vols., 1986
New American Dictionary of Music. 1991

New Palgrave Dictionary of Money and Finance. 1992
Oxford English Dictionary. 20 vols., 1989
Oxford Thesaurus. 1992
Roget's International Thesaurus. 1992
Webster's Third New International Dictionary. 1961

E. Encyclopedias
Academic American Encyclopedia. 1993
Collier's Encyclopedia. 24 vols., 1993
Encyclopedia Americana. 1993
The New Encyclopaedia Britannica. 1987, 1990
Random House Encyclopedia. 1990
World Book Encyclopedia. 22 vols., 1993

F. Periodical Indexes
Applied Science and Technology Index. Since 1958
Art Index. Since 1929
Bibliographic Index: A Cumulative Bibliography of Bibliographies.
    Since 1938
Book Review Digest. Since 1905
Business Periodicals Index. Since 1958
Education Index. Since 1929
General Science Index. Since 1978
Humanities Index. Since 1974
Index to Book Reviews in the Humanities. Since 1960
Industrial Arts Index. 1913–1957. (Superseded by *Applied Science
    and Technology Index* and *Business Periodicals Index.* Since
    1958)
International Index to Periodicals. 1907–1964. (Superseded
    by *Social Sciences and Humanities Index.* Since 1965)
International Nursing Index. Since 1966
MLA [Modern Language Association] *International Bibliography.*
    Since 1963
The Music Index. Since 1949
New York Times Index. Since 1851
Nineteenth Centry Readers' Guide, 1890–1899. 1945
Poole's Index to Periodical Literature, 1802–1906. 1945
Public Affairs Information Service Bulletin. Since 1915
Readers' Guide to Periodical Literature. Since 1900
Social Sciences and Humanities Index. 1965–1974. (Superseded
    by *Social Sciences Index* and *Humanities Index.* 1974)
Social Sciences Index. Since 1974.
Technical Book Review Index. Since 1917
United States Catalog: Books in Print. Since 1928
Vertical File Index. Since 1935

II. SCIENCE AND TECHNOLOGY

A. General
Great Events from History—Science and Technology Series. 1991
The Great Scientists. 12 vols., 1989
McGraw-Hill Encyclopedia of Science and Technology. 20 vols., 1992
The New Illustrated Science and Invention Encyclopedia. 26 vols., 1989
Science and Technology Desk Reference. 1993
Van Nostrand's Scientific Encyclopedia. 1989

B. Agriculture
Agricultural Handbook. 1988
Agriculture Dictionary. 1991
Biological and Agricultural Index. Since 1916
Information Sources of Agriculture and Horticulture. 1992
Yearbook of Agriculture. Since 1894

C. Biology
Atlas of Endangered Species. 1991
Biological Abstracts. Since 1926
Biological and Agricultural Index. Since 1916
Encyclopedia of Human Biology. 1991
Gray's Anatomy. 1989
Grzimek's Encyclopedia of Mammals. 1989
Information Sources in the Life Sciences. 1987
Marshall Cavendish International Wildlife Encyclopedia. 1990
Progress in Biophysics and Biophysical Chemistry. (Since 1950.
     Now *Progress in Biophysics and Molecular Biology*)
Visual Dictionary of the Human Body. 1991

D. Chemistry
Chemical Abstracts. Since 1907
Chemical Information Sources. 1991
Dictionary of Biochemistry and Molecular Biology. 1989
The Elements. 1991
Handbook of Chemistry and Physics. Since 1914
Handbook of Industrial Chemical Additives. 1991
Hawley's Condensed Chemical Dictionary. 1993
Lange's Handbook of Chemistry. 1992

E. Computer Sciences
Computer Catalogs. 1992
Computer Glossary. 1991
Computer Professionals Quick Reference. 1992
Dictionary of Computer Terms. 1992

Macmillan Encyclopedia of Computers. 1992
The New Hackers Dictionary. 1991

F. Electronics
American Electrician's Handbook. 1992
Encyclopedia of Electronics. 1990
HarperCollins Dictionary of Electronics. 1991
The Lineman's and Cableman's Handbook. 1992

G. Energy
Chambers' Nuclear Energy and Radiation Dictionary. 1992
Energy Research Abstracts. Since 1976
Energy Update. 1991
International Petroleum Encyclopedia. 1992

H. Engineering
Applied Science and Technology Index. Since 1958
ASM Engineered Materials Reference Book. 1989
Civil Engineers Reference Book. 1989
Engineering Index. Since 1884
Eshbach's Handbook of Engineering Fundamentals, 4th ed., 1990
Industrial Engineering Terminology. 1991
Sweet's Catalog. Since 1976
Who's Who in Engineering. Since 1977

I. Environmental Studies
Environmental Abstracts. Since 1971
The Green Almanac. 1991
HarperCollins Dictionary of Environmental Science. 1992
Nature Directory. 1991

J. Geology
Concise Oxford Dictionary of Earth Sciences. 1990
Glossary of Geology, 3rd ed. 1987
Handbook of Minerology. 1990
McGraw-Hill Encyclopedia of the Geological Sciences. 1988
Mineral Reference Manual. 1991
Weather Almanac. 1987

K. Health and Physical Education
Consumer Health and Nutrition Index. Since 1985
Cumulative Index to Nursing and Allied Health Literature.
   Since 1977
Essential Guide to Vitamins and Minerals. 1992
Marshall Cavendish Encyclopedia of Family Health. 12 vols., 1991
National Health Directory. 1992
Physical Education Index. Since 1978

Sourcebook on Food and Nutrition. 1982
Sports Rule Encyclopedia. 1990

L. Mathematics
Biographical Dictionary of Mathematics, 4 vols. 1991
A Dictionary of Statistical Terms. 1990
Encyclopedic Dictionary of Mathematics. 1987
Handbook of Differential Equations. 1989
HarperCollins Dictionary of Mathematics. 1991
Mathematical Journals: An Annotated Guide. 1992
The Numbers You Need. 1992

M. Medicine
Glossary of Medical Terminology. 1992
Index Medicus. Since 1927
Information Services in the Medical Sciences. 1992
The Merk Manual. Since 1899
Physicians' Desk Reference. Since 1947

N. Physics
Encyclopedia of Physics. 1990
Handbook of Chemistry and Physics. Since 1914
Macmillan Dictionary of Physics. 1986
Magill's Survey of Science: Physical Science Series. 1992
Reviews of Modern Physics. Since 1929

III. SOCIAL SCIENCES

A. General
*Handbook of Research on Social Studies Teaching
    and Learning.* 1991
An International Encyclopedia of the Social Sciences. 17 vols., 1968
Public Affairs Information Service. Since 1915
Social Science Encyclopedia. 1985
Social Science Reference Sources: A Practical Guide. 1990
Social Sciences Index. Since 1974

B. Business
Business Information: How to Find It, How to Use It. 1992
Business Information Sourcebook. 1991
Business Periodicals Index. Since 1958
Commodity Year Book. Since 1939
A Concise Dictionary of Business. 1990
Dun's Business Month. Since 1893
Encyclopedia of Business Information Sources. 1992

Foreign Commerce Yearbook. Since 1933
Moody's Manual of Investments. Since 1929
Standard and Poor's Corporation Records. Since 1928
Standard and Poor's Register of Corporations, Directors
    and Executives, United States and Canada. Since 1928
Survey of Current Business. Since 1921
Thomas' Register of American Manufacturers. Since 1905
Wall Street Journal Index. Since 1958

C. Criminology
Crime in the U.S. Since 1930
Criminal Justice Abstracts. Since 1977
Criminal Justice Periodical Index. Since 1975
Criminology: A Reader's Guide. 1991
Dictionary of Crime. 1992
Encyclopedia of Police Science. 1989
Encyclopedia of World Crime. Since 1989

D. Economics
Economics Desk Companion. 1992
Encyclopedic Dictionary of Economics. 1991
Handbook of Economic Cycles. 1991
A Lexicon of Economics. 1991
MIT Dictionary of Modern Economics. 1992
World Economic Survey. Since 1945

E. Education
American Educators Encyclopedia. 1991
A Critical Dictionary of Educational Concepts. 1990
Current Index to Journals in Education. Since 1969
Digest of Educational Statistics. Since 1962
Directory of American Scholars. Since 1942
Education Index. Since 1929
Encyclopedia of Educational Research. 1992
Encyclopedia of Higher Education. 1992
ERIC Resources in Education. Since 1966

F. Ethnic Studies
Conflict and Culture: A Literature Review and Bibliography. 1992
Dictionary of American Immigration History. 1990
Dictionary of Race and Ethnic Relations. 1988
Encyclopedia of World Cultures. 1991
Handbook of North American Indians. Since 1978
Hispanic Almanac. 1990
People Atlas. 1991
World Directory of Minorities. 1990

G. Geography
Climates of the States. Since 1974
Concise Oxford Dictionary of Geography. 1992
National Geographic Index. Since 1899
Rand McNally World Atlas. 1992
The Weather Almanac. 1987
Who Was Who in World Exploration. 1992
World Survey of Climatology. Since 1969

H. Health
Consumer Health and Nutrition Index. Since 1985
Cumulative Index to Nursing and Allied Health Literature.
  Since 1977
Essential Guide to Vitamins and Minerals. 1992
Home Health Care: An Annotated Bibliography. 1992
Marshall Cavendish Encyclopedia of Family Health. 12 vols., 1991
National Health Directory. 1992
Sourcebook on Food and Nutrition. 1982

I. History
American Destiny. 10 vols., 1975
American Historical Review. Since 1905
Cambridge History of Latin America. 1984
Cambridge Medieval History. 8 vols., 1911–1936
Concise Dictionary of World History. 1983
Dictionary of Amercan History. 8 vols., 1976
Dictionary of Historical Terms. 1990
Encyclopedia of Asian History. 1988
Facts on File Encyclopedia of the 20th Century. 1991
Great Events from History: Ancient and Medieval Series. 1972
Historical Abstracts. Since 1955
History of American Life: A Social, Cultural, and Economic Analysis. 13 vols., 1929–1944
New Cambridge Modern History. 14 vols., since 1957
Peoples' Chronology. 1992
This Day in American History. 1990
Timetables of History. 1991
The World and Its People. 19 vols., 1988

J. Political Science
American Political Science Review. Since 1906
Atlas of World Affairs. 1991
Congressional Record. Since 1873
Dictionary of Politics. 1992
Facts on File World Political Almanac. 1992
HarperCollins Dictionary of American Government and Politics.
  1992

Index to Legal Periodicals. Since 1909
Municipal Year Book. Since 1934
Political Handbook of the World. Since 1928
Public Affairs Information Service Bulletin. Since 1915
Statesman's Yearbook. Since 1964

K. Physical Education
Great Athletes. 1992
College Admissions Index of Majors and Sports, 1992-93. 1992
Encyclopedia of North American Sports History. 1992
Sports Fan's Connection: An All-Sports-In-One-Directory. 1992
Sports Illustrated 1992 Sports Almanac. 1991

L. Psychology
American Journal of Psychology. Since 1887
Encyclopedia of Learning and Memory. 1992
Encyclopedia of Occultism and Parapsychology. 1991
Encyclopedia of Psychology. 4 vols., 1984
Encyclopedia of Schizophrenia and the Psychotic Disorders. 1992
Encyclopedic Dictionary of Psychology. 1991
Marshall Cavendish Encyclopedia of Personal Relationships. 1990
Mental Measurements Yearbook. Since 1938
Psychological Abstracts. Since 1927
Psychological Bulletin. Since 1904

M. Social Work
Adoption Directory. 1989
Assistance and Benefits Information Directory. 1992
Encyclopedia of Child Abuse. 1989
Encyclopedia of Social Work. 1987
Social Work Dictionary. 1991

N. Sociology
American Journal of Sociology. Since 1895
American Sociological Review. Since 1936
Encyclopedia of Sociology. 1992
Handbook of Sociology. 1988
Sociological Abstracts. Since 1953

IV. HUMANITIES

A. Art and Architecture
American Art Directory. Since 1898
Art Index. Since 1929
Encyclopedia of World Art. 15 vols. With Supplements, 1959
Fine Art Index. 1992

HarperCollins Dictionary of Art Terms and Techniques. 1991
Illustrated Encyclopedia of Architects and Architecture. 1991
New International Illustrated Encyclopedia of Art. 24 vols., 1967
Who's Who in American Arts. Since 1937

B. Foreign Languages
Facts on File English/Spanish Visual Dictionary. 1992
International Encyclopedia of Linguistics. 4 vols., 1992
Oxford Guide to the French Language. 1992
Random House Portuguese Dictionary. 1991
Vocabulary of Soviet Society and Culture. 1992
Webster's New World Hebrew Dictionary. 1992
The World's Major Languages. 1987

C. Language
Dickson's Word Treasury. 1992
A Dictionary of Linguistics and Phonetics. 1991
Handbook of Good English. 1991
International Encyclopedia of Linguistics. 4 vols., 1992
Linguistics Encyclopedia. 1991
Oxford Companion to the English Language. 1992

D. Literature
Abstracts of English Studies. Since 1958
American Authors, 1600–1900. 1938
American Literature. Since 1929
Black Literature Criticism. 1992
Book Review Digest. Since 1905
British Writers. 8 vols., 1984
Cambridge Guide to English Literature. 1983
Cambridge History of American Literature. 3 vols., 1972
Cambridge History of English Literature. 15 vols., 1907–1933
Columbia Dictionary of Modern European Literature. 1980
Contemporary Authors. Since 1962
Contemporary Literary Criticism. Since 1973
Cyclopedia of Literary Characters. 1990
Dictionary of Concepts in Literary Criticism and Theory. 1992
Dictionary of Fictional Characters. 1991
Dictionary of Literary Biography. Since 1978
Essay and General Literature Index. Since 1900
Fiction Catalog. Since 1908
Granger's Index to Poetry. 1990
Handbook to Literature. 1986
Humanities Index. Since 1974
Macmillan Home Book of Proverbs, Maxims and Phrases. 1965
Magill's Critical Survey of Long Fiction. 8 vols., 1991

Magill's Critical Survey of Poetry. 8 vols., 1982
Magill's Critical Survey of Short Fiction. 7 vols., 1993
Masterplots. 12 vols., 1976
New History of French Literature. 1989
Oxford Companion to American Literature. 1983
Oxford Companion to Classical Literature. 1989
Oxford Companion to English Literature. 1985
PMLA [Publications of the Modern Language Association].
   Since 1921
*Poetry Explication: A Checklist of Interpretation Since 1925
   of British and American Poems Past and Present.* 1980
Short Story Index. 5 vols., 1950, 1973 (Supplements Since 1974)
Twentieth Century Literary Criticism. Since 1978
Twentieth Century Short Story Explication. Since 1977
World Literature Criticism. 1992
Writer's Handbook. Since 1936

E. Journalism
Bibliographical Dictionary of American Journalism. 1989
Journalism: A Guide to the Reference Literature. 1990
The 1992–1993 Guide to Newspaper Syndications. 1992
A Sourcebook of American Literary Journalism. 1992
Ulrich's International Periodicals Directory. Since 1932

F. Mass Communications
Broadcasting and Cable Market Place. 1992
Broadcasting Cablecasting Yearbook. Since 1982
Broadcasting Yearbook. Since 1982
Communication Abstracts. Since 1978
Communications Standard Dictionary. 1989
Facts on File Dictionary of Film and Broadcast Terms. 1991
Longman Dictionary of Mass Media and Communication. 1982
Telecommunications Systems and Services Directory. Since 1983
Television and Cable Factbook. Since 1946
TV Encyclopedia. 1991
World's News Media: A Comprehensive Reference Guide. 1991

G. Music and Dance
Contemporary Musicians. Since 1989
Dance Handbook. 1988
Dance Magazine. Since 1926
Dance World. Since 1966
Great Song Thesaurus. 1989
Illustrated History of Popular Music. Since 1989
The International Cyclopedia of Music and Musicians. 1985
Music Business Handbook and Career Guide. 1990

Music Index. Since 1949
New Grove Dictionary of American Music. 4 vols., 1986
New Grove Dictionary of Musical Instruments. 3 vols., 1984
New Grove Dictionary of Music and Musicians. 20 vols., 1980
New Grove Dictionary of Opera. 4 vols., 1992
New Oxford Companion to Music. 2 vols., 1983
New Oxford History of Music. Since 1986

H. Philosophy

Concise Encyclopedia of Western Philosophy and Philosophers. 1991
Dictionary of the History of Ideas. 4 vols., 1973
Encyclopedia of Ethics. 1992
Encyclopedia of Philosophy. 8 vols., 1967
Journal of Philosophy. Since 1904
Macmillan Illustrated Encyclopedia of Myths and Legends. 1989
Philosopher's Index. Since 1967
Philosophical Review. Since 1892
World Philosophy. 5 vols., 1982

I. Religion

Bible Atlases and Concordances. (A variety of titles is available)
Concise Dictionary of Cults and Religions. 1991
Dictionary of Judaism and Christianity. 1991
Dictionary of Religion and Philosophy. 1987
Eliade Guide to World Religions. 1991
Encyclopedia of American Religions. 1989
Encyclopedia Judaica. 16 vols., 1972
Encyclopedia of Religion. 16 vols., 1987
Encyclopedia of Religion and Ethics. 13 vols., 1959
The Golden Bough: A Study in Magic and Religion. 12 vols., 1907–1915
History of the Church. 10 vols., 1987
International Bibliography of the History of Religions. Since 1954
New Catholic Encyclopedia. 15 vols., 1967
New Schaff-Herzog Encyclopedia of Religious Knowledge. 13 vols., 1949–1950
Religious Information Sources: A World Guide. 1992
Religious Leaders of America. 1991
Who's Who of World Religions. 1992
Yearbook of American Churches. Since 1916

J. Speech

American Orators Before 1900. 1987
Speeches of the American Presidents. 1988
Tuttle Dictionary of Quotations for Speeches. 1992

K. Theater
American Musical Theater: A Chronicle. 1992
American Theatre History: An Annotated Bibliography. 1992
Back Stage Theater Guide. 1991
Dramatic Criticism Index. 1972
International Dictionary of Theatre. 1992
Magill's Critical Survey of Drama. 6 vols., 1985
McGraw-Hill Encyclopedia of World Drama. 5 vols., 1984
Play Index. 1992
Theatrical Designers: An International Biographical Dictionary.
   1992

L. Women's Studies
Dictionary of Feminist Theory. 1990
Directory of Financial Aids for Women. 1991
Women's Studies Abstracts. Since 1972
Women's Studies Encyclopedia. Since 1989
Women Who Ruled. 1990

V. VOCATIONAL STUDIES

A. Aviation
Aerospace Facts and Figures. Since 1945
Cambridge Air and Space Dictionary. 1990
Dictionary of Aviation. 1991
Jane's All the World's Aircraft. Since 1909
World Aviation Directory. Since 1940

B. Fashion
Historical Encyclopedia of Costumes. 1988
Conran Directory of Design. 1985
Fashion in the Western World: 1500–1990. 1992
Who's Who in Fashion. 1988

C. Interior Design
Encyclopedia of Arts and Crafts. 1989
Contemporary Designers. 1990
Penguin Dictionary of Decorative Arts. 1989
Interior Design. Since 1932
Sotheby's Concise Encyclopedia of Furniture. 1989

D. Medical and Allied Health
American Medical Association Encyclopedia of Medicine. 1989
American Nursing: A Biographical Dictionary. 1992
Complete Drug Reference. 1992

Index Medicus. Since 1927
Merck Manual. Since 1899
Medical School Admission Requirements. 1993-94.
Mosby's Medical, Nursing, and Allied Health Dictionary. 1990
Physicians' Desk Reference. Since 1947
Textbook of Medicine. 1982

E. Office Technology
Elseirer's Dictionary of Office Automation: In Four Languages.
  1991
Professional Secretaries International Complete Office Handbook.
  1992
Secretary's Handbook. 1988
Secretary's Standard Reference Manual and Guide. 1978
The Trainer's Resource. Since 1981
Van Nostrand Reinhold Dictionary of Information Technology. 1989
Webster's New World Secretarial Handbook. 1989

F. Travel and Tourism Management
Dictionary of Hospitality, Travel and Tourism. 1990
Fodor's Travel Guides. (By country) Since 1936
Hotel and Motel Redbook. Since 1886
Hotel and Travel Index. Since 1938
Travel Dictionary. 1990

G. Recreation
Campground and Trailer Park Directory. Since 1984
Lincoln Library of Sports Champions. 1989
National Parks: The Family Guide. 1991
Parks Directory of the United States. 1992
U.S. Outdoor Atlas and Recreation Guide. 1992

Reference Words and Abbreviations

Knowing the words and abbreviations usually found in reference and scholarly materials will make searching for and recording information easier because you will understand them. You may want to use some of them in your own note taking, and some are appropriate for documentation and citation.

Geographical names have limited use, because the states where publishers are located are not shown in either the MLA Works Cited or text documentation. However, if you use material from outside the United States, whether print or nonprint (such as a film), you must indicate the country of origin. Sometimes that will be shown by a beginning capital letter and an ending period, as in Can. (Canada) or Gt. Brit. (Great Britain). Some countries are shown only by two capitals: NZ (New Zealand) and UK (United Kingdom). Canadian provinces are also indicated by two capitals, as in BC (British Columbia) and NB (New Brunswick).

Religious and literary works considered classics are often abbreviated, especially when titles are frequently repeated. Books of the Bible, including the OT (Old Testament) and NT (New Testament) are usually abbreviated; dictionaries often contain such lists. Chief among classical works commonly abbreviated are those by Chaucer and Shakespeare. For example, Chaucer's CT (*Canterbury Tales*) and its various sections, such as Pard T (The Pardoner's Tale), MkT (The Monk's Tale), and WBT (The Wife of Bath's Tale) are often abbreviated in scholarly works. Among Shakespeare's plays, you can easily recognize most of the abbreviations, such as JC (*Julius Caesar*), Oth (*Othello*), Ado (*Much Ado About Nothing*), and H5 (*Henry V*). His sonnets are often referred to as Son., followed by a number or an opening line.

There is a **trend *away* from using foreign terms**, especially Latin ones. Even the once-popular "ibid." and "op. cit." are no longer recommended for your own documentation, although you may encounter them in your reading of other materials. Also, even when some of these abbreviations for foreign words or phrases *are* used, they are not put in italics or underlined despite the custom of doing so in other kinds of writing.

Here, then, are some of the more widely used scholarly and reference words and their abbreviations.

abbr.	abbreviation
abr.	abridged
AD	*anno Domini* ("in the year of our Lord," or after Christ)— used before numerals for a year, as in AD 1776
adapt.	adapted by, or adaptation
anon.	anonymous
BC	before Christ—used after numerals for a year, as in 79 BC
BCE	before the common era (analogous to BC but used to designate time in calendars, such as the Hebrew calendar, that do not reckon time according to the life of Jesus)
bibliog.	bibliography, or bibliographer, or bibliographic, or bibliographical
biog.	biography, or biographer, or biographical
©	copyright
c. or ca.	*circa* ("about")—used with approximate dates
CE	common era—used to describe time in calendars, such as the Hebrew calendar, that do not reckon time according to the life of Jesus; analogous to AD
cf.	*confer* ("compare with")
ch. or chap.	chapter
chor.	choreographer, or choreographed by
col., cols.	column(s)
comp.	compiled by, or compiler
cond.	conductor, or conducted by
Cong.	U. S. Congress
Cong. Rec.	*Congressional Record*
Const.	U.S. Constitution
dir.	director, or directed by
diss.	dissertation
dist.	distributor, or distributed by
ed., eds.	edited by, or edition, or editor(s)
e.g.	*exempli gratia* ("for example")
enl.	enlarged
esp.	especially
et al.	*et alii* ("and others")—always abbreviated
etc.	*et cetera* ("and so forth")
ex.	example
f., ff.	following page(s)
fig., figs.	figure(s)
fn.	footnote
fwd.	foreword
GPO	Government Printing Office, Washington, D.C.
H. Doc.	House of Representatives Document
HR	U.S. House of Representatives

ibid.	*ibidem* ("in the same place")
i.e.	*id est* ("that is")
illus.	illustrated, or illustrations, or illustrator
intl.	international
introd.	introduction, or introduced by
l., ll.	line(s)
ms., mss.	manuscript(s)
narr.	narrator, or narrated by
NB	*nota bene* ("mark or note well")—take notice
n.d.	no date of publication available
n.p.	no publisher available; no place of publication given
n.p., n. pag.	no pagination shown
op. cit.	*opere citato* ("in the work cited")
orig.	original or originally
p., pp.	page(s)
passim	*passim* ("throughout")—here and there in the work
perf.	performer, or performed by
pref.	preface
prod.	producer, or produced by
pseud.	pseudonym
pub. or publ.	publisher, or published by, or publication
qtd.	quoted in
rept.	report, or reported by
rev.	revised by, or revision; reviewed by, or review—usually spelled out if confusion is possible
rpt.	reprint, or reprinted by
S	U.S. Senate
S. Doc.	Senate Document
S. Rept.	Senate Report
S. Res.	Senate Resolution
sic	so, or thus (usually within square brackets; otherwise, in parentheses)
supp.	supplement
tr., trans.	translator, or translated by, or translation
v.	*vide* ("see" or consult)
viz.	*videlicet* ("namely")
vol., vols.,	volume(s)
writ.	writer, or written by

Index

Abbreviations:
  of commonly used terms,
    291–93
  in notes, 112
Abstract, 228
Abstracting services, 76–77
Accuracy in notes, 112–13
Acknowledgments:
  location of, 186–87, 191–92
  note numbering system,
    194
  of direct play quotations,
    174
  of direct poetry quotations,
    173–74
  of direct prose quotations,
    166–68, 171–73
  of ideas, 186
  of maps, charts, diagrams,
    pictures, 191–92
  of sources, 4, 186–201
Alphabetizing:
  in library sources, 35,
    37–38
  in sources (APA) 252
  in works cited (MLA) 203
  of note cards, 131
Analyzing as approach, 48–49
Annotation:
  defined, 226
  examples of, 226–27
  in preliminary citations, 113
  in works cited, 226–227
APA (American Psychological
    Association):
  documentation forms,
    247–251
  endnotes, 50, 251
  format, 247–48
  in-text documentation,
    249–51
  notes, 251
  page numbering, 248

quotations, 249
reference forms, 248–49,
    251–56
sample paper, 257–71
title page, 248
typing customs, 247–48
Appendix, 227–28, 251
Approach, finding an, 47–52,
    140–41
  wording an, 52
Approaches to subject:
  analysis, 48
  analyzing, 47–53
  comparing and contrasting,
    50
  criticizing, 49
  decision about, 129
  evaluating, 49
  examining, 48–49
  overall organization,
    140–41
  persuading, 51–52
  relating, 50–51
  wording of, 52–53
Argument as approach, 51–52
Assigned topics, 19
Audience:
  importance of, 10–11
  writing for, 10–11, 18,
    41–42, 155
Audiotapes, 98, 99
Audiovisual materials. See
    Nonprint
Author:
  catalog card, 35, 77–78
  in reference works, 209
  of encyclopedia article, 69
  on words cited card, 59,
    60–61
  reliability, 107, 110
Author-date system:
  documentation, 272–73
  references. See APA

Background as opening, 161
Bad endings, 178–79
Bad openings, 161–62
Beginning of papers, 156–61
Between-line documentation,
    272
Bias in writing, 156
Bibliography:
  aiding topic choice, 20, 25
  defined, 202
  source of information, 25,
    67, 69
  See also Preliminary
    citations; Works cited
Body of paper, 162–75
Books:
  endnotes for, 194–96
  publication information
    about, 62–65
  works cited forms for,
    204–208
Booklets, as sources of
    information, 87
Borrowed ideas,
    acknowledging, 186
Brackets, square, 118–19

Card catalog, 26, 77–78
  customs, 31–38
  dictionary, 26
  divided, 26
  explained, 33–34
  order of entries, 35–38
  source of ideas, 31
Catalog systems:
  Dewey Decimal, 32, 34
  Library of Congress, 32–33
Cause to effect, organization
    by 140
CDs, preliminary citation,
    98–99
Central idea. See Thesis
    statement

Challenging assumption as
opening, 158–59
Choosing a subject. *See*
Narrowing topics; Topics
Citations. *See* Preliminary
citations
Clarifying subject as
opening, 157
Clustering, 43, 141–42
Coherence in writing, 163–64
Combination notes, 126
Comment notes, 125–30, 175,
193, 225
Common knowledge, 106
Comparing and contrasting:
as approach, 50
as organization, 138–39
Completeness in notes,
113–14
Computer:
aids to outlining, 152
as information sources,
84–87
catalogs, 77–78
databases, 84–87
drafting on, 155
editing, 182–83
for notes, 127–28
revision, 182–83
searches, 38
spell checker, 182
style analyses, 183
word processing, 155
works cited, 217
Conclusion reached as
ending, 178
Concrete wording, 165
Content organization. *See*
Organization of content
Continuous pagination,
66–67
Controversial topics, 18
Copying without
acknowledgment, 5
See also Plagiarism
Critical thinking, 10, 47
Criticizing, as approach, 49

Database:
defined, 84
how it operates, 84–86
preliminary citations from,
86–87
Decimal outline, 148
Dewey Decimal classification,
31–32, 34
Dictionary catalog, 26
Discipline, self, 13
Divided catalog, 26
Documentation:
APA forms, 249–52
author and dates, 272–73

between lines, 172
content of, 186
conventions of, 187–93
endnotes, 193–201
footnotes, 172
forms of, 149–51, 272–74
full in text, 173
in endnotes, 196–97
in multiple volumes, 190
in parenthesis, 166
in text, 166–75
in various disciplines, 272
location of, 186, 187–88
MLA forms, 187–93,
193–94, 194–201
of books in endnotes,
193–94
of figures, 191
of quotations, 190
of visuals, 191–92, 199–200
nonprint materials, 191,
199–201
numbering sources,
273–74
parenthetical, 166–75,
188–93
punctuation of, 188–89
work quoted in another,
190
Documented paper, 2
Documented report, 2
Double submission, 39
Drafting paper, 8, 154–55
Drama, quotations from
174–75

Editing, 8, 180–81, 182–83
Effect to cause, organization
by, 140
Ellipsis, 118
Emphasis in writing, 164–65
Encyclopedia:
general, 68–69
in choosing a topic, 24
in works cited, 68–69, 211
source of research ideas, 24
subject, 69
Ending paper, 175–79
Endnotes, 193–94, 194–201,
225–26
subsequent references
in, 200–01
Evaluating:
as approach, 49
information, 7, 109–10,
source materials, 108–10
Examining as approach,
48–49

Fact:
as opening, 160
defined, 111, 112–13   ·

Field-of-study topics:
aids to choosing, 19–29
card catalog, 26
course materials, 22
defined, 14
encyclopedias, 24–25
online catalog, 26
periodical indexes, 27
personal interests, 28–29
taking stock, 19
textbook, 20–22
vocation, 28
Figures, 191
Filing system, card catalog,
35, 37–38
Films, 94–97, 218
Filmstrips, 94, 95, 219
First page of paper:
APA style, 257
MLA style, 230
First references, forms of:
books, 195–97
nonprint sources, 199–200
other print sources, 197–99
periodicals, 196–97
Five Ws, 44–46
Focusing on a subject, 42–47
Footnotes, location of, 272
Foreign words in notes, 120
Free association, 42–43
Free choice topics, 29–31
Freewriting, 42

General reference
information, 54–57
General to particular,
organization by, 139
Good openings, 157–61
Good writing, 155–56,
162–70
Government publications:
sources of information,
74–76
works cited forms, 216
Grouping ideas on note cards,
130

Hanging indentation form,
60, 203, 251
Headings on research paper
pages:
APA, 249, 257
MLA, 223–24, 232

Identification, personal on
paper, 223
Illustrative material, 191–92,
225
Importance of research paper,
9–10
Indentation:
in APA reference, 251

Indentation (*continued*):
  in endnotes, 195
  in works cited, 60, 205
Indexes:
  as sources of information,
    71–73, 78
  conventions of, 78–80
  of journals, 80–82
  of magazines, 80
  of newspapers, 82, 84
Inferences, 112–13
Information:
  adequate, 41
  collecting, 54–99
  evaluating, 7, 108–10
  integrating in writing,
    165–71
  primary sources of, 55
  recording, 100–28
  secondary sources of, 56
Integrating resources, 165–70
Interlibrary loan, 88
Interpolations in notes,
    118–19
Interviews:
  as research source, 91–92
  works cited form for,
    92–93, 215
In-text documentation, 273
Investigative report, 2
Italics in quotes, 118

Journals, 80, 82–83
  indexes for, 80–82
  publication information,
    65–67, 210

Key words. *See* Slug lines
Known to unknown,
    organization by, 138

Laser discs, 99
Lectures:
  as sources of information,
    92–93
  preliminary citation, 93
  references for, 199
Legibility of notes, 112
Length:
  of outline, 143
  of research paper, 6, 40
Letters:
  as information source, 88
  documenting, 198
  works cited form for, 216
Library cataloging customs,
    31–38
Library of Congress
    classification, 32–33
Library report, 2
Limitations of topic, 40–42
Linking as ending, 178

Magazine articles:
  publication information,
    65–67
  works cited, 210
Magazine indexes, 78–80
Managing time, 13
Mapping, 141, 143
Materials as criterion to
    determine subject, 41
Mechanics of writing, 181,
    182
Music, works cited, 219–220

Names:
  in card catalog, 37
  in writing, 156
Narrowing topics, 40–47
Natural sciences,
    documentation forms
    for, 270
"Neutral" subjects, 36
Newspaper:
  indexes, 82–84
  publication information, 67,
    211
Nonprint media:
  as source of information,
    90–99
  documenting sources, 191
  in endnotes, 199–201
  preliminary citations for,
    89–99
  "publication" information,
    89
  works cited forms for,
    215–220
Note cards:
  abbreviations on, 112
  accuracy in, 112
  completeness, 113
  content of, 121
  conventions of, 114–20
  evaluation of, 129–130
  form, 113–14
  identification on, 117
  kinds of, 120–26
  legibility of, 112
  number of, 126–27
  previewing for 107–11
  qualities of, 111–14
  quotations on, 114–18
  source notation on, 100,
    113–14
Notes:
  accuracy of, 111, 112
  combination, 126
  comment, 125
  completeness, 113–14
  conventions of, 114–20
  evaluation of, 129–30
  kinds of, 120–26
  legibility of, 112

location of, 193–94, 244
  paraphrase, 122–23
  personal ideas, 119, 125
  poetry, 116–18
  qualities of good, 111
  quotations on, 115–16,
    123–25
  summary, 121–22
  with documentation, 100,
    113–14
  words omitted from, 118
Note numbering system, 194
Note taking:
  general information, 111–27
  poetry, 116–18
  quotation, 115–16
  quotation acknowledgment,
    113–14, 114–18
  quotation within quotation,
    116
Numbering sources for
    documentation, 273–74

Online (computer) catalog,
    26, 77–78
  See also Card catalog
Openings of research paper:
  bad, 161–62
  good, 157–61
Opinion, 4, 5, 112–13
Order of material, 141–46,
    150–52
Organization and overall
    approach:
  by time, 138
  cause to effect, 140
  comparison and contrast,
    138–39
  general to particular, 139
  known to unknown, 138
  methods of, 137–40
  of content, 137–53
  of ideas, 7–8, 129–52
  visual, 141–43
Original work, 3, 4–5
  See also Plagiarism
Outline
  characteristics of, 144–47
  computer aids to, 152
  conventions of, 148–50
  decimal, 148
  defined, 142–43
  divisions, 144
  evolution of, 135–37
  explained, 142–52
  forms for, 147–48, 149, 150
  indentation system, 150
  information in, 143–46
  in presentation, 232
  length of, 143
  order of importance in,
    144–46

paragraph, 147–48
parallel phrasing, 150
punctuation in, 149, 150
reason for, 143
relation to thesis statement,
142
relationship of ideas, 145–46
revising, 142, 150–52
sample of, 230–31
sentences in, 147
spacing, 149, 150, 224,
230–31
subordination, 144, 145,
152–53
symbols on note cards, 152
symbols used, 148–49
topic, 147
types of, 147–48
typing, 224
Overworked topics, 18

Page numbering in research
paper, 223, 224, 226, 232,
248, 258
Pagination in periodicals,
65–67
Pamphlets:
as source of information,
73, 87
works cited form for, 198,
213
Paradox as opening, 159
Paragraph indentation form
for endnotes, 195
Paragraph outline, 147–48
Paraphrase notes, 122–23
Parenthetical documentation,
166–75, 187–93
identifying sources in,
189–191
using notes with, 175
Particular to general,
organization by, 139
Peer evaluation, 42, 153
Periodical articles:
publication information
about, 57, 78, 84
works cited forms for,
65–67, 201, 210–12
Periodical indexes:
as sources of information,
78, 80–85
conventions of, 78–80
for choosing a topic, 27
Periodicals:
continuous paging, 66–67
in endnotes, 196–98
page numbering, 65–67
paging by issue, 65–66
volume year, 66
Personal comment
notes, 125

Personal interest in choosing
topics, 28–29
Personal inventory, 28
Personal opinion, 6, 112–13
Persuasion. See Argument as
an approach
Photocopying, 127
Plagiarism, 5, 100–06, 187
avoiding, 100, 101, 186–201
in notes, 102–06
of words and ideas, 101
unconscious, 100, 102–06,
114
Plays:
documentation of, 116–17
in works cited, 212–19
Poetry:
documentation, 116–17
forms in notes, 116–17
in works cited, 209
quotations, 116–17
Polls, 93–94
Preface of paper, 228
Preliminary citations:
author unit, 60–61
books, 54–55, 62–65
cards, 54–55
computer databases, 84–87
content of, 59
conventions of, 59–67,
70–88, 91–98
defined, 54, 56
encyclopedias, 68–69
forms for, 59–67, 70–88,
91–98
newspapers, 67
nonprint, 89–99
publication information,
62–68
radio and TV, 90
titles, 61–62
uses for, 55
Presentation form:
abstract, 228
annotations, 226
appendix, 227–28
comment notes, 225
endnotes, 225–26
fastening pages, 228
first pages, 223
general information,
222–228
illustrations, 225
outline, 224
page numbering, 223
preface, 228
proofreading, 221–222
statement of purpose, 228
synopsis, 228
text, 224
title page, 223–224
typing, 222

works cited, 226
word processing, 222
Preview reading, 107
Primary sources:
defined, 55
importance of, 55
location of, 55
Printed aids to choosing topic,
20–25
Problem to solution,
organization by, 139–40
Procrastination, 13
Process log, 11–12
Process of research paper,
6–9
Proofreading, 221–22
Prose quotation, 172–73
Publication information:
for books, 62–65
for evaluation, 113–14
in nonprint, 89–90
in works cited, 62–63
magazines and journals,
65–67
newspapers, 67
Publishers' names:
in works cited, 63–65
streamlining, 63–65
Punctuation:
for quotations, 115–19,
171–75
in parenthetical
documentation, 188–89
of quotations within
quotations, 171–72

Qualities of writing, 162–71
Question to answer
organization, 139–40
Questionnaires, 93–94
Quotations:
acknowledging, 171–175,
249
as ending, 176–77
as opening, 159–60
do not constitute research
paper, 5
of drama, 174–75
of poetry, 114–15, 116–18,
173–74
of prose, 182
on notes, 114–18, 123–25
punctuation of, 115–19,
171–75
within quotations, 171–72,
190
words omitted from, 118

Radio programs:
as source of information, 90
works cited forms, 90–91,
215, 218

Reading for notes, 107–08, 110–11
Reference forms, APA, 251–56
Reference words and abbreviations, 291–93
Reference works available in libraries, 69–77
  general, 277–79
  humanities, 285–89
  science and technology, 280–82
  social sciences, 282–85
  vocational studies, 289–90
Relating:
  as an approach, 50–51
  as an opening, 158
Reports, 2
Research:
  academic, 2
  applied, 1
  business, 1
  defined, 1–2
  market, 2
  pure, 1
  scholarly, 1, 2
  sources of information, 54–59, 68–99
  technical, 1
Research paper:
  audience, 10–11
  bases of, 6–9
  characteristics of, 3–4
  comment notes, 225
  defined, 2, 3–4, 4–6
  endnotes, 225–26
  importance of, 9–10
  length of, 6, 40
  outline of, 142–53
  page numbering, 223
  participant in, 10
  personal advantages of, 4, 9–10
  process log, 11–12
  readers of, 10–11
  steps to, 6–9
  title page, 223
  titles, 53, 183–85
  works cited customs, 203
  writing, 154–81
Resource information:
  documenting, 171–74, 186–201
  integration with text, 165–71
Return to statement, as ending, 176
Reusing research paper, 17
Reminder as ending, 176
Revising:
  computer aids to, 182–83

outline, 142–46, 150–52
writing, 8, 179–81

Sample research paper:
  APA, 257–71
  MLA, 229–46
Scanning for notes, 108
Search strategy, 56–57
Search strategy record, 58–59
Secondary sources:
  defined, 56
  location of, 56
"See also" listings, 35
Selecting general topic, 14–35
Selecting research subject, 40–53
Sentence outline, 147
Sentence structure, 180–81
Simple to complex organization, 138
Single source topics, 17
Skills from research, 9–10
Skim reading, 107–08
Slug lines, 114, 152
Sources:
  credibility, 109–11
  evaluating, 108–11
  of notes, 113–14
Sources of information:
  abstracting services, 76–77
  additional, 82–89
  bibliographies, 57, 69–70
  card catalog, 77–78
  computer database, 84–87
  directories, 70
  encyclopedias, 68–69, 70
  evaluating, 108–11
  government publications, 74–76
  identifying in documentation, 189–91
  indexes, 71–73, 78–84
  journal indexes, 80, 82–83
  magazine indexes, 80–81
  newspaper indexes, 80–81
  nonprint, 90–99
  online catalog, 77–78
  periodical indexes, 78–84
  primary, 55
  secondary, 56
  vertical file, 73–74
Spacing in parenthetical documentation 188–89
Speeches:
  as source of information, 92–93
  preliminary citations, 94
  works cited, 216–17
Specialized library collections, 88
Specifics in writing, 165

Spelling, 181, 182
Square brackets, use of, 118–19
Statement of purpose, 228
Stating position:
  as ending, 176–78
  as opening, 157–58
Statistics as opening, 160
Style of writing, 155–56, 180–81
Structuring strategies, 48–53, 136–141, 141–43
Subdividing, 43–44
Subject:
  choosing, 6–7
  defined, 14
  different from topic, 14
  focusing on, 42–47
Subjects. See Narrowing topics; Topics
Subject subdivisions in catalog, 32, 38
Subsequent reference forms in endnotes, 200–01
Summary:
  in notes, 121–22
  is not a research paper, 4
Supporting statement, 164
Survey as information, 93–94
Synopsis, 230
Synthesis, 3

Tables, 191–92, 225
Television programs:
  as sources of information, 90
  works cited forms for, 90–91, 215
Term paper, 2
Text of paper, 224
Textbook for topic ideas, 19, 20–23
Thesis statement:
  defined, 131–34
  evolution of, 134–35
  functions of, 133
  not a question, 134
  not a title, 133
  not a topic, 133
Third person, 155
Time:
  management, 13
  organization by, 138
  studying, 11
  thinking, 11
Title card, 33–34
Title page of paper, 223–24, 232, 248, 257
Titles:
  conventions of, 184–85
  for research paper, 53, 183–85

in card catalog, 33–34
in taking notes, 120
Titles in works cited, 61–62
Topic outline, 147
Topics:
  assigned, 14, 19
  choosing, 14–37
  controversial, 18
  defined, 14
  field-of-study, 14, 19–29
  free choice, 15, 29–31
  good, 15–16
  narrowing, 40–51
  neutral, 18
  originality of, 17
  overlap, 17, 39
  sources available, 16
  to avoid, 16, 18
  unfruitful, 17, 18
Typing:
  annotations, 228–29
  of endnotes, 225–26
  of outline, 224
  of quotations, 171–74
  of research paper, 222, 224
  of resource list, 251–256
  of text, 224
  of works cited, 202–220
  parenthetical
    documentation, APA,
    249–51
  parenthetical
    documentation, MLA,
    189–92

Unity in writing, 163–64

Vertical file material, 73–74
Video, interactive, 99
Videocassettes, 99
Visuals, documenting, 191–92,
  225

Word choices, 180–81
Word processing, 222
Works cited:
  contents of, 61–69, 202
  conventions in research
    paper, 203
  defined, 202
  for periodicals, 210–12
  forms for books, 204–09
  general information,
    202–20
  in research paper, 202–20,
    245–46
  nonprint sources, 215–20
  other print sources, 212–15
  page numbering, 203
  typing, 204–20, 226
Works cited cards:
  conventions of, 60–68, 203,
    204–20
  for books, 60–65
  for encyclopedias, 68–69,
    70
  for indexes, 78–83
  for periodicals, 60–62,
    65–67

forms of, 59–65, 70–88,
  90–99
from databases, 84–86
nonprint materials, 89–99
publication information,
  62–68
Writing:
  bias in, 156
  body of paper, 162–79
  coherence, 163–64
  concreteness, 165
  documentation in, 8,
    166–75, 186–201
  drafting, 8, 154–55
  editing, 9
  emphasis, 164–65
  endings, 175–79
  integrating information,
    165–71
  mechanics, 179, 180–81,
    181
  openings, 157–61
  outline forms, 141–43,
    147–48
  proofreading, 181–83, 221–22
  qualities of, 163–65
  revision, 9, 179, 180–83
  sentence structure, 180–81
  specificity, 165
  style, 155–56
  support, 164
the paper, 8, 162–79
unity, 163–64
  word choice, 180–81